An Unauthorized Biography of J. Edgar Hoover

Victoria Hockfield

The role of the book within our culture is changing. The change is brought on by new ways to acquire & use content, the rapid dissemination of information and real-time peer collaboration on a global scale. Despite these changes one thing is clear--"the book" in it's traditional form continues to play an important role in learning and communication. The book you are holding in your hands utilizes the unique characteristics of the Internet -- relying on web infrastructure and collaborative tools to share and use resources in keeping with the characteristics of the medium (user-created, defying control, etc.)--while maintaining all the convenience and utility of a real book.

Contents

Articles

Legacy   **209**

References

J. Edgar Hoover

J. Edgar Hoover

John Edgar Hoover

J. Edgar Hoover
1st Director of the Federal Bureau of Investigation

In office
March 22, 1935 – May 2, 1972

President	Franklin D. Roosevelt Harry S. Truman Dwight D. Eisenhower John F. Kennedy Lyndon B. Johnson Richard Nixon
Preceded by	Office created (was BOI director)
Succeeded by	L. Patrick Gray

6th Director of the Bureau of Investigation

In office
May 10, 1924 – March 22, 1935

President	Calvin Coolidge Herbert Hoover Franklin D. Roosevelt

Preceded by	William J. Burns
Succeeded by	Became FBI director
Born	January 1, 1895 Washington, DC
Died	May 2, 1972 (aged 77) Washington, DC
Religion	Presbyterian
Signature	

John Edgar Hoover (January 1, 1895 – May 2, 1972) was the first Director of the Federal Bureau of Investigation (FBI) of the United States. Appointed director of the Bureau of Investigation—predecessor to the FBI—in 1924, he was instrumental in founding the FBI in 1935, where he remained director until his death in 1972. Hoover is credited with building the FBI into a large and efficient crime-fighting agency, and with instituting a number of modern innovations to police technology, such as a centralized fingerprint file and forensic laboratories.

Late in life, and after his death, Hoover became an increasingly controversial figure. His critics have accused him of exceeding the jurisdiction of the FBI. He used the FBI to harass political dissenters and activists, to amass secret files on political leaders, and to collect evidence using illegal methods. It is because of Hoover's long and controversial reign that FBI directors are now limited to 10-year terms.

Early life and education

J. Edgar Hoover was born on New Year's Day 1895 in Washington, DC, to Anna Marie (née Scheitlin; 1860–1938), who was descended from a line of Swiss mercenaries, and Dickerson Naylor Hoover, Sr. (1856–1921), of English and German ancestry. Annie's uncle had been the Swiss honorary consul general to the United States. Hoover grew up in the Eastern Market. He worked at the Library of Congress during college and, in 1917, obtained a law degree from George Washington University. While a law student, Hoover became interested in the career of Anthony Comstock, the New York City US Postal Inspector, who waged prolonged campaigns against fraud and vice (including pornography and information on birth control) a generation earlier.

FBI career

During World War I, Hoover found work with the Justice Department. He was soon promoted to head of the Enemy Aliens Registration Section. In August 1919, he became head of the new General Intelligence Division of the Bureau of Investigation within the Justice Department (see the Palmer Raids). From there, in 1921, he rose in the Bureau of Investigation to deputy head, and in 1924, the Attorney General made him the acting director. On May 10, 1924, Hoover was appointed by President Calvin Coolidge to be the sixth director of the Bureau of Investigation, following President Warren Harding's death and in response to allegations that the prior director, William J. Burns, was involved in the Teapot Dome scandal. When Hoover took over the Bureau of Investigation, it had approximately 650 employees, including 441 Special Agents.

J. Edgar Hoover in 1924

Hoover was noted as sometimes being capricious in his leadership; he frequently fired FBI agents, singling out those whom he thought "looked stupid like truck drivers" or he considered to be "pinheads". He also relocated agents who had displeased him to career-ending assignments and locations. Melvin Purvis was a prime example; he was one of the most effective agents in capturing and breaking up 1930s gangs and received substantial public recognition, but a jealous Hoover maneuvered him out of the FBI.

Gangster wars

In the early 1930s, an epidemic of bank robberies in the Midwest was orchestrated by colorful criminal gangs who took advantage of superior firepower and fast getaway cars to avoid arrest. Many of these desperadoes, particularly John Dillinger (who became famous for leaping over bank cages and his repeated escapes from jails and police traps), frequently made headlines. The fact that the robbers frequently took stolen cars across state lines (a federal offence) gave Hoover and his men the authority to pursue them. Things did not go as planned however, and there were some embarrassing foul-ups on the part of the FBI, particularly clashes with the Dillinger gang. A raid on a summer lodge named "Little Bohemia" in Manitowish Waters, Wisconsin, left an agent and a hapless civilian bystander dead, along with others wounded. All the gangsters escaped. Hoover realized that his job was now on the line, and he pulled out all stops to capture the culprits. In late July 1934, Purvis, the Director of Operations in the Chicago office, received a tip on Dillinger's whereabouts. The tip paid off when Dillinger was located and killed outside the Biograph Theater.

In the same period, there were numerous Mafia shootings as a result of Prohibition, while Hoover continued to deny the very existence of organized crime. Frank Costello helped encourage this view by feeding Hoover, "an inveterate horseplayer" known to send Special Agents to place $100 bets for him, tips on sure winners through their mutual friend, gossip columnist Walter Winchell. Hoover went on to say the Bureau had "much more important functions" than arresting bookmakers and gamblers.

Due to several highly publicized captures or shootings of outlaws and bank robbers including Dillinger, Alvin Karpis, and Machine Gun Kelly, the Bureau's powers were broadened and it was re-named the Federal Bureau of Investigation in 1935. In 1939, the FBI became pre-eminent in the field of domestic intelligence. Hoover made changes, such as expanding and combining fingerprint files in the Identification Division to compile the largest collection of fingerprints ever. Hoover also helped to greatly expand the FBI's recruitment and create the FBI Laboratory, a division established in 1932 to examine evidence found by the FBI.

Investigation of subversion and radicals

Hoover was concerned about subversion, and under his leadership, the FBI spied upon tens of thousands of suspected subversives and radicals. Hoover tended to exaggerate the dangers of these "subversives", and many times overstepped his bounds in his pursuit of eliminating that perceived threat.

The FBI investigated rings of German saboteurs and spies starting in the late 1930s, and had primary responsibility for counterespionage. The first arrests of German agents were made in 1938, and continued throughout World War II. In the Quirin affair during World War II, when German U-boats set two small groups of Nazi agents ashore in Florida and Long Island to cause acts of sabotage within the country, the members of these teams were apprehended only after one of the would-be saboteurs contacted the FBI, confessed everything, and then betrayed the other seven men. President Harry Truman wrote in his memoirs: "The country had reason to be proud of and have confidence in our security agencies. They had kept us almost totally free of sabotage and espionage during World War II". [citation needed].

The FBI participated in the Venona Project, a pre-World War II joint project with the British to eavesdrop on Soviet spies in the UK and the United States. It was not initially realized that espionage was being committed, but due to multiple wartime Soviet use of one-time pad ciphers, which are normally unbreakable, redundancies were created, enabling some intercepts to be decoded, which established the espionage. Hoover kept the intercepts—America's greatest counterintelligence secret—in a locked safe in his office, choosing not to inform President Truman, Attorney General J. Howard McGrath, or two Secretaries of State—Dean Acheson and General George Marshall—while they held office. He informed the Central Intelligence Agency (CIA) of the Venona Project in 1952.

According to documents declassified in 2007, Hoover maintained a list of 12,000 Americans suspected of disloyalty with the intention of detaining them, and doing so by suspending the writ of habeas corpus. Hoover submitted his plan to Truman at the outbreak of the Korean War, but there is no evidence that Truman accepted the plan.

COINTELPRO years

Main article: COINTELPRO

In 1956, Hoover was becoming increasingly frustrated by Supreme Court decisions that limited the Justice Department's ability to prosecute people for their political opinions, most notably, Communists. At this time he formalized a covert "dirty tricks" program under the name COINTELPRO.

This program remained in place until it was revealed to the public in 1971, and was the cause of some of the harshest criticism of Hoover and the FBI. COINTELPRO was first used to disrupt the Communist Party, and later organizations such as the Black Panther Party, Martin Luther King, Jr.'s SCLC, the Ku Klux Klan, the American Nazi Party and others. Its methods included infiltration, burglaries, illegal wiretaps, planting forged documents and spreading false rumors about key members of target organizations. Some authors have charged that COINTELPRO methods also included inciting violence and arranging murders. In 1975, the activities of COINTELPRO were investigated by the "*United States Senate Select Committee to Study Governmental Operations with Respect to Intelligence Activities*" called the Church Committee after its chairman, Senator Frank Church (D-Idaho) and these activities were declared illegal and contrary to the Constitution. Hoover amassed significant power by collecting files containing large amounts of compromising and potentially embarrassing information on many powerful people, especially politicians. According to Laurence Silberman, appointed Deputy Attorney General in early 1974, FBI Director Clarence M. Kelley thought such files either did not exist or had been destroyed. After *The Washington Post* broke a story in January 1975, Kelley searched and found them in his outer office. The House Judiciary Committee then demanded that Silberman testify about them.

In 1956, several years before he targeted King, Hoover had a public showdown with T.R.M. Howard, a civil rights leader from Mound Bayou, Mississippi. During a national speaking tour, Howard had criticized the FBI's failure to thoroughly investigate the racially motivated murders of George W. Lee, Lamar Smith, and Emmett Till. Hoover wrote an open letter to the press singling out these statements as "irresponsible."

Response to Mafia and civil rights groups

In the 1950s, evidence of Hoover's unwillingness to focus FBI resources on the Mafia became grist for the media and his many detractors, after famed reporter Jack Anderson[citation needed] exposed the immense scope of the Mafia's organized crime network, a huge threat Hoover had long downplayed. Hoover's retaliation and continual harassment of Anderson lasted into the 1970s. His moves against people who maintained contacts with subversive elements, some of whom were members of the civil rights movement, also led to accusations of trying to undermine their reputations. The treatment of

Martin Luther King, Jr. and actress Jean Seberg are two cited examples. [*citation needed*]

Hoover personally directed the FBI investigation into the assassination of President John F. Kennedy. In 1964, just days before Hoover testified in the earliest stages of the Warren Commission hearings, President Lyndon B. Johnson waived for Hoover the then-mandatory U.S. government service retirement age of seventy, allowing Hoover to remain the FBI Director "for life." The House Select Committee on Assassinations issued a report in 1979 critical of the performance by the FBI, the Warren Commission as well as other agencies. The report also criticized what it characterized as the FBI's reluctance to thoroughly investigate the possibility of a conspiracy to assassinate the president.

Late career and death

Presidents Harry Truman, John F. Kennedy, and Lyndon B. Johnson each considered dismissing Hoover as FBI Director, but all of them ultimately concluded that the political cost of doing so would be too great.

Hoover maintained strong support in Congress until his death in 1972 from a heart attack (reported the day after as the effects of high blood pressure.) Operational command of the Bureau passed to Associate Director Clyde Tolson. Soon thereafter, President Richard Nixon appointed L. Patrick Gray, a Justice Department official with no FBI experience, as Acting Director, with W. Mark Felt remaining as Associate Director. Being passed over to head the FBI is said[*citation needed*] to have contributed to Felt's decision to become the informant later referred to as "Deep Throat".

Legacy

Hoover was a consultant to Warner Brothers on a 1959 theatrical film about the FBI, *The FBI Story*, and in 1965 on Warner Brothers' long-running spin-off television series, *The F.B.I.* Hoover personally made sure that Warner Brothers would portray the FBI more favorably than other crime dramas of the times.

In 1979 there was a large increase in conflict in the House Select Committee on Assassinations (HSCA) under Senator Richard Schweiker, which had re-opened the investigation into the assassination of President Kennedy, reported that Hoover's FBI "failed to investigate adequately the possibility of a conspiracy to assassinate the President". The HSCA further reported that Hoover's FBI "was deficient in its sharing of information with other agencies and departments".

The FBI Headquarters in Washington, DC is named after Hoover. Because of the controversial nature of Hoover's legacy, there have been periodic proposals to rename it. In 2001, Senator Harry Reid sponsored an amendment to strip Hoover's name from the building. "J. Edgar Hoover's name on the FBI building is a stain on the building", Reid said. However, the Senate never adopted the amendment.

Personal life

Sexuality

Since the 1940s, rumors have circulated that Hoover was homosexual. It has been suggested that Clyde Tolson, an associate director of the FBI who was Hoover's heir, may have been his lover.

Clyde Tolson (left) and Hoover relaxing on the beach in Los Angeles, 1939

Some authors have dismissed the rumors about Hoover's sexuality and his relationship with Tolson in particular as unlikely, while others have described them as probable or even "confirmed", and still others have reported the rumors without stating an opinion. Hoover described Tolson as his alter ego: the men not only worked closely together during the day, but also took meals, went to night clubs and vacationed together. This closeness between the two men is often cited as evidence that they were lovers, though some FBI employees who knew them, such as Mark Felt, say that the relationship was merely "brotherly".

Tolson inherited Hoover's estate and moved into his home, having accepted the American flag that draped Hoover's casket. Tolson is buried a few yards away from Hoover in the Congressional Cemetery. Attorney Roy Cohn, an associate of Hoover during the 1950s investigations of Communists and himself a closeted homosexual, opined that Hoover was too frightened of his own sexuality to have anything approaching a normal sexual or romantic relationship.

In his 1993 biography *Official and Confidential: The Secret Life of J Edgar Hoover,* journalist Anthony Summers quoted a witness, "society divorcee" Susan Rosenstiel, (who later served time at Rikers Island for perjuring herself in a 1971 case) who claimed to have seen Hoover engaging in cross-dressing in the 1950s; she claimed that on two occasions she witnessed Hoover wearing a fluffy black dress with flounces and lace, stockings, high heels and a black curly wig, at homosexual orgies.

In 1958 the bisexual millionaire distiller and philanthropist Lewis Solon Rosenstiel asked Susan [Rosenstiel], his fourth wife, if—having been previously married to another bisexual man for nine years—she had ever seen "a homosexual orgy". Although she had once surprised her sixty-eight-year-old husband in bed with his attorney, Roy Cohn, Susan told Summers that she had never before been invited to view sex between men. With her consent, the couple went one day, soon after this odd question, to Manhattan's Plaza Hotel. Cohn, a former aide to Senator Joseph McCarthy and a Republican power broker, met them at the door. As she and her husband entered the suite, "Susan said, she recognized a third man: J. Edgar Hoover", director of the Federal Bureau of Investigation (FBI), whom she had met previously at her New York City

Upper East Side townhouse. Hoover, Lewis had explained, gave him access to influential politicians; he returned these favors, in part, by paying the director's gambling debts.

Summers also said that the Mafia had blackmail material on Hoover, and that as a consequence, Hoover had been reluctant to aggressively pursue organized crime. Although never corroborated, the allegation of cross-dressing has been widely repeated, and "J. Edna Hoover" has become the subject of humor on television, in movies and elsewhere. In the words of author Thomas Doherty, "For American popular culture, the image of the zaftig FBI director as a Christine Jorgensen wanna-be was too delicious not to savor." Skeptics of the cross-dressing story point to Susan Rosenstiel's poor credibility and say recklessly indiscreet behavior by Hoover would have been totally out of character whatever his sexuality. Most biographers consider the story of Mafia blackmail to be unlikely in light of the FBI's investigations of the Mafia. Along these lines, Truman Capote, who helped spread salacious rumors about Hoover, once remarked that he was more interested in making Hoover angry than determining whether the rumors were true.

Hoover hunted down and threatened anyone who made insinuations about his sexuality. He also spread destructive, unsubstantiated rumors that Adlai Stevenson was gay to damage the liberal governor's 1952 Presidential Campaign. His extensive secret files contained surveillance material on Eleanor Roosevelt's alleged lesbian lovers, speculated to be acquired for the purpose of blackmail.

The opening of Soviet archives revealed evidence that there was a Soviet campaign to discredit the United States which used allegations of homosexuality to discredit Hoover. Hoover's biographer Richard Hack reported that Hoover was romantically linked to actress Dorothy Lamour in the late 1930s and early 1940s, and that after Hoover's death, Lamour did not deny rumors that she had had an affair with Hoover in the years between her two marriages. Hack additionally reports that during the 1940s and 1950s, Hoover so often attended social events with Lela Rogers, the divorced mother of dancer and actress Ginger Rogers, that many of their mutual friends assumed the pair would eventually marry.

A Freedom of Information Act request filed by the *Washington Post* revealed that longtime Hollywood lobbyist Jack Valenti, a special assistant and confidant to President Lyndon Johnson, was investigated by Hoover's FBI in 1964. The investigation, which was carried out despite Valenti's two-year marriage to Johnson's personal secretary, focused on rumors that he was having a gay relationship with a commercial photographer friend.

Promiscuous OSS agent Mary Bancroft, mistress of both Allen Dulles and Henry Luce and daughter of a former publisher of The Wall Street Journal may have made an unsuccessful pass at J. Edgar for she calls him "... that Virgin Mary in pants."

Masonic connections

Hoover was a "devoted" Freemason and was coroneted a 33rd Degree Scottish Rite Freemason in the Southern Scottish Rite Jurisdiction. He was raised a Master Mason on November 9, 1920, in Federal Lodge No. 1, Washington, DC, just two months before his 26th birthday. During his 52 years with the Craft, he received medals, awards and decorations. Eventually in 1955, he was coroneted a Third Degree Inspector General Honorary and awarded the Scottish Rite's highest recognition, the Grand Cross of Honour in 1965 by the Southern Masonic Jurisdiction. Today a J. Edgar Hoover room exists within the House of the Temple. The room contains many of Hoover's personal papers and records.

Honors

- In 1938, Hoover received an honorary doctorate from Oklahoma Baptist University during the commencement exercises at which he was the speaker.
- In 1950, Britain's King George VI awarded Hoover an honorary knighthood in the Order of the British Empire. This entitled him to the postnominal letters KBE, but not to the use of the title "Sir" (because he was not a British citizen).
- In 1955, Hoover received the National Security Medal from President Eisenhower.
- In 1966, he received the Distinguished Service Award from President Lyndon B. Johnson for his service as director of the FBI.
- The FBI headquarters in Washington, DC, is named the J. Edgar Hoover Building.
- On Hoover's death, Congress voted its permission for his body to lie in state in the Capitol Rotunda, an honor that, at the time, had been accorded to twenty-one other Americans.
- Congress also voted that a memorial book be published to honor Hoover's memory. *J. Edgar Hoover: Memorial Tributes in the Congress of the United States and Various Articles and Editorials Relating to His Life and Work* was published in 1974.

Portrayals

J. Edgar Hoover has been portrayed many times in the media. Some notable portrayals include:

- In the 1971 Woody Allen movie *Bananas*, J. Edgar Hoover was portrayed by African-American actress, Dorothi Fox.
- Broderick Crawford and James Wainwright portrayed Hoover in the Larry Cohen film *The Private Files of J. Edgar Hoover* (1977).
- Hoover was portrayed by actor Dolph Sweet in the TV Miniseries *King* (1978).
- Hoover was portrayed by actor Ernest Borgnine in the TV-movie *Blood Feud* (1983).
- Hoover was portrayed by actor Vincent Gardenia in the TV-movie *Kennedy* (1983).
- Hoover was portrayed by actor Treat Williams in the TV-movie *J. Edgar Hoover* (1987).
- Hoover was portrayed by actor Kevin Dunn in the movie *Chaplin* (1992).

- Hoover was portrayed by actor Pat Hingle in the TV-movie *Citizen Cohn* (1992).
- Hoover was portrayed by actor Richard Dysart, both in the TV-movie *Marilyn & Bobby: Her Final Affair* (1993) and in Mario Van Peebles' 1995 film *Panther*.
- Hoover was portrayed by actor Bob Hoskins in the Oliver Stone drama *Nixon* (1995).
- Hoover was portrayed by Canadian actor David Fredericks in two episodes of *The X-Files*, as well as on its sister show *Millennium*.
- Hoover was originally portrayed by Eric Jordan Young in the musical *Dillinger, Public Enemey Number One*.
- Hoover was portrayed by actor Billy Crudup in the Michael Mann film *Public Enemies* (2009).
- In an *Animaniacs* short parodying World War II propaganda, Yakko, Wakko, and Dot are collecting silk stockings for the effort and Hoover comes to eagerly collect them personally.
- In the video game *Call of Cthulhu: Dark Corners of the Earth*, Hoover leads the raid on the Innsmouth gold refinery.
- Hoover serves as a major antagonist in James Ellroy's *Underworld USA Trilogy*.
- The character "J. Eager Believer" appears in the Firesign Theatre parody, *J-Men Forever*.
- Hoover serves as a major antagonist in John Birmingham's *Axis of Time Trilogy*.

Film

A biopic of Hoover's life is being made for release in 2012. The screenplay was written by Dustin Lance Black and it is being directed by Clint Eastwood. Leonardo DiCaprio is expected to play Hoover.

See also

- Anti-communism
- Federal Bureau of Investigation
- G-Man (slang)
- McCarthyism

Writings

J. Edgar Hoover was the nominal author of a number of books and articles. Although it is widely believed that all of these were ghostwritten by FBI employees, Hoover received the credit and royalties.

- Hoover, J. Edgar (1938). *Persons In Hiding* [1]. Gaunt Publishing. ISBN 1-56169-340-5.
- Hoover, J. Edgar (1958). *Masters of Deceit: The Story of Communism in America and How to Fight It* [2]. Kessinger Publishing. ISBN 1-4254-8258-9.
- Hoover, J. Edgar (1962). *A Study of Communism* [3]. Holt Rinehart & Winston. ISBN 0-03-031190-X.

Sources

- Ackerman, Kenneth D. (2007). *Young J. Edgar: Hoover, the Red Scare, and the Assault on Civil Liberties*. Carroll & Graf. ISBN 978-0-78671-775-0.
- Beverly, William (2003). *On the Lam; Narratives of Flight in J. Edgar Hoover's America*. University Press of Mississippi. ISBN 1-57806-537-2.
- Carter, David (2003). *Stonewall: The Riots That Sparked The Gay Revolution*. New York: St. Martin's Griffin. ISBN 978-0312342692.
- Charles, Douglas (2007). *J. Edgar Hoover and the Anti-interventionists: FBI Political Surveillance and the Rise of the Domestic Security State, 1939–1945*. Ohio State University Press. ISBN 978-0814210611.
- Garrow, David J. (1981). *The FBI and Martin Luther King, Jr., From 'Solo' to Memphis*. W.W.Norton. ISBN 0-393-01509-2.
- Gentry, Curt (1991). *J. Edgar Hoover: The Man and the Secrets*. Plume. ISBN 0-452-26904-0.
- Lowenthal, Max (1950). *The Federal Bureau of Investigation*. Greenwood Publishing Group. ISBN 0837157552.
- Powers, Richard Gid (1986). *Secrecy and Power: The Life of J. Edgar Hoover*. Free Press. ISBN 0029250609.
- Schott, Joseph L. (1975). *No Left Turns: The FBI in Peace & War*. Praeger. ISBN 0-275-33630-1.
- Stove, Robert J. (2003). *The Unsleeping Eye: Secret Police and Their Victims*. Encounter Books. ISBN 1-893554-66-X.
- Summers, Anthony (2003). *Official and Confidential:The Secret Life of J. Edgar Hoover*. Putnam Publishing Group. ISBN 0-399-13800-5.
- Swearingen, M. Wesley. *FBI Secrets An Agent's Expose*.
- Theoharis, Athan (1993). *From the Secret Files of J. Edgar Hoover*. Ivan R. Dee. ISBN 1-56663-017-7.

External links

- J. Edgar Hoover [4] at Find a Grave
- StraightDope.com [5] – 'The Straight Dope: Was J. Edgar Hoover a crossdresser?'
- Voices of Democracy [6] - 'Speech Before the House Committee on Un-American Activities 26 March 1947'
- *"American Gangster:* J. Edgar Hoover & COINTELPRO" [7] by Alan Kurtz (Blogcritics)
- Time.com [8] - 'The Truth about Hoover', December 22, 1975
- Wall Street Journal [9] – 'Hoover's Institution', Laurence H. Silberman, July 20, 2005
- Assassination Records Review Board [10] – Final Report: 1998
- Zpub.com [11] – 'J. Edgar Hoover Biography'
- J. Edgar Hoover's Watching You [12] - slideshow by *Life magazine*
- Yardley, Jonathan (June 26, 2004). "'No Left Turns': The G-Man's Tour de Force" [13]. *A review of the book "No Left Turns"* (Washington Post). Retrieved May 5, 2010.

Federal Bureau of Investigation

Federal Bureau of Investigation	
Common name	Federal Bureau of Investigation
Abbreviation	FBI
Seal of the Federal Bureau of Investigation	
Motto	*Fidelity, Bravery, Integrity*
Agency overview	
Formed	1908
Employees	33,652 (July 31, 2009)
Annual budget	7.9 billion USD (2010)
Legal personality	Governmental: Government agency
Jurisdictional structure	
Federal agency(Operations jurisdiction)	United States
Legal jurisdiction	As per operations jurisdiction.
Governing body	United States Congress
Constituting instrument	United States Code Title 28 Part II Chapter 33 [1]
General nature	• Federal law enforcement • Civilian agency
Operational structure	
Headquarters	J. Edgar Hoover Building, Washington, D.C.
Sworn members	13,249 (July 31, 2009)

Unsworn members	19,460 (July 31, 2009)
Agency executives	• Robert S. Mueller III, Director • Timothy P. Murphy, Deputy Director • List of FBI Directors, Other directors
Child agencies	• FBI Academy • FBI Laboratory • Criminal Justice Information Services (CJIS) • Critical Incident Response Group (CIRG) • Counterterrorism Division (CTD) • FBI Police (FBIP)
Major units	
Field offices	56: List of FBI Field Offices

Notables	
People	• John Edgar Hoover, Director, for being the founding director • William Mark Felt, former Federal Agent, for whistle blowing, Watergate scandal • Joseph Leo Gormley, Forensic Scientist, for expert testimony
Significant Operations	• COINTELPRO • Special Intelligence Service

Website
http://www.fbi.gov/
this information

The **Federal Bureau of Investigation (FBI)** is an agency of the United States Department of Justice that serves as both a federal criminal investigative body and an internal intelligence agency. The FBI has investigative jurisdiction over violations of more than 200 categories of federal crime. Its motto is the backronym of FBI, "Fidelity, Bravery, Integrity".

The FBI's headquarters, the J. Edgar Hoover Building, is located in Washington, D.C.. Fifty-six field offices are located in major cities throughout the United States as well as over 400 resident agencies in smaller cities and towns across the country. More than 50 international offices called "legal attachés" are in U.S. embassies worldwide.

Mission and priorities

In the fiscal year 2010, the FBI's total budget was approximately $7.9 billion, including $618 million in program increases to counter-terrorism, computer intrusions, surveillance, weapons of mass destruction, white-collar crime, and training programs.

The FBI was established in 1908 as the Bureau of Investigation (BOI). Its name was changed to the Federal Bureau of Investigation (FBI) in 1935.

The FBI's main goal is to protect and defend the United States against terrorist and foreign intelligence threats, to uphold and enforce the criminal laws of the United States, and to provide leadership and criminal justice services to federal, state, municipal, and international agencies and partners.

Currently, the FBI's top investigative priorities are:

1. Protect the United States from terrorist attack (see counter-terrorism);
2. Protect the United States against foreign intelligence operations and espionage (see counter-intelligence);
3. Protect the United States against cyber-based attacks and high-technology crimes (see cyber-warfare);
4. Combat public corruption at all levels;
5. Protect civil rights;
6. Combat transnational/national criminal organizations and enterprises (see organized crime);
7. Combat major white-collar crime;
8. Combat significant violent crime;
9. Support federal, state, local and international partners;
10. Upgrade technology for successful performance of the FBI's mission.

In August 2007, the top categories of lead criminal charges resulting from FBI investigations were:

1. Bank robbery and incidental crimes (107 charges)
2. Drugs (104 charges)
3. Attempt and conspiracy (81 charges)
4. Material involving sexual exploitation of minors (53 charges)
5. Mail fraud – frauds and swindles (51 charges)
6. Bank fraud (31 charges)
7. Prohibition of illegal gambling businesses (22 charges)
8. Fraud by wire, radio, or television (20 charges)
9. Hobbs Act (Robbery and extortion affecting interstate commerce) (17 charges)
10. Racketeer Influenced and Corrupt Organizations Act (RICO)-prohibited activities (17 charges)

Indian reservations

Serious crime, endemic in Indian Country, on Indian reservations, has historically been required by the 1885 Major Crimes Act, 18 U.S.C. §§1153, 3242, and court decisions to be investigated by the federal government, usually the Federal Bureau of Investigation, and prosecuted by United States Attorneys of the United States federal judicial district in which the reservation lies.

> The FBI has criminal jurisdiction in "Indian Country" (the official name for the program) for major crimes under the "Indian Country" Crimes Act (Title 18, United States Code, Section 1152), the Indian Country Major Crimes Act (Title 18, United States Code, Section 1153), and the Assimilative Crimes Act (Title 18, United States Code, Section 13). The 1994 Crime Act expanded federal criminal jurisdiction in Indian Country in such areas as guns, violent juveniles, drugs, and domestic violence. Under the Indian Gaming Regulatory Act, the FBI has jurisdiction over any criminal act directly related to casino gaming. The FBI also investigates civil rights violations, environmental crimes, public corruption, and government fraud occurring in "Indian Country."

The FBI does not specifically list crimes in Indian country as one of its priorities. Often serious crimes have been either poorly investigated or prosecution has been declined. Tribal courts were limited to sentences of one year or less, until on July 29, 2010 the Tribal Law and Order Act was enacted which in some measure reforms the system permitting tribal courts to impose sentences of up to three years provided proceedings are recorded and additional rights are extended to defendants.

Indian reservations often use their own investigative agency for crimes within its reservations, the Bureau of Indian Affairs, which is under the the US Department of the Interior.

Legal authority

The FBI's mandate is established in Title 28 of the United States Code (U.S. Code), Section 533, which authorizes the Attorney General to "appoint officials to detect... crimes against the United States." Other federal statutes give the FBI the authority and responsibility to investigate specific crimes.

J. Edgar Hoover began using wiretapping in the 1920s during

FBI badge and gun

Prohibition to arrest bootleggers. A 1927 case in which a bootlegger was caught through telephone tapping went to the United States Supreme Court, which ruled that the FBI could use wiretaps in its investigations and did not violate the Fourth Amendment as unlawful search and seizure as long as the FBI did not break in to a person's home to complete the tapping. After Prohibition's repeal, Congress passed the 1934 Communications Act, which outlawed non-consensual phone tapping, but allowed bugging. In another Supreme Court case, the court ruled in 1939 that due to the 1934 law, evidence the FBI obtained by phone tapping was inadmissible in court. A 1967 Supreme Court decision overturned the 1927 case allowing bugging, after which Congress passed the Omnibus Crime Control and Safe Streets Act, allowing public authorities to tap telephones during investigations, as long as they obtain a warrant beforehand.

The FBI's chief tool against organized crime is the Racketeer Influenced and Corrupt Organizations (RICO) Act. The FBI is also charged with the responsibility of enforcing compliance of the United States Civil Rights Act of 1964 and investigating violations of the act in addition to prosecuting such violations with the United States Department of Justice (DOJ). The FBI also shares concurrent jurisdiction with the Drug Enforcement Administration (DEA) in the enforcement of the Controlled Substances Act of 1970.

The USA PATRIOT Act increased the powers allotted to the FBI, especially in wiretapping and monitoring of Internet activity. One of the most controversial provisions of the act is the so-called *sneak and peek* provision, granting the FBI powers to search a house while the residents are away, and not requiring them to notify the residents for several weeks afterwards. Under the PATRIOT Act's provisions the FBI also resumed inquiring into the library records of those who are suspected of terrorism (something it had supposedly not done since the 1970s).

In the early 1980s, Senate hearings were held to examine FBI undercover operations in the wake of the Abscam controversy, which had allegations of entrapment of elected officials. As a result in following years a number of guidelines were issued to constrain FBI activities.

A March 2007 report by the inspector general of the Justice Department described the FBI's "widespread and serious misuse" of national security letters, a form of administrative subpoena used to demand records and data pertaining to individuals. The report said that between 2003 and 2005 the FBI had issued more than 140,000 national security letters, many involving people with no obvious connections to terrorism.

Information obtained through an FBI investigation is presented to the appropriate U.S. Attorney or Department of Justice official, who decides if prosecution or other action is warranted.

The FBI often works in conjunction with other Federal agencies, including the U.S. Coast Guard (USCG) and U.S. Customs and Border Protection (CBP) in seaport and airport security, and the National Transportation Safety Board in investigating airplane crashes and other critical incidents. Immigration and Customs Enforcement (ICE) is the only other agency with the closest amount of investigative power. In the wake of the September 11 attacks, the FBI maintains a role in most federal criminal investigations.

History

Beginnings: The Bureau of Investigation

In 1886, the Supreme Court, in *Wabash, St. Louis & Pacific Railway Company v. Illinois,* found that the states had no power to regulate interstate commerce. The resulting Interstate Commerce Act of 1887 created a Federal responsibility for interstate law enforcement. The Justice Department made little effort to relieve its staff shortage until the turn of the century, when Attorney General Charles Joseph Bonaparte reached out to other agencies, including the Secret Service, for investigators. But the Congress forbade this use of Treasury employees by Justice, passing a law to that effect in 1908. So the Attorney General moved to organize a formal Bureau of Investigation (BOI or BI), complete with its own staff of special agents. The Secret Service provided the Department of Justice 12 Special Agents and these agents became the first Agents in the new BOI. Thus, the first FBI agents were actually Secret Service agents. Its jurisdiction derived from the Interstate Commerce Act of 1887. The FBI grew out of this force of special agents created on July 26, 1908 during the presidency of Theodore Roosevelt. Its first official task was visiting and making surveys of the houses of prostitution in preparation for enforcing the "White Slave Traffic Act," or Mann Act, passed on June 25, 1910. In 1932, it was renamed the United States Bureau of Investigation. The following year it was linked to the Bureau of Prohibition and rechristened the Division of Investigation (DOI) before finally becoming an independent service within the Department of Justice in 1935. In the same year, its name was officially changed from the Division of Investigation to the present-day Federal Bureau of Investigation, or FBI.

The J. Edgar Hoover Directorship

The Director of the BOI, J. Edgar Hoover, became the first FBI Director and served for 48 years combined with the BOI, DOI, and FBI. After Hoover's death, legislation was passed limiting the tenure of future FBI Directors to a maximum of ten years. The Scientific Crime Detection Laboratory, or the FBI Laboratory, officially opened in 1932, largely as a result of Hoover's efforts. Hoover had substantial involvement in most cases and projects the FBI handled during his tenure.

J. Edgar Hoover, FBI Director from 1924 to 1972.

During the "War on Crime" of the 1930s, FBI agents apprehended or killed a number of notorious criminals who carried out kidnappings, robberies, and murders throughout the nation, including John Dillinger, "Baby Face" Nelson, Kate "Ma" Barker, Alvin "Creepy" Karpis, and George "Machine Gun" Kelly.

Other activities of its early decades included a decisive role in reducing the scope and influence of the Ku Klux Klan. Additionally, through the work of Edwin Atherton, the FBI claimed success in apprehending an entire army of Mexican neo-revolutionaries along the California border in the 1920s.

The FBI and national security

Beginning in the 1940s and continuing into the 1970s, the Bureau investigated cases of espionage against the United States and its allies. Eight Nazi agents who had planned sabotage operations against American targets were arrested, six of whom were executed (*Ex parte Quirin*). Also during this time, a joint US/UK code breaking effort (Venona)—with which the FBI was heavily involved—broke Soviet diplomatic and intelligence communications codes, allowing the US and British governments to read Soviet communications. This effort confirmed the existence of Americans working in the United States for Soviet intelligence. Hoover was administering this project but failed

Lester J. Gillis, also known as "Baby Face" Nelson.

to notify the Central Intelligence Agency (CIA) until 1952. Another notable case is the arrest of Soviet spy Rudolf Abel in 1957. The discovery of Soviet spies operating in the US allowed Hoover to pursue his longstanding obsession with the threat he perceived from the American Left, ranging from Communist Party of the United States of America (CPUSA) union organizers to American liberals with no revolutionary aspirations whatsoever.

The FBI and the civil-rights movement

During the 1950s and 1960s, FBI officials became increasingly concerned about the influence of civil rights leaders. In 1956, for example, Hoover took the rare step of sending an open letter denouncing Dr. T.R.M. Howard, a civil rights leader, surgeon, and wealthy entrepreneur in Mississippi who had criticized FBI inaction in solving recent murders of George W. Lee, Emmett Till, and other blacks in the South. The FBI carried out controversial domestic surveillance in an operation it called the COINTELPRO, which was short for *"CO*unter-*INTEL*ligence *PRO*gram." It aimed at investigating and disrupting dissident political organizations within the United States, including both militant and non-violent organizations, including the Southern Christian Leadership Conference, a leading civil rights organization.

Martin Luther King, Jr. was a frequent target of investigation. The FBI found no evidence of any crime, but attempted to use tapes of King involved in sexual activity for blackmail. In his 1991 memoirs, *Washington Post* journalist Carl Rowan asserted that the FBI had sent at least one anonymous letter to King encouraging him to commit suicide.

In March 1971, a Media, Pennsylvania FBI resident office was robbed; the thieves took secret files and distributed them to a range of newspapers including the *Harvard Crimson*. The files detailed the FBI's extensive COINTELPRO program, which included investigations into lives of ordinary citizens—including a black student group at a Pennsylvania military college and the daughter of Congressman Henry Reuss of Wisconsin. The country was "jolted" by the revelations, and the actions were denounced by members of Congress including House Majority Leader Hale Boggs. The phones of some members of Congress, including Boggs, had allegedly been tapped.

The FBI and Kennedy's assassination

When President John F. Kennedy was shot and killed, the jurisdiction fell to the local police departments until President Lyndon B. Johnson directed the FBI to take over the investigation. To ensure that there would never be any more confusion over who would handle homicides at the federal level, Congress passed a law that put investigations of deaths of federal officials within FBI jurisdiction.

The FBI and organized crime

In response to organized crime, on August 25, 1953, the Top Hoodlum Program was created. It asked all field offices to gather information on mobsters in their territories and to report it regularly to Washington for a centralized collection of intelligence on racketeers. After the Racketeer Influenced and Corrupt Organizations Act, or RICO Act, took effect, the FBI began investigating the former Prohibition-organized groups, which had become fronts for crime in major cities and even small towns. All of the FBI work was done undercover and from within these organizations using the provisions provided in the RICO Act and these groups were dismantled. Although Hoover initially denied the existence of a National Crime Syndicate in the United States, the Bureau later conducted operations against known organized crime syndicates and families, including those headed by Sam Giancana and John Gotti. The RICO Act is still used today for all organized crime and any individuals that might fall under the Act.

However, in 2003 a congressional committee called the FBI's organized crime informant program "one of the greatest failures in the history of federal law enforcement." Protecting an informant, the FBI allowed four innocent men to be convicted of murder while protecting a in March 1965. Three of the men were sentenced to death (which was later reduced to life in prison). The fourth defendant was sentenced to life in prison, where he spent three decades. In July 2007, U.S. District Judge Nancy Gertner in Boston found the bureau helped convict the four men of the March 1965 gangland murder of Edward "Teddy" Deegan. The U.S. Government was ordered to pay $100 million in damages to the four defendants.

Notable post-Hoover reorganizations

Special FBI teams

In 1984, the FBI formed an elite unit to help with problems that might arise at the 1984 Summer Olympics, particularly terrorism and major-crime. The formation of the team arose from the 1972 Summer Olympics at Munich, Germany when terrorists murdered Israeli Athletes. The team was named Hostage Rescue Team (HRT) and acts as the FBI lead for a national SWAT team in related procedures and all counter terrorism cases. Also formed in 1984 was the *Computer Analysis and Response Team* (CART). The end of the 1980s and the early part of the 1990s saw the reassignment of over 300 agents from foreign counter intelligence duties to violent crime, and the designation of violent crime as the sixth national priority. But with reduced cuts to other well-established departments, and because terrorism was no longer considered a threat after the end of the Cold War, the FBI became a tool of local police forces for tracking fugitives who had crossed state lines, a felony. The FBI Laboratory also helped develop DNA testing, continuing the pioneering role in identification that began with its fingerprinting system in 1924.

Notable efforts in the 1990s

Between 1993 and 1996, the FBI increased its counter-terrorism role in the wake of the first 1993 World Trade Center bombing in New York, New York and the Oklahoma City bombing in 1995, and the arrest of the Unabomber in 1996. Technological innovation and the skills of FBI Laboratory analysts helped ensure that all three of these cases were successfully prosecuted, but the FBI was also confronted by a public outcry in this period, which still haunts it today. In the early and late 1990s, the FBI role in the Ruby Ridge and Waco incidents caused an uproar over the killings. During the 1996 Summer Olympics in Atlanta, Georgia, the FBI was also criticized for its investigation on

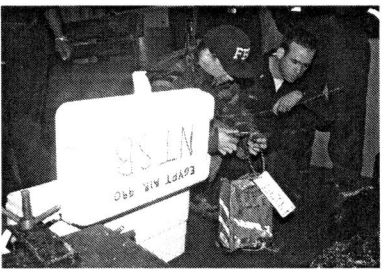

An FBI Agent tags the cockpit voice recorder from EgyptAir Flight 990 on the deck of the USS *Grapple* (ARS 53) at the crash site on November 13, 1999.

the Centennial Olympic Park bombing. It has settled a dispute with Richard Jewell, who was a private security guard at the venue, along with some media organizations, in regards to the leaking of his name during the investigation. After Congress passed the *Communications Assistance for Law Enforcement Act* (CALEA, 1994), the *Health Insurance Portability and Accountability Act* (HIPAA, 1996), and the *Economic Espionage Act* (EEA, 1996), the FBI followed suit and underwent a technological upgrade in 1998, just as it did with its CART team in 1991. Computer Investigations and Infrastructure Threat Assessment Center (CITAC) and the National Infrastructure Protection Center (NIPC) were created to deal with the increase in Internet-related problems, such as computer viruses, worms, and other malicious programs that might unleash havoc in the US. With these developments, the FBI increased its electronic surveillance in public safety and national security investigations, adapting to how telecommunications advancements changed the nature of such problems.

September 11th attacks

Within months of the September 11 attacks in 2001, FBI Director Robert Mueller, who had only been sworn in 1 week before the attacks, called for a re-engineering of FBI structure and operations. In turn, he made countering every federal crime a top priority, including the prevention of terrorism, countering foreign intelligence operations, addressing cyber security threats, other high-tech crimes, protecting civil rights, combating public corruption, organized crime, white-collar crime, and major acts of violent crime.

In February 2001, Robert Hanssen was caught selling information to the Russians. It was later learned that Hanssen, who had reached a high position within the FBI, had been selling intelligence since as early as 1979. He pleaded guilty to treason and received a life sentence in 2002, but the incident led many to question the security practices employed by the FBI. There was also a claim that Robert Hanssen might have contributed information that led to the September 11, 2001 attacks.

The 9/11 Commission's final report on July 22, 2004 stated that the FBI and Central Intelligence Agency (CIA) were both partially to blame for not pursuing intelligence reports which could have prevented the September 11, 2001 attacks. In its most damning assessment, the report concluded that the country had "not been well served" by either agency and listed numerous recommendations for changes within the FBI. While the FBI has acceded to most of the recommendations, including oversight by the new Director of National Intelligence, some former members of the 9/11 Commission publicly criticized the FBI in October 2005, claiming it was resisting any meaningful changes.

On July 8, 2007 the *Washington Post* published excerpts from UCLA Professor Amy Zegart's book *Spying Blind: The CIA, the FBI, and the Origins of 9/11*. The article reported that government documents show the CIA and FBI missed 23 potential chances to disrupt the terrorist attacks of September 11, 2001. The primary reasons for these failures included: agency cultures resistant to change and new ideas; inappropriate incentives for promotion; and a lack of cooperation between the FBI, CIA and the rest of the United States Intelligence Community. The article went on to also blame the FBI's decentralized structure which prevented effective communication and cooperation between different FBI offices. The article also claimed that the FBI has still not evolved into an effective counterterrorism or counterintelligence agency, due in large part to deeply ingrained cultural resistance to change within the FBI. For example, FBI personnel practices continue to treat all staff other than Special Agents as support staff, categorizing Intelligence Analysts alongside the FBI's auto mechanics and janitors.

Organizational structure

The FBI is organized into five functional branches and the Office of the Director, which contains most administrative offices. Each branch is managed by an Executive Assistant Director. Each office and division within the branch is managed by an Assistant Director.

- Office of the Director

  - Office of Congressional Affairs
  - Office of Equal Employment Opportunity Affairs
  - Office of the General Counsel
  - Office of Integrity and Compliance
  - Office of the Ombudsman
  - Office of Professional Responsibility
  - Office of Public Affairs
  - Inspection Division
  - Facilities and Logistics Services Division
  - Finance Division
  - Records Management Division
  - Resource Planning Office
  - Security Division

- National Security Branch

  - Counterintelligence Division
  - Counterterrorism Division
  - Directorate of Intelligence
  - Weapons of Mass Destruction Directorate

- Criminal, Cyber, Response, and Services Branch

  - Criminal Investigative Division
  - Cyber Division (Director: Gordon M Snow)
  - Critical Incident Response Group
  - Office of International Operations (Director: Joseph M. Demarest)
  - Office of Law Enforcement Coordination

- Human Resources Branch

  - Training Division
  - Human Resources Division

- Science and Technology Branch

  - Criminal Justice Information Services Division
  - Laboratory Division
  - Operational Technology Division

- Special Technologies and Applications Office
- Information and Technology Branch
  - Information Technology Operations Division
  - Office of IT Policy & Planning
  - Office of IT Program Management
  - Office of IT Systems Development
  - Office of the Chief Knowledge Officer

Infrastructure

The FBI is headquartered at the J. Edgar Hoover Building in Washington, D.C., with 56 field offices in major cities across the United States. The FBI also maintains over 400 resident agencies across the United States, as well as over 50 legal attachés at United States embassies and consulates. Many specialized FBI functions are located at facilities in Quantico, Virginia, as well as in Clarksburg, West Virginia. The FBI is in process of moving its Records Management Division, which processes Freedom of Information Act (FOIA) requests, to Winchester, Virginia.

J. Edgar Hoover Building, FBI Headquarters

The FBI Laboratory, established with the formation of the BOI, did not appear in the J. Edgar Hoover Building until its completion in 1974. The lab serves as the primary lab for most DNA, biological, and physical work. Public tours of FBI headquarters ran through the FBI laboratory workspace before the move to the J. Edgar Hoover Building. The services the lab conducts include *Chemistry, Combined DNA Index System* (CODIS), *Computer Analysis and Response, DNA Analysis, Evidence Response, Explosives, Firearms and Tool marks, Forensic Audio, Forensic Video, Image Analysis, Forensic Science Research, Forensic Science Training, Hazardous*

FBI Mobile Command Center, Washington Field Office

Materials Response, Investigative and Prospective Graphics, Latent Prints, Materials Analysis, Questioned Documents, Racketeering Records, Special Photographic Analysis, Structural Design, and *Trace Evidence.* The services of the FBI Laboratory are used by many state, local, and international agencies free of charge. The lab also maintains a second lab at the FBI Academy.

The FBI Academy, located in Quantico, Virginia, is home to the communications and computer laboratory the FBI utilizes. It is also where new agents are sent for training to become FBI Special

Agents. Going through the twenty-one week course is required for every Special Agent. It was first opened for use in 1972 on 385 acres (1.6 km²) of woodland. The Academy also serves as a classroom for state and local law enforcement agencies who are invited onto the premiere law enforcement training center. The FBI units that reside at Quantico are the *Field and Police Training Unit, Firearms Training Unit, Forensic Science Research and Training Center, Technology Services Unit* (TSU), *Investigative Training Unit, Law Enforcement Communication Unit, Leadership and Management Science Units* (LSMU), *Physical Training Unit, New Agents' Training Unit* (NATU), *Practical Applications Unit* (PAU), the *Investigative Computer Training Unit* and the "College of Analytical Studies."

In 2000, the FBI began the Trilogy project to upgrade its outdated information technology (IT) infrastructure. This project, originally scheduled to take three years and cost around $380 million, ended up going far over budget and behind schedule. Efforts to deploy modern computers and networking equipment were generally successful, but attempts to develop new investigation software, outsourced to Science Applications International Corporation (SAIC), were a disaster. Virtual Case File, or VCF, as the software was known, was plagued by poorly defined goals, and repeated changes in management. In January 2005, more than two years after the software was originally planned for completion, the FBI officially abandoned the project. At least $100 million (and much more by some estimates) was spent on the project, which was never operational. The FBI has been forced to continue using its decade-old Automated Case Support system, which is considered woefully inadequate by IT experts. In March 2005, the FBI announced it is beginning a new, more ambitious software project code-named Sentinel expected for completion by 2009.

Carnivore was an electronic evesdropping software system implemented by the Federal Bureau of Investigation during the Clinton administration that was designed to monitor email and electronic communications. After prolonged negative coverage in the press, the FBI changed the name of its system from "Carnivore" to the more benign-sounding "DCS1000." DCS is reported to stand for "Digital Collection System"; the system has the same functions as before. The Associated Press reported in mid-January 2005 that the FBI essentially abandoned the use of Carnivore in 2001, in favor of commercially available software, such as NarusInsight.

The Criminal Justice Information Services (CJIS) Division, located in Clarksburg, West Virginia. It is the youngest division of the FBI only being formed in 1991 and opening in 1995. The complex itself is the length of three football fields. Its purpose is to provide a main repository for information. Under the roof of the CJIS are the programs for the *National Crime Information Center* (NCIC), *Uniform Crime Reporting* (UCR), *Fingerprint Identification, Integrated Automated Fingerprint Identification System* (IAFIS), *NCIC 2000*, and the *National Incident-Based Reporting System* (NIBRS). Many state and local agencies use these systems as a source for their own investigations and contribute to the database using secure communications. FBI provides these tools of sophisticated identification and information services to local, state, federal, and international law enforcement agencies.

FBI is in charge of National Virtual Translation Center which provides "timely and accurate translations of foreign intelligence for all elements of the Intelligence Community."

Evidence processing controversies

In the 1990s, it turned out that the fingerprint unit of the FBI's crime lab had repeatedly done shoddy work. In some cases, the technicians, given evidence that actually cleared a suspect, reported instead that it proved the suspect guilty. Many cases had to be reopened when this pattern of errors was discovered.

FBI agents from the Washington Field Office with a tactical vehicle standing by for the 2009 Presidential Inauguration

Faulty bullet lead analysis testimony

For over 40 years, the FBI crime lab in Quantico believed lead in bullets had unique chemical signatures, and that by breaking them down and analyzing them, it was possible to match bullets, not only to a single batch of ammunition coming out of a factory, but to a single box of bullets. The National Academy of Sciences conducted an 18-month independent review of comparative bullet-lead analysis. In 2003, its National Research Council published a report calling into question 30 years of FBI testimony. It found the model the FBI used for interpreting results was deeply flawed and that the conclusion that bullet fragments could be matched to a box of ammunition so overstated, that it was misleading under the rules of evidence. One year later, the FBI decided to stop doing bullet lead analysis.

Of over 2,500 cases using this analysis, there are potentially hundreds or thousands where FBI lab technicians provided forensic testimony at criminal trials. In each case, the testimony was wrong and misleading. The U.S. Government has a legal obligation to notify defendants about any information that might help prove their innocence, even after they have been convicted. Only the FBI can identify the cases in which bullet lead analysis was performed, yet it has resisted releasing that information.

As a result of the *60 Minutes/Washington Post* investigation in November 2007, (two years later) the bureau said it will identify, review, and release all of the pertinent cases, and notify prosecutors about cases in which faulty testimony was given.

Personnel

As of December 31, 2009, the FBI had a total of 33,652 employees. That includes 13,412 special agents and 20,420 support professionals, such as intelligence analysts, language specialists, scientists, information technology specialists, and other professionals.

The Officer Down Memorial Page provides the biographies of 57 FBI officers killed in the line of duty from 1925 to 2009.

Hiring process

In order to apply to become an FBI agent, an applicant must be between the ages of 23 and 37. However, due to the decision in Robert P. Isabella v. Department of State and Office of Personnel Management, 2008 M.S.P.B. 146, preference eligible veterans may apply after age 37. In 2009, the Office of Personnel Management issued implementation guidance on the Isabella decision: OPM Letter [2] The applicant must also hold American citizenship, have a clean record, and hold a four-year bachelors degree. All FBI employees require a Top Secret (TS) security clearance, and

Agents in training on the FBI Academy firing range

in many instances, employees need a higher level, TS/SCI clearance. In order to get a security clearance, all potential FBI personnel must pass a series of Single Scope Background Investigations (SSBI), which are conducted by the Office of Personnel Management. Special Agents candidates also have to pass a Physical Fitness Test (PFT) that includes a 300-meter run, one-minute sit-ups, maximum push-ups, and a 1.5-mile (2.4 km) run. There is also a polygraph test personnel have to pass, with questions including possible drug use.

After potential special agent candidates are cleared with TS clearance and the Form SF-312 non-disclosure agreement is signed, they attend the FBI training facility located on Marine Corps Base Quantico in Virginia. Candidates spend approximately 21 weeks at the FBI Academy, where they receive over 500 classroom hours and over 1,000 simulated law enforcement hours to train. Upon graduation, new FBI Special Agents are placed all around the country and the world, depending on their areas of expertise. Professional support staff works out of one of the many support buildings the FBI maintains. However, any Agent or Support staff member can be transferred to any location for any length of time if their skills are deemed necessary at one of the FBI field offices or one of the 400 resident agencies the FBI maintains.

BOI and FBI directors

Main article: Director of the Federal Bureau of Investigation

FBI Directors are appointed by the President of the United States. They must be confirmed by the United States Senate and serve ten-year terms unless they resign or are fired by the President before their term is up. J. Edgar Hoover, appointed by Calvin Coolidge in 1924, was by far the longest-serving FBI Director, serving until his death in 1972. In 1968, Congress passed legislation as part of the Omnibus Crime Control and Safe Streets Act Pub.L. 90-351, June 19, 1968, 82 Stat. 197 that specified a 10-year term limit for future FBI Directors, as well as requiring Senate confirmation of appointees. As the incumbent, this legislation did not apply to Hoover, only to his successors. The current FBI Director is Robert Mueller, who was appointed in 2001 by George W. Bush.

The FBI director is responsible for the day-to-day operations at the FBI. Along with his deputies, the director makes sure cases and operations are handled correctly. The director also is in charge of making sure the leadership in any one of the FBI field offices are manned with qualified agents. Before the Intelligence Reform and Terrorism Prevention Act was passed in the wake of the September 11 attacks, the FBI director would brief the President of the United States on any issues that arise from within the FBI. Since then, the director now reports to the Director of National Intelligence (DNI) who in turn reports to the President.

Weapons

An FBI Special Agent is issued a Glock Model 22 or 23 pistol in .40 S&W caliber upon successful completion of their training at the FBI Academy. The Glock Model 27 in .40 S&W caliber is authorized as a secondary weapon. Special Agents are authorized to purchase and qualify with the Glock Model 21 in .45 ACP caliber for duty carry. Special Agents of the FBI HRT (Hostage Rescue Team) are issued the Springfield Model 1911A1 .45 ACP Pistol. (*See article FBI Special Weapons and Tactics Teams*) The FBI has a list of authorized weapons for duty carry. The FBI also issues the SIG Sauer P228.

Publications

The FBI Law Enforcement Bulletin is published monthly by the FBI *Law Enforcement Communication Unit*, with articles of interest to state and local law enforcement personnel. First published in 1932 as *Fugitives Wanted by Police*, the FBI Law Enforcement Bulletin covers topics including law enforcement technology and issues, such as crime mapping and use of force, as well as recent criminal justice research, and Vi-CAP alerts, on wanted suspects and key cases.

The FBI also publishes some reports for both law enforcement personnel as well as regular citizens covering topics including law enforcement, terrorism, cybercrime, white-collar crime, violent crime, and statistics. However, the vast majority of Federal government publications covering these topics are published by the Office of Justice Programs agencies of the United States Department of Justice, and disseminated through the National Criminal Justice Reference Service.

Crime statistics

In the 1920s, the FBI began issuing crime reports by gathering numbers from local police departments. Due to limitations of this system found during the 1960s and 1970s—victims often simply did not report crimes to the police in the first place—the Department of Justice developed an alternate method of tallying crime, the victimization survey.

Uniform Crime Reports

Main article: Uniform Crime Reports

The Uniform Crime Reports (UCR) compile data from over 17,000 law enforcement agencies across the country. They provide detailed data regarding the volume of crimes to include arrest, clearance (or closing a case), and law enforcement officer information. The UCR focuses its data collection on violent crimes, hate crimes, and property crimes. Created in the 1920s, the UCR system has not proven to be as *uniform* as its name implies. The UCR data only reflect the most serious offense in the case of connected crimes and has a very restrictive definition of rape. Since about 93% of the data submitted to the FBI is in this format, the UCR stands out as the publication of choice as most states require law enforcement agencies to submit this data.

Preliminary Annual *Uniform Crime Report* for 2006 was released on June 4, 2006. The report shows violent crime offenses rose 1.3%, but the number of property crime offenses decreased 2.9% compared to 2005.

National Incident Based Reporting System

Main article: National Incident Based Reporting System

The National Incident Based Reporting System (NIBRS) crime statistics system aims to address limitations inherent in UCR data. The system used by law enforcement agencies in the United States for collecting and reporting data on crimes. Local, state, and federal agencies generate NIBRS data from their records management systems. Data is collected on every incident and arrest in the Group A offense category. The Group A offenses are 46 specific crimes grouped in 22 offense categories. Specific facts about these offenses are gathered and reported in the NIBRS system. In addition to the Group A offenses, eleven Group B offenses are reported with only the arrest information. The NIBRS system is in greater detail than the summary-based UCR system. As of 2004, 5,271 law enforcement agencies submitted NIBRS data. That amount represents 20% of the United States population and 16% of the crime statistics data collected by the FBI.

FBI files on specific persons

It is possible to obtain a copy of an FBI file on oneself, on a living person who gives you permission to do so, or on a deceased individual, through the U.S. Freedom of Information Act. The FBI has generated files on numerous celebrities including Elvis Presley, Frank Sinatra, John Denver, John Lennon, Jane Fonda, Groucho Marx, Charlie Chaplin, MC5, Lou Costello, Sonny Bono, Bob Dylan, Michael Jackson, Mickey Mantle, and Gene Autry. The FBI also profiled Jack the Ripper in 1988 but his identity still remains unproven today. To quote Howard Zinn, "if I found that the FBI did not have any dossier on me, it would have been tremendously embarrassing and I wouldn't have been able to face my friends."

Media portrayal

Main article: FBI portrayal in the media

The FBI has been frequently depicted in popular media since the 1930s. The Bureau has participated to varying degrees, which has ranged from direct involvement in the creative process itself in order to present the FBI in a favorable light, to providing consultation on operations and closed cases.

Notable people

- Edwin Atherton
- Ed Bethune
- J. Edgar Hoover
- Richard Miller
- Loy F. Weaver
- William Mark Felt
- John P. O'Neill
- Melvin Purvis
- Joseph D. Pistone
- Sue Thomas

See also

- Bureau of Alcohol, Tobacco, Firearms, and Explosives (ATF)
- Drug Enforcement Administration (DEA)
- FBI Honorary Medals
- Federal law enforcement in the United States
- Immigration and Customs Enforcement (ICE)
- Law enforcement in the United States
- State bureau of investigation

- United States Marshals Service
- United States Secret Service (USSS)
- U.S. Diplomatic Security Service (DSS)
- FBI Victims Identification Project

Further reading

- HSI BOOK Government HSI Files
- Charles, Douglas M. (2007). *J. Edgar Hoover and the Anti-interventionists: FBI Political Surveillance and the Rise of the Domestic Security State, 1939–1945*. Columbus, Ohio: The Ohio State University Press. ISBN 0814210619.
- Kessler, Ronald (1993). *The FBI: Inside the World's Most Powerful Law Enforcement Agency*. Pocket Books Publications. ISBN 0-6717-8657-1.
- Powers, Richard Gid (1983). *G-Men, Hoover's FBI in American Popular Culture*. Southern Illinois University Press. ISBN 0-8093-1096-1.
- Sullivan, William (1979). *The Bureau: My Thirty Years in Hoover's FBI*. Norton. ISBN 0-393-01236-0.
- Theoharis, Athan G.; John Stuart Cox (1988). *The Boss: J. Edgar Hoover and the Great American Inquisition*. Temple University Press. ISBN 0-87722-532-X.
- Theoharis, Athan G.; Tony G. Poveda, Susan Rosenfeld, Richard Gid Powers (2000). *The FBI: A Comprehensive Reference Guide*. Checkmark Books. ISBN 0-8160-4228-4.
- Theoharis, Athan G. (2004). *The FBI and American Democracy: A Brief Critical History*. Kansas: University Press. ISBN 0-7006-1345-5.
- Tonry, Michael (ed.) (2000). *The Handbook of Crime & Punishment*. Oxford University Press. ISBN 0-19-514060-5.
- Trahair, Richard C. S. (2004). *Encyclopedia of Cold War Espionage, Spies, and Secret Operations*. Ballentine: Greenwood Press. ISBN 0-313-31955-3.
- Williams, David (1981). "The Bureau of Investigation and its Critics, 1919–1921: the Origins of Federal Political Surveillance" [3]. *Journal of American History* (Organization of American Historians) **68** (3): 560–579. doi:10.2307/1901939 [4].

External links

- Official FBI website [5]
- Church Committee Report [6], Vol. 6, "Federal Bureau of Investigation." 1975 congressional inquiry into American intelligence operations.
- FBI Disclosures under Freedom of Information Act [7]
- Official FBI Recruiting [8]
- Federal Bureau of Investigation at FAS.org [9]
- The FBI ...Past, Present & Future [10]

Geographical coordinates: 38°53′40″N 77°01′28″W

Early Life and Education

Eastern Market, Washington, D.C.

Eastern Market	
U.S. National Register of Historic Places	
Location:	7th and C Streets, SE, Washington, D.C.
Coordinates:	38°53'11"N 76°59'48"W
Built/Founded:	1871
Architect:	Adolf Cluss, Snowden Ashford
Architectural style(s):	Italianate
Governing body:	Local
Added to NRHP:	May 27, 1971
NRHP Reference#:	71000998

The **Eastern Market** is a public market in the Capitol Hill neighborhood of Washington, D.C., housed in a 19th century brick building. It is located on 7th Street SE, a few blocks east of the U.S. Capitol between North Carolina Avenue SE and C Street SE. The Eastern Market is on the National Register of Historic Places. Badly damaged by an early-morning fire on April 30, 2007, the market building reopened on June 26, 2009.

Eastern Market also marks a smaller community within the Capitol Hill neighborhood by serving as an anchor point for other nearby stores and restaurants. It is served by a nearby eponymous stop on the Washington Metro Blue and Orange Lines.

History

The Eastern Market was designed by Adolf Cluss and was in continuous operation as a public market from 1873 until April 30, 2007. It was the first in a larger city-owned public market system, initiated to urbanize Washington, make orderly provision for the distribution of goods to its residents, and serve as a magnet to draw residents. The Market was expanded in 1908 with the addition of the Center and North Halls designed by Snowden Ashford. At the start of the 20th century, the Eastern Market was recognized as the unofficial "town center" of Capitol Hill. It is the last of the city's public markets still in operation.

Interior of Eastern Market

The market nearly closed because of competition from grocery store chains and a decline in neighborhood investment. Local residents fought to keep it open, and the area has since been revitalized. Eastern Market continues to host a thriving farmers' market. Fresh meats, baked goods and cheeses are sold from indoor stalls, and fresh produce is sold outside along the tent-covered sidewalk. Artisans and antiques dealers also sell their goods outside the market on weekends, making Eastern Market a popular stop for locals as well as tourists. The Market 5 Gallery organizes art shows, music and theater performances, and craft sales at the Eastern Market.

About

Eastern Market is part of ward 6 of DC's 8 wards. Tommy Wells is the current councilman of the area. Nestled in what is known as the Capitol Hill neighborhood. This is the area bounded by North and South Capitol Streets on the west, 15th street on the east and H street on the north and by the Southeast southwest Freeway. Working adults, singles and families with young children largely populate the neighborhood of town houses. This is an old fashioned neighborhood where residents can do their shopping on a daily basis. Currently managed under the guidance of interim manager Barry Margeson. The flea market of Eastern Market has one of the most diverse markets in the nation. It host up to 100 exhibitors from five continents.

The market participates in a host of holiday and seasonal events to attract visitors, award prices and offer certificates and include those who live in the area into the community. Presently Eastern Market is being met with proposals for renovation. The goal of the renovation plan is to link 8th street's [Barrack Row] and Eastern Market in order to create a community gathering space.

Beyond the Flea Market. Eastern Market is also known for its cultural attractions, which include the Folger Shakespeare Library and theater and the Library of Congress.

Eastern Market has been featured in scenes of movies including Body of Lies (2008) and Mercury Rising (1998).

2007 fire

Eastern Market was badly damaged by an early-morning 3-alarm fire on April 30, 2007. The heaviest damage was in the South Hall of the market, the portion occupied by vendors' stalls, where the roof suffered a partial collapse. *The Washington Post* has described the South Hall as "gutted so badly that birds can now fly in through the front windows and out the back ones." Following the fire, Washington D.C. Mayor Adrian Fenty promised to rebuild the market. The outdoor weekend market was disrupted but never closed. Many of the food vendors re-opened for business within weeks of the fire, selling their products outside of the building. In August 2007, the city completed a temporary market annex, known as the "East Hall," on the opposite side of 7th Street, on the grounds of Hine Junior High School. This housed the vendors until the reopening of the market building, with a ribbon-cutting on June 26, 2009.

Fire damage inside the South Hall

The origin of the fire is officially filed as "undetermined". However, former D.C. fire investigators Gerald Pennington and Greg Bowyer have suggested the fire was deliberately set by suspect Joel Ramos.

Post 2007 fire

Eastern Market reopened its doors the summer of 2009 after two years of reconstruction work. On March 9, 2010 the renovation of the market received the Outstanding Project Award from the Structural Engineering Association of Metropolitan Washington in April. The Market has already received an "Honor Award" in the design category and has been recognized as a National Finalist by the American Counsel of Engineering Companies of Metropolitan Washington.

Interior of Eastern Market in 2010

The restoration process was a detailed and challenging effort to re-purpose and salvage various components of the critically damaged building. Among many innovative improvements, the historic roof was restored and state of the art equipment was installed. The design allowed the previously hidden historic skylight to be reintroduced as a prominent architectural feature of the new Eastern Market South Hall. Renovation was overseen by the [Department of Real Estate Services] and coordinated with Robert Silman Associates and Quinn Evans Architects.

Mayor Adrian Fenty moved to have 7th street through fare in front of the market closed to vehicle traffic on the weekends to function as a "pedestrian plaza."

External links

- Eastern Market Official Website [1]
- Eastern Market historical landmark, at the National Park Service site [2]
- Eastern Market Community Advisory Committee site [3]
- Save Eastern Market [4], a website dedicated to news and information about the fire and rebuilding effort
- YouTube video [5] HD video of the Eastern Market shortly after re-opening
- http://www.voiceofthehill.com/FRONT-PAGE/Eastern-Market-set-to-reopen-June-26
- http://www.easternmarket.net/

Library of Congress

Library of Congress	
Established	1800
Location	Washington, D.C.
Branches	N/A
Collection	
Size	21,814,555 cataloged books in the Library of Congress classification system 11,701,147 books in large type and raised characters, incunabula (books printed before 1501), monographs and serials, music, bound newspapers, pamphlets, technical reports, and other printed material, and 109,029,796 items in the nonclassified (special) collections 142,544,498 total Items
Access and use	
Circulation	Library does not publicly circulate
Population served	535 members of the United States Congress, their staff, and members of the public
Other information	
Budget	$613,496,414
Director	James H. Billington (Librarian of Congress)
Staff	3,624
Website	http://www.loc.gov

The **Library of Congress** is the research library of the United States Congress, *de facto* national library of the United States, and the oldest federal cultural institution in the United States. Located in three buildings in Washington, D.C., it is the largest library in the world by shelf space and number of books. The head of the Library is the Librarian of Congress, currently James H. Billington.

The Library of Congress was established by Congress in 1800, and was housed in the United States Capitol for most of the 19th century. After much of the original collection had been destroyed during the War of 1812, Thomas Jefferson sold 6487 books, his entire personal collection, to the library in 1815. After a period of decline during the mid-19th century the Library of Congress began to grow rapidly in both size and importance after the American Civil War, culminating in the construction of a separate library building and the transference of all copyright deposit holdings to the Library. During the rapid expansion of the 20th century the Library of Congress assumed a preeminent public role, becoming a "library of last resort" and expanding its mission for the benefit of scholars and the American people.

The Library's primary mission is researching inquiries made by members of Congress through the Congressional Research Service. Although it is open to the public, only Members of Congress, Supreme Court justices and other high-ranking government officials may check out books. As the *de facto* national library, the Library of Congress promotes literacy and American literature through projects such as the American Folklife Center, American Memory, Center for the Book and Poet Laureate.

History

Construction of the Thomas Jefferson Building, from July 8, 1888 to May 15, 1894.

Origins and Jefferson's contribution (1800–1851)

The Library of Congress was established on April 24, 1800, when President John Adams signed an Act of Congress providing for the transfer of the seat of government from Philadelphia to the new capital city of Washington. Part of the legislation appropriated $5,000 "for the purchase of such books as may be necessary for the use of Congress ..., and for fitting up a suitable apartment for containing them...." Books were ordered from London and the collection, consisting of 740 books and 30 maps, was housed in the new Capitol. Although the collection covered a variety of topics, the bulk of the materials were legal in nature, reflecting Congress' role as a maker of laws.

Thomas Jefferson played an important role in the Library's early formation, signing into law on January 26, 1802 the first law establishing the structure of the Library of Congress. The law established the presidentially appointed post of Librarian of Congress and a Joint Committee on the Library to regulate and oversee the Library, as well as giving the president and vice president the ability to borrow books. The Library of Congress was destroyed in August 1814, when invading British troops set fire to the Capitol building and the small library of 3,000 volumes within.

Within a month, former President Jefferson offered his personal library as a replacement. Jefferson had spent 50 years accumulating a wide variety of books, including ones in foreign languages and volumes of philosophy, science, literature, and other topics not normally viewed as part of a legislative library, such as cookbooks, writing that, "I do not know that it contains any branch of science which Congress would wish to exclude from their collection; there is, in fact, no subject to which a Member of Congress may not have occasion to refer." In January 1815, Congress accepted Jefferson's offer, appropriating $23,950 for his 6,487 books.

Weakening (1851–1865)

The antebellum period was difficult for the Library. During the 1850s the Smithsonian Institution's librarian Charles Coffin Jewett aggressively tried to move that organization towards becoming the United States' national library. His efforts were blocked by the Smithsonian's Secretary Joseph Henry, who advocated a focus on scientific research and publication and favored the Library of Congress' development into the national library. Henry's dismissal of Jewett in July 1854 ended the Smithsonian's attempts to become the national library, and in 1866 Henry transferred the Smithsonian's forty thousand-volume library to the Library of Congress.

On December 24, 1851 the largest fire in the Library's history destroyed 35,000 books, about two–thirds of the Library's 55,000 book collection, including two–thirds of Jefferson's original transfer. Congress in 1852 quickly appropriated $168,700 to replace the lost books but not for the acquisition of new materials. This marked the start of a conservative period in the Library's administration under Librarian John Silva Meehan and Joint Committee Chairman James A. Pearce, who worked to restrict the Library's activities. In 1857, Congress transferred the Library's public document distribution activities to the Department of the Interior and its international book exchange program to the Department of State. Abraham Lincoln's political appointment of John G. Stephenson as Librarian of Congress in 1861 further weakened the Library; Stephenson's focus was on non-library affairs, including service as a volunteer aide-de-camp at the battles of Chancellorsville and Gettysburg during the American Civil War. By the conclusion of the war, the Library of Congress had a staff of seven for a collection of 80,000 volumes. The centralization of copyright offices into the United States Patent Office in 1859 ended the Library's thirteen year role as a depository of all copyrighted books and pamphlets.

Spofford's expansion (1865–1897)

The Library of Congress inside the U.S. Capitol Building c. 1890

The Library of Congress reasserted itself during the latter half of the 19th century under Librarian Ainsworth Rand Spofford, who directed the Library from 1865 to 1897. Aided by an overall expansion of the federal government and a favorable political climate, Spofford built broad bipartisan support for the Library as a national library and a legislative resource, began comprehensively collecting Americana and American literature, and led the construction of a new building to house the Library, and transformed the Librarian of Congress position into one of strength and independence. Between 1865 and 1870, Congress appropriated funds for the construction of the Thomas Jefferson Building, placed all copyright registration and deposit activities under the Library's control, and restored the Library's international book exchange. The Library also acquired the vast libraries of both the Smithsonian and historian Peter Force, strengthening its scientific and Americana collections significantly. By 1876, the Library of Congress had 300,000

volumes and was tied with Boston Public Library as the nation's largest library. When the Library moved from the Capitol building to its new headquarters in 1897, it had over 840,000 volumes, 40% of which had been acquired through copyright deposit.

A year before the Library's move to its new location, the Joint Library Committee held a session of hearings to assess the condition of the Library and plan for its future growth and possible reorganization. Spofford and six experts sent by the American Library Association, including future Librarian of Congress Herbert Putnam and Melvil Dewey of the New York State Library, testified before the committee that the Library should continue its expansion towards becoming a true national library. Based on the hearings and with the assistance of Senators Justin Morrill of Vermont and Daniel Voorhees of Indiana, Congress more than doubled the Library's staff from

Some of the Library of Congress' holdings awaiting shelving inside the newly opened Thomas Jefferson Building

42 to 108 and established new administrative units for all aspects of the Library's collection. Congress also strengthened the office of Librarian of Congress to govern the Library and make staff appointments, as well as requiring Senate approval for presidential appointees to the position.

Post-reorganization (1897–1939)

Main Library of Congress building at the start of the 20th century

The Library of Congress, spurred by the 1897 reorganization, began to grow and develop more rapidly. Spofford's successor John Russell Young, though only in office for two years, overhauled the Library's bureaucracy, used his connections as a former diplomat to acquire more materials from around the world, and established the Library's first assistance programs for the blind and physically disabled. Young's successor Herbert Putnam held the office for forty years from 1899 to 1939, entering into the position two years before the Library became the first in the United States to hold one million volumes. Putnam focused his efforts on making the Library more accessible and useful for the public and for other libraries. He instituted the interlibrary loan service, transforming the Library of Congress into what he referred to as a "library of last resort". Putnam also expanded Library access to "scientific investigators and duly qualified individuals" and began publishing primary sources for the benefit of scholars.

Putnam's tenure also saw increasing diversity in the Library's acquisitions. In 1903 he persuaded President Theodore Roosevelt to transfer by executive order the papers of the Founding Fathers from the State Department to the Library of Congress. Putnam expanded foreign acquisitions as well, including the 1904 purchase of a four-thousand volume library of Indica, the 1906 purchase of G. V.

Yudin's eighty-thousand volume Russian library, the 1908 Schatz collection of early opera librettos, and the early 1930s purchase of the Russian Imperial Collection, consisting of 2,600 volumes from the library of the Romanov family on a variety of topics. Collections of Hebraica and Chinese and Japanese works were also acquired. Congress even took the initiative to acquire materials for the Library in one occasion, when in 1929 Congressman Ross Collins of Mississippi successfully proposed the $1.5 million purchase of Otto Vollbehr's collection of incunabula, including one of four remaining perfect vellum copies of the Gutenberg Bible.

In 1914 Putnam established the Legislative Reference Service as a separative administrative unit of the Library. Based in the Progressive era's philosophy of science as a problem-solver, and modeled after successful research branches of state legislatures, the LRS would provide informed answers to Congressional research inquiries on almost any topic. In 1965 Congress passed an act allowing the Library of Congress to establish a trust fund board to accept donations and endowments, giving the Library a role as a patron of the arts. The Library received the donations and endowments of prominent individuals such

A copy of the Gutenberg Bible on display at the Library of Congress

as John D. Rockefeller, James B. Wilbur and Archer M. Huntington. Gertrude Clarke Whittall donated five Stradivarius violins to the Library and Elizabeth Sprague Coolidge's donations paid for a concert hall within the Library of Congress building and the establishment of an honorarium for the Music Division. A number of chairs and consultantships were established from the donations, the most well-known of which is the Poet Laureate Consultant.

The Library's expansion eventually filled the Library's Main Building despite shelving expansions in 1910 and 1927, forcing the Library to expand into a new structure. Congress acquired nearby land in 1928 and approved construction of the Annex Building (later the John Adams Building) in 1930. Although delayed during the Depression years, it was completed in 1938 and opened to the public in 1939.

Modern history (1939–)

When Putnam retired in 1939, President Franklin D. Roosevelt appointed Archibald MacLeish as his successor. Occupying the post from 1939 to 1944 during the height of World War II, MacLeish became the most visible Librarian of Congress in the Library's history. MacLeish encouraged librarians to oppose totalitarianism on behalf of democracy; dedicated the South Reading Room of the Adams Building to Thomas Jefferson, commissioning artist Ezra Winter to paint four themed murals for the room; and established a "democracy alcove" in the Main Reading Room of the Jefferson Building for important documents such as the Declaration, Constitution and Federalist Papers. Even the Library of Congress assisted during the war effort, ranging from the storage of the Declaration of Independence and the United States Constitution in Fort Knox for safekeeping to researching weather data on the Himalayas for Air Force pilots. MacLeish resigned in 1944 to become Assistant Secretary of State, and President Harry Truman appointed Luther H. Evans as Librarian of Congress. Evans, who served until 1953, expanded the Library's acquisitions, cataloging and bibliographic services as much as the fiscal-minded Congress would allow, but his primary achievement was the creation of Library of Congress Missions around the world. Missions played a variety of roles in the postwar world: the mission in San Francisco assisted participants in the meeting that established the United Nations, the mission in Europe acquired European publications for the Library of Congress and other American libraries, and the mission in Japan aided in the creation of the National Diet Library.

Erotica, mural painting by George Randolph Barse (1861–1938) in the Library of Congress

Elihu Vedder's *Minerva of Peace mosaic*

Evans' successor L. Quincy Mumford took over in 1953. Mumford's tenure, lasting until 1974, saw the initiation of the construction of the James Madison Memorial Building, the third Library of Congress building. Mumford directed the Library during a period of increased educational spending, the windfall of which allowed the Library to devote energies towards establishing new acquisition centers abroad, including in Cairo and New Delhi. In 1967 the Library began experimenting with book preservation techniques through a Preservation Office, which grew to become the largest library research and conservation effort in the United States. Mumford's administration also saw the last major public debate about the Library of Congress' role as both a legislative library and a national library. A 1962 memorandum by Douglas Bryant of the Harvard University Library, compiled at the request of Joint Library Committee chairman Claiborne Pell, proposed a number of institutional reforms, including expansion of national activities and services and various organizational changes, all of which would shift the Library more towards its national role over its legislative role. Bryant even suggested possibly changing the name of the Library of Congress, which was rebuked by Mumford as "unspeakable violence to tradition". Debate continued within the library community until the Legislative Reorganization Act of 1970 shifted the Library back towards its legislative roles, placing greater focus on research for Congress and congressional committees and renaming the Legislative Reference Service to the Congressional Research Service.

After Mumford retired in 1974, Gerald Ford appointed Daniel J. Boorstin as Librarian. Boorstin's first challenge was the move to the new Madison Building, which took place between 1980 and 1982. The move released pressures on staff and shelf space, allowing Boorstin to focus on other areas of Library administration such as acquisitions and collections. Taking advantage of steady budgetary growth, from $116 million in 1975 to over $250 million by 1987, Boorstin actively participated in enhancing ties with scholars, authors, publishers, cultural leaders, and the business community. His active and prolific role changed the post of Librarian of Congress so that by the time he retired in 1987, the *New York Times* called it "perhaps the leading intellectual public position in the nation." Ronald Reagan appointed James H. Billington as the thirteenth Librarian of Congress in 1987, a post he holds as of 2010. Billington took advantage of new technological advancements and the Internet to link the Library to educational institutions around the country in 1991. The end of the Cold War also enabled the Library to develop relationships with newly open Eastern European nations, helping them to establish parliamentary libraries of their own.

In the mid-1990s, under Billington's leadership, the Library of Congress began to pursue the development of what it called a "National Digital Library," part of an overall strategic direction that has been somewhat controversial within the library profession. In late November 2005, the Library announced intentions to launch the World Digital Library, digitally preserving books and other objects from all world cultures. In April 2010, it announced plans to archive all public communication on Twitter, including all communication since Twitter's launch in March 2006.

Holdings

The collections of the Library of Congress include more than 32 million cataloged books and other print materials in 470 languages; more than 61 million manuscripts; the largest rare book collection in North America, including the rough draft of the Declaration of Independence, a Gutenberg Bible (one of only four perfect vellum copies known to exist); over 1 million US government publications; 1 million issues of world newspapers spanning the past three centuries; 33,000 bound newspaper volumes; 500,000 microfilm reels; over 6,000 comic book titles; films; 4.8 million maps; sheet music; 2.7 million sound recordings; more than 13.7 million prints and photographic images including fine and popular art pieces and architectural drawings; the Betts Stradivarius; and the Cassavetti Stradivarius.

Library of Congress, Thomas Jefferson Building

The Library developed a system of book classification called Library of Congress Classification (LCC), which is used by most US research and university libraries, although most public libraries continue to use the Dewey decimal system[citation needed].

The Library serves as a legal repository for copyright protection and copyright registration, and as the base for the

The Great Hall interior

United States Copyright Office. Regardless of whether they register their copyright, all publishers are required to submit two complete copies of their published works to the Library if requested—this requirement is known as *mandatory deposit*. Parties wishing not to publish, need only submit one copy of their work. Nearly 22,000 new items published in the U.S. arrive every business day at the Library. Contrary to popular belief, however, the Library does not retain all of these works in its permanent collection, although it does add an average of 10,000 items per day. Rejected items are used in trades with other libraries around the world, distributed to federal agencies, or donated to schools, communities, and other organizations within the United States. As is true of many similar libraries, the Library of Congress retains copies of every publication in the English language that is deemed significant.

The Library of Congress states that its collection fills about 745 miles (1,199 km), while the British Library reports about 388 miles (625 km) of shelves. The Library of Congress holds about 130 million items with 29 million books against approximately 150 million items with 25 million books for the British Library.

The Library of Congress is usually quoted as occupying, if digitized and stored as plain text, 20 petabytes of information (10 in other quotations), based on the amount of cataloged books in the Library of Congress classification system (20 million in 2007) and estimating one megabyte of text per book. This leads many people to conclude that 20 petabytes is equivalent to the entire holdings of the Library, but this is misleading because the Library contains many items in addition to books, such as manuscripts, photographs, maps, and sound recordings, that, if digitized, would amount to much more information. The Library currently has no plans for systematic digitization of any significant portion of its books.

The Library makes millions of digital objects, comprising tens of petabytes, available at its American Memory site. American Memory is a source for public domain image resources, as well as audio, video, and archived Web content. Nearly all of the lists of holdings, the *catalogs* of the library, can be consulted directly on its web site. Librarians all over the world consult these catalogs, through the Web or through other media better suited to their needs, when they need to catalog for their collection a book published in the United States. They use the Library of Congress Control Number to make sure of the exact identity of the book.

The Library of Congress also provides an online archive of the proceedings of the U.S. Congress at THOMAS, including bill text, Congressional Record text, bill summary and status, the Congressional Record Index, and the United States Constitution.

The Library also administers the National Library Service for the Blind and Physically Handicapped, a talking and braille library program provided to more than 766,000 Americans.

Buildings of the Library

The Library of Congress is physically housed in three buildings on Capitol Hill and a conservation center in rural Virginia. The Library's Capitol Hill buildings are all connected by underground passageways, so that a library user need pass through security only once in a single visit. The library also has off-site storage facilities for less commonly-requested materials.

Jefferson Building

Thomas Jefferson Building

Main article: Thomas Jefferson Building

The Thomas Jefferson Building is located between Independence Avenue and East Capitol Street on First Street SE. It first opened in 1897 as the main building of the Library and is the oldest of the three buildings. Known originally as the Library of Congress Building or Main Building, it took its present name on June 13, 1980.

Madison Building

John Adams Building

Main article: John Adams Building

The John Adams Building is located between Independence Avenue and East Capitol Street on 2nd Street SE. It opened in 1938 as an annex to the main building. Between April 13, 1976 and June 13, 1980, the John Adams Building was known as the Thomas Jefferson Building.

James Madison Memorial Building

Main article: James Madison Memorial Building

The James Madison Memorial Building is located between First and Second Streets on Independence Avenue SE. It opened on May 28, 1980 as the new headquarters of the Library. The James Madison Memorial Building also serves as the official memorial to James Madison. It houses, among other materials, the Law Library of Congress.

Packard Campus for Audio-Visual Conservation

Main article: National Audio-Visual Conservation Center

The Packard Campus for Audio-Visual Conservation is the Library of Congress's newest building, opened in 2007 and located in Culpeper, Virginia. It was constructed out of a former Federal Reserve storage center and Cold War bunker. The campus is designed to act as a single site to store all of the library's movie, television, and sound collections. It is named to honor David Woodley Packard, whose Packard Humanities Institute oversaw design and construction of the facility.

Using the Library

The library is open to the general public for academic research and tourists. Only those who are issued a Reader Identification Card may enter the reading rooms and access the collection. The Reader Identification Card is available in the Madison building to persons who are at least 16 years of age upon presentation of a government issued picture identification (e.g. driver's license, state ID card or passport). However, only members of Congress, Supreme Court Justices, their staff, Library of Congress

Library of Congress reading room

staff and certain other government officials can actually remove items from the library buildings. Members of the general public with Reader Identification Cards must use items from the library collection inside the reading rooms only; they cannot remove library items from the reading rooms or the library buildings.

Since 1902, libraries in the United States have been able to request books and other items through interlibrary loan from the Library of Congress if these items are not readily available elsewhere. Through this, the Library of Congress has served as a "library of last resort", according to former Librarian of Congress Herbert Putnam.

Librarians of Congress

The **Librarian of Congress** is the head of the Library of Congress, appointed by the President of the United States with the advice and consent of the Senate. He serves as the chief librarian of all the sections of the Library of Congress. One of the responsibilities of the Librarian of Congress is to appoint the U.S. Poet Laureate.

1. John J. Beckley (1802–1807)
2. Patrick Magruder (1807–1815)
3. George Watterston (1815–1829)
4. John Silva Meehan (1829–1861)
5. John Gould Stephenson (1861–1864)
6. Ainsworth Rand Spofford (1864–1897)
7. John Russell Young (1897–1899)
8. Herbert Putnam (1899–1939)
9. Archibald MacLeish (1939–1944)
10. Luther H. Evans (1945–1953)
11. Lawrence Quincy Mumford (1954–1974)
12. Daniel J. Boorstin (1975–1987)

13. James H. Billington (1987–present)

Annual events

- Archives Fair
- Fellows in American Letters of the Library of Congress
- Davidson Fellows Reception
- Founder's Day Celebration
- Gershwin Prize for Popular Song
- Judith P. Austin Memorial Lecture
- The National Book Festival

See also

- American Folklife Center
- British Library
- Congressional Research Service
  - Federal Research Division
- Documents Expediting Project
- Law Library of Congress
- Library of Congress Classification
- Library of Congress Country Studies
- Library of Congress Living Legend
- Library of Congress Subject Headings
- List of librarians
- List of national libraries
- MARC standards
- National Archives and Records Administration
- National Film Registry
- National Recording Registry
- Poet Laureate Consultant in Poetry to the Library of Congress
- Project MINERVA
- The Feleky Collection
- United States Copyright Office
- United States Senate Library
- World Digital Library

External links

- The Library of Congress website [1]
    - American Memory [2]
    - History of the Library of Congress [3]
    - Search the Library of Congress catalog [4]
    - thomas.loc.gov [5], legislative information
- Library Of Congress Meeting Notices and Rule Changes [6] from The Federal Register RSS Feed [7]
- Library of Congress photos on Flickr [8]
- Outdoor sculpture [9] at the Library of Congress
- Standards, The Library of Congress [10]
- Works by the Library of Congress [11] at Project Gutenberg
- Library of Congress [12] at FamilySearch Research Wiki for genealogists

Geographical coordinates: 38°53′19″N 77°00′17″W

George Washington University

The George Washington University	
Motto	Deus Nobis Fiducia (*God in our trust*)
Established	February 9, 1821
Type	Private
Endowment	$1.011 billion
Chairman	W. Russell Ramsey
President	Steven Knapp
Provost	Steven R. Lerman
Academic staff	2,062
Students	24,531
Undergraduates	10,813
Postgraduates	13,718
Location	Washington, D.C., U.S.
Campus	Urban — Foggy Bottom; Suburban — Mount Vernon; Rural — Ashburn
Colors	Buff and Blue
Nickname	Colonials
Mascot	George, the Colonial
Website	www.gwu.edu [1]

The George Washington University (**GW**, **GWU**, or **George Washington**) is a private, coeducational comprehensive research university located in Washington, D.C. The university was chartered by an Act of Congress on February 9, 1821 as The Columbian College in the District of Columbia. It is the largest university in the nation's capital. It is renowned for its programs in international affairs, political science, law, and medicine.

History

Founding and early history

George Washington, the University's namesake.

The first American president George Washington had long argued for the creation of a university in the District of Columbia. In his will, he bequeathed fifty shares of the Potomac Company to support such an institution. He wrote, "I give and bequeath in perpetuity the fifty shares which I hold in the Potomac Company (under the aforesaid Acts of the Legislature of Virginia) towards the endowment of a University to be established within the limits of the District of Columbia, under the auspices of the General Government, if that Government should incline to extend a fostering hand towards it." The shares turned out not to be worth very much, but Washington's idea for a university continued.

Baptist missionary and leading minister Luther Rice raised funds to purchase a site for a college to educate citizens in Washington, D.C. A large building was constructed on College Hill, which is now known as Meridian Hill, and on February 9, 1821, President James Monroe approved the congressional charter creating the non-denominational *Columbian College in the District of Columbia*. The first commencement in 1824 was considered an important event for the young city of Washington, D.C.. In attendance were President Monroe, John C. Calhoun, Henry Clay, Marquis de Lafayette, and other dignitaries. During the Civil War, most students left to join the Confederacy and the college's buildings were used as a hospital and barracks. Walt Whitman was among many of the volunteers to work on the campus. After the Civil War in 1873, Columbian College became the Columbian University and moved to an urban downtown location centered on 15th and H streets, NW. In 1904, Columbian University changed its name to *The George Washington University* in an agreement with the George Washington Memorial Association. The university relocated its principal operations to Foggy Bottom in 1912.

The George Washington University, like much of Washington, D.C., traces many of its origins back to the Freemasons. The Bible that the presidents of the university use to swear an oath on upon inauguration is the Bible of Freemason George Washington. Freemasonry symbols are prominently displayed throughout the campus including the foundation stones of many of the university buildings. The Freemasons feel a special bond in helping the school throughout its history financially.

Expansion

The majority of the present infrastructure and financial stability at GW is due to the tenures of Presidents Cloyd Heck Marvin, Lloyd Hartman Elliott, and Stephen Joel Trachtenberg. In the 1930s, the University was the center for theoretical physics. The cosmologist George Gamow produced critical work on the Big Bang Theory at GW in the 1930s and 1940s. In one of the most important moments in the 20th century, Niels Bohr announced that Otto Hahn had successfully split the atom on January 26, 1939 at the Fifth Washington Conference on theoretical physics in the Hall of Government. During the Vietnam War era, Thurston Hall, an undergraduate

The historic 1925 F Street Club currently serves as the President's Residence. IMF buildings are seen behind it.

dormitory housing 875 students was (according to campus folklore) a staging ground for Student Anti-War Demonstrations (at 1900 F Street NW, the building is 3 blocks from the White House). In 1996, the university purchased the Mount Vernon College for Women in the city's Palisades neighborhood that became the school's coeducational Mount Vernon Campus. The campus was first utilized in 1997 for women only, but became co-educational in a matter of years. The Mount Vernon campus is now totally integrated into the GW community, serving as a complement to the Foggy Bottom campus. In December 2006, the university named Johns Hopkins University provost Steven Knapp its next president. He began his presidency on August 1, 2007.

Campuses

Main articles: Campuses of George Washington University and George Washington University Residence Halls

Foggy Bottom

The Midcampus Walk, through Professor's Gate, leading to Monroe Court and Kogan Plaza.

The main GW campus consists of 43-acres in historic Foggy Bottom and is located a few blocks from the White House and the National Mall. Barring a few outlying buildings, the boundaries of campus are delineated by (running clockwise from Washington Circle) Pennsylvania Avenue, 19th Street, E Street, Virginia Avenue, 24th Street, and New Hampshire Avenue. The University owns much of the property in Foggy Bottom and leases it to various tenants, including the World Bank and the International Monetary Fund. Other nearby institutions include the Harry S. Truman Building (Department of State headquarters), John F. Kennedy Center for the Performing Arts, United States Institute of Peace, Watergate complex, and the embassies of Saudi Arabia, Mexico, Spain, Uruguay, and Bosnia and Herzegovina.

The university has a significant presence in the area. Signs indicating the relative location of various university buildings can be found on almost every street corner. The student union (the Marvin Center), several residence halls, the Media and Public Affairs building, Academic Center and other major academic buildings are located within a three-block radius of University Yard (the original quadrangle on campus).

The nearby area surrounding George Washington's main library, Gelman Library, forms the hub of the campus. The seven-story library building contains over two million volumes and is constructed in the Brutalist architectural style of the 1970s. It features a concrete façade punctuated by windows that are divided by projecting vertical slabs. For most of the year, parts of the library are open 24 hours day, seven days per week for use by students, faculty and staff. The library's upper level is home to the National Security

Lisner Auditorium

Archive, a research institution that publishes declassified U.S. government files concerning selected topics of American foreign policy. It was a National Security Archive Freedom of Information Act request that eventually made the Central Intelligence Agency's so-called "Family Jewels" public.

Close to the library is Lisner Auditorium and a large open area between them is known as Kogan Plaza. Southeast of the plaza and located near Monroe Hall and Hall of Government is the Monroe Court, a landscaped area with a large fountain. The Foggy Bottom–GWU Washington Metro station is located at the intersection of 23rd and I Streets NW due south of Washington Circle, and provides access to the Orange and Blue lines. The University Hospital is located next to the Metro station entrance.

The Foggy Bottom campus contains most of the residential dormitories in which GW students live. The most notable include: Ivory Tower, Thurston Hall, Madison Hall, Potomac House, Fulbright Hall, Mitchell Hall, Crawford Hall, Schenley Hall, Munson Hall, Jacqueline Bouvier Kennedy Onassis Hall, Phillips-Amsterdam Hall, The West End and the newest residence, South Hall, among others.

In late 2007, construction began on a large mixed-use residential, office and retail development located on the site of the old GW Hospital (Square 54) and just east of the Foggy Bottom-GWU Metrorail station. It was the second-largest undeveloped lot in the District of Columbia at the time of initial construction activity.

Mount Vernon

In 1999, the university acquired the 23-acre Mount Vernon College for Women and renamed it **The George Washington University - Mount Vernon Campus**.

Nicknamed "The Vern," students at this campus are the neighbors of the Embassy of Germany in Washington in the Foxhall area. The campus is served by a 24-hour shuttle service known as the "Vern Express." Although its dormitories are fully co-educational, the campus' legacy as a former women's college has been retained with the Elizabeth Somers Women's Leadership Program, a residential-academic program for first-year female undergraduate students. The Mount Vernon campus also hosts the university's outdoor varsity sports.[citation needed]

The Mount Vernon campus is being heavily promoted by the university to attract more students. Events such as the Fountain Fling provide an incentive for students to explore and use the facilities on campus. The Mount Vernon Campus also offers special services such as free DVD rentals and better catering services. The university also developed the campus to house more freshmen with a new residence hall.

The GW Virginia Science and Technology Campus

The George Washington University also operates a research and graduate campus in Ashburn, Virginia (near Dulles International Airport) and several other graduate satellite education centers including the Alexandria Graduate Education Center in Alexandria, the Graduate Education Center in Arlington, and the Hampton Roads Center in Newport News. The Virginia Science and Technology Campus campus hosts more than a dozen research centers, labs, and institutes including the National Crash Analysis Center.

Organization

University

The George Washington University is governed by a Board of Trustees and the president who are in charge of managing the institution as a whole and providing a vision for the future. The current Chairman of the Board is W. Russell Ramsey. Ramsey is a business entrepreneur who is known as the co-founder of Friedman, Billings, Ramsey Group, a top investment bank in the United States. He is currently the chairman, CEO, and CIO of Ramsey Asset Management. The current President is Steven Knapp who was the provost at Johns Hopkins University before being chosen by the Board of Trustees in 2007. Knapp is the sixteenth president of the university. There is currently no student representative on the Board, a perennially contentious issue in Student Association elections. In 2004 students voted in support of representation onto the Board of Trustees.[citation needed]

In the *Chronicle of Higher Education* survey of college presidents' salaries for 2007-08, then-President Stephen Trachtenberg topped the nation with a compensation of $3.7 million.

Schools and colleges

GW is organized into twelve schools and colleges, each with a different dean and organization.

Undergraduate & Graduate Schools of The George Washington University					
Columbian College of Arts and Sciences	School of Media and Public Affairs	School of Business	Elliott School of International Affairs	School of Public Health and Health Services	School of Engineering and Applied Science

Graduate Schools of The George Washington University				
George Washington University Graduate School of Political Management	Trachtenberg School of Public Policy and Public Administration	George Washington University Medical School	George Washington University Law School	Graduate School of Education & Human Development

The Columbian College of Arts and Sciences (CCAS) is the oldest and largest college in the university. It was founded in 1821; at the beginning of the university's history, there was no distinction between this college and the university. The School of Media and Public Affairs (SMPA), and the Trachtenberg School of Public Policy and Public Administration (SPPPA) belong to this college, although they are run separately. The Columbian College was among the first American institutions to grant a Doctor of Philosophy (Ph.D.), in 1888. The Columbian College is notable for its academic diversity. Nonetheless, the student body lacks ethnic diversity in line with the general public. While blacks constitute 55% of the population of the District of Columbia, and 12.1% of the nation as a whole, they constitute only 2.3% of the undergraduate population.

The historic Old President's Office features a time capsule with letters from former President George W. Bush and Speaker of the House Dennis Hastert.

The School of Media and Public Affairs (SMPA), which, although run separately, belongs to the Columbian College of Arts in Sciences. It offers two undergraduate degrees, Journalism and Mass Communication and Political Communication and a master's degree in Media and Public Affairs. It is housed in the same building as the Graduate School of Political Management. The Public Affairs Project at GWU, part of SMPA, is responsible for the creation and production of the PBS special, Planet Forward. [School of Media and Public Affairs (SMPA) is one of the few schools in the country, and GWU was the first, to offer a Bachelor's Degree in political communication. The program boasts a faculty of retired and current professionals- including CNN correspondents, journalists, political analysts, and campaign professionals.

The School of Medicine and Health Sciences (SMHS) or simply the George Washington School of Medicine, was founded in 1824 due to the need for doctors in the District of Columbia. In 1981, the Medical Center became the center of the national spotlight when President Ronald Reagan was rushed to the emergency room after an attempted assassination. The emergency room area was later renamed the Ronald Reagan Institute of Emergency Medicine, and other politicians, such as former Vice President Dick Cheney, come to GW for routine and emergency procedures. Cheney and wife Lynne Cheney then helped to start the Richard B. and Lynne V. Cheney Cardiovascular Institute in 2006. Others include former First Lady Laura Bush who was treated for a pinched nerve a few years ago. An associate school in the university is the School of Public Health and Health Services (SPHHS).

University Yard with Corcoran Hall on the left and the Media and Public Affairs Building on the right, across H Street.

George Washington University Law School was established in 1826 and is the oldest law school in the District of Columbia. Supreme Court Justices William Strong, David J. Brewer, and John Marshall Harlan were among those who served on its faculty. Chief Justice John Roberts, Justice Samuel Alito, and Justice Antonin Scalia presided over its moot court in 2006, 2007, and 2009, respectively.

The Graduate School of Education & Human Development (GSEHD) officially started in 1909. The school is composed of three distinct academic departments, and it is one of the largest schools within GW. U.S. News & World Report rated the graduate program in the top 20, and was 5th overall in total research expenditures.

The School of Engineering and Applied Science (SEAS) was founded on October 1, 1884 as the Corcoran Scientific School of Columbian University. The school separated from the Columbian College in 1962 and was one of the first to accept women for degree candidacy in engineering and has awarded the most engineering doctoral degrees to women in the country. The bazooka was invented at the SEAS in 1942.

The Elliott School of International Affairs (ESIA) was founded in 1898 as the School of Comparative Jurisprudence and Diplomacy. Under President Lloyd Elliott, the school separated from Columbian College. On September 3, 2005, alumnus Colin Powell opened a new complex for this school at 1957 E Street NW in front of the Department of State.

The Elliott School building, at 1957 E St NW, was opened in 2003 with a ceremony featuring then United States Secretary of State and alumnus, Colin Powell.

The George Washington School of Business was established in 1928 with a $1 million gift by the Masonic Supreme Council of the Scottish Rite for the Southern Jurisdiction. The part-time MBA program or "Professional MBA," is a flexible format program and is currently ranked 26th in the nation by *US News and World Report*.

On February 6, 2006, the Chairman and CEO of FedEx, Frederick Smith, opened a new complex for the school called Duquès Hall.

The School of Business is located in the Ric & Dawn Duquès Hall, named after graduate Ric Duques.

During the Trachtenberg Presidency, the university created several professional schools. Some schools founded during his era were the College of Professional Studies, and the Graduate School of Political Management.

Academics

Admission

GW received more than 21,135 applications and admitted 6,655 students for the class of 2014, or approximately 31.5% of applicants. GW Law is ranked 20th in the country.

Students at GW participate in a variety of educational opportunities. There are 9,700 full-time undergraduates studying in 87 majors with 1,500 in business, 500 in engineering, 2,000 in international affairs, 700 in communications and media, 800 in sciences and math, 2,900 in social sciences, and 1,300 in arts, languages, and humanities. Nearly 900 students participate in GW's Study Abroad Programs each semester in 50 countries. Additionally, about 125 entering students each fall join the University Honors Program community of 500 students.

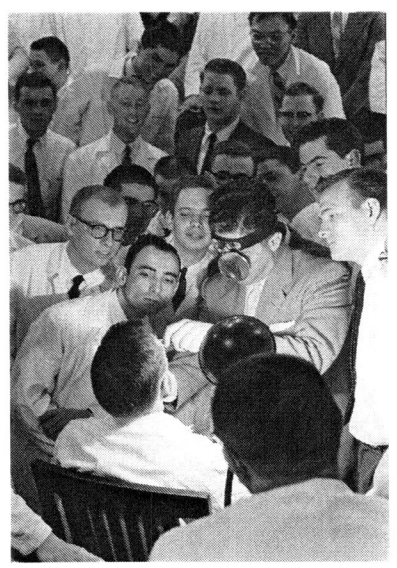

Medical school students in class (1958)

The George Washington University has been ranked by The Princeton Review in the Top 10 for the following categories:

- Most Politically Active
- Dorms Like Palaces
- Great College Towns
- Best in the Northeast

In discussing the University's U.S. News national university ranking, which is currently ranked at 51st in the nation, President Trachtenberg explained why its ranking was inconsequential: "I sometimes help my wife cook, and I stand there and watch, and she looks at a recipe in a book, and she says, 'Hmm, three pinches of salt, I think that's going to be too salty,' and she only puts two pinches in," he said. "You can't go by what some magazine tells you life is supposed to be about." However, U.S. News data and research director Bob Morse has claimed that, although the University may publicly downplay its status, it privately lobbied the magazine to expand its rankings beyond 150 schools. "The idea that they didn't care about the rankings—they might not care to actually publicize it, but they cared enough to encourage us to do the rankings the way we are printing them now," Morse said. "Their position was, 'We'd rather let people know we are listed 8th.' I'm sure they thought that would be helpful to them."

Demographics of student body

	Undergraduate	Graduate	U.S.
Black	6.9%	9.3%	12.8%
Asian	10.2%	8.9%	4.4%
White	58.0%	54.7%	66.7%
Hispanic	6.6%	4.2%	15.1%
Unspecified	12.5%	12.1%	N/A
Native American	0.3%	0.7%	1.0%
International student	5.4%	10.0%	N/A
Men	44.4%	45.1%	N/A
Women	55.6%	54.9%	N/A

Tuition

At the George Washington University, tuition is guaranteed to remain at the freshman rate for up to ten continuous (full time) semesters of attendance at the university. Tuition has risen 58 percent over the past seven years. Tuition for the 2009-2010 year is $41,610, while the combined room and board is approximately $10,000 for incoming freshmen. The tuition rate only applies to the incoming Class of 2013 and will not increase for those students for up to 10 semesters. Although GW is the third most expensive school in the United States of America, it also gives the most need-based financial aid.

Research

Main article: Research at The George Washington University

There are major research institutions that many students utilize like the Library of Congress, the National Institutes of Health, the Carnegie Institute, the Thomas Jefferson National Accelerator Facility, and the National Geographic Society. Many think tanks nearby provide students with every opportunity to participate in research projects with professors and advisors.

Student life

The university is located in downtown D.C., near the Kennedy Center, embassies, and other cultural events. There are many student organizations at the University. GW has a Division I athletics program that includes men's baseball, basketball, cross country, golf, gymnastics, women's lacrosse, rowing, soccer, women's softball, squash, swimming & diving, tennis, women's volleyball, and water polo.

Colonials athletics teams compete in the Atlantic 10 Conference. While only a Division II program, the Men's and Women's Rugby Teams both compete in the Potomac Rugby Union and have had much recent success.

GW has a NROTC program on campus.

Student organizations and government

Most student organizations are run through the Student Association (SA). The SA is fashioned after the federal government with an executive, legislative, and judicial branch. Some SA presidents have been successful after college, such as former SA president Edward "Skip" Gnehm, who was the Ambassador to Kuwait during the Gulf War and received the Presidential Distinguished Service Award and two Presidential Meritorious Service Awards.

There are over 300 registered student organizations on campus. The largest student organization on campus claiming a membership approaching 2000, the GW College Democrats have hosted speakers such as CNN contributor Donna Brazile and former DNC Chairman Howard Dean among numerous others. Likewise, the GW College Republicans [2], one of the largest CR chapters in the nation, have been visited by politicians like John Ashcroft former Florida Governor Jeb Bush and former President George W. Bush. The International Affairs Society (IAS) runs the university's award winning Model United Nation's team, in addition to hosting yearly high school and middle school Model UN conferences on campus. GW's Student Global AIDS Campaign (SGAC) is one of the most active chapters in the country [citation needed] due to the high amount of AIDS cases in Washington, D.C. The GW Chapter of STAND: A Student Anti-Genocide Coalition, or GW STAND, was formed in 2003 and works with the United States Holocaust Memorial Museum and the Genocide Intervention Network on information about genocide in Darfur. The Global Language Group, or Global Languages, is a non-profit organization that offers over 150 free classes in 50 languages.

There are chapters of many varied academic groups at the University. The local chapter of the Society of Physics Students was at one time under the auspices of world-renowned scientists like George Gamow, Ralph Asher Alpher, Mario Schoenberg and Edward Teller, who have all taught at the university. The Enosinian Society, founded in 1822, is one of the university's oldest student organizations. Invited speakers included Daniel Webster.

There are multiple news sources on campus: the twice-weekly newspaper The *GW Hatchet*, founded in 1904, The GW Patriot [3], a journal of politics and campus culture noted for its blog and *The Daily Colonial*, an online newsmagazine founded in 2004. There is also an online only student-run radio station, WRGW, that is in its 79th year and campus television station GWTV broadcasts on campus cable channel 6 and on its website.

Controversies

The Program Board had, in years past, scheduled an X-rated film to show as part of their semester series. The film was usually partnered with a discussion of the First Amendment or a seminar on the sociological underpinnings of pornography. One year in the mid-1990s, "Porn Night" garnered national press coverage along with an ensuing protest. The film shown that night was *John Wayne Bobbitt Uncut*. The organized protest brought together College Republicans with College Democrats, Christians, Jews and Muslims and a bevy of diverse student organizations to speak out against pornography. A number of university administrators appeared that night to show their support of the students' right to assemble - on one hand to view the movie and on the other to protest using student fees to show the film in the first place.

A number of posters in October 2007 surfaced at GW satirizing the "Islamofascism Awareness Week," which was assumed to have been from the GW Young American's Foundation. On October 9, The Daily Colonial reported that the posters were not the work of the YAF, but rather an attempt to discredit the YAF for their involvement in promoting the Islamo-Fascism Awareness Week. Later that day, seven students advocating against alleged racism inherent in Islamo-Fascism Awareness Week emailed their statement of responsibility regarding the posters to the GW Hatchet. While YAF and other conservative groups demanded that the students be expelled, the university's judicial services found the students in violation of only GW's postering policy and the students were put on disciplinary probation and fined $25 for the satirical fliers.

In January 2009, a member of the GW College Democrats desecrated GW Young America's Foundation crucifixes that were being stored in the College Republicans' office after a pro-life event. The controversy, exposed by Pat Dollard and The GW Patriot [3], resulted in disciplinary action against a member of the College Democrats.

Environmental sustainability

GWU received a B on the College Sustainability Report Card for 2010, an improvement over the University's 2009 grade of C+. The school is reaching for a higher rating by updating facilities with energy efficient technologies.

Some students have criticized GW's recent initiatives as specifically designed as answers to questions on sustainability reports. GW keeps the lights on in all academic buildings, even when there are no classes and overnight. In addition, only 1 of 106 University Police Department's vehicles is a hybrid and GW does not count the 13 Mount Vernon Campus Express buses toward its sustainability totals.

Greek life

GW has a Greek community of over 2200 students (22 percent of the undergraduate population).

There are 16 recognized men's social fraternity chapters on campus, including Alpha Epsilon Pi, Beta Theta Pi, Delta Tau Delta, Kappa Alpha Order, Kappa Sigma, Lambda Chi Alpha, Phi Kappa Psi, Phi Sigma Kappa, Pi Kappa Alpha, Pi Kappa Phi, Sigma Chi, Sigma Nu, Sigma Phi Epsilon , Tau Kappa Epsilon, Theta Delta Chi, and Zeta Beta Tau.

There are 10 Panhellenic sororities on campus, including Alpha Delta Pi, Alpha Epsilon Phi, Alpha Phi, Chi Omega, Delta Gamma, Kappa Kappa Gamma, Pi Beta Phi, Sigma Delta Tau, Sigma Kappa, and Phi Sigma Sigma.

Six National Pan-Hellenic Council (NPHC) fraternities and sororities exist on campus: Alpha Phi Alpha, Alpha Kappa Alpha, Delta Sigma Theta, Kappa Alpha Psi, Omega Psi Phi, and Zeta Phi Beta.

Other Greek-life exist on campus in the form of multicultural, professional, community-serviced based and honor groups: Alpha Phi Alpha, Alpha Kappa Psi, Delta Sigma Pi, Mu Sigma Upsilon, Order of Omega, Phi Beta Kappa, Omicron Delta Kappa, Tau Beta Pi, Iota Nu Delta, Lambda Upsilon Lambda , Lambda Pi Chi, Phi Alpha Delta, Pi Delta Psi, Kappa Phi Lambda, Sigma Psi Zeta, Delta Phi Epsilon, Theta Tau,an Islamic-interest frat, Phi Sigma Pi, Alpha Chi Sigma, Alpha Phi Omega, Sigma Pi Sigma, Alpha Omega Epsilon, Xi Delta Pi, and Epsilon Sigma Alpha.

Athletics and spirit programs

Main article: George Washington Colonials

George Washington University is a member of the Atlantic 10 Conference and most of its teams play at the NCAA Division I level. All indoor sports play at the Smith Center on the Foggy Bottom campus. The outdoor events are held at the Mount Vernon campus Athletic Complex. The university's colors are buff and blue (buff being a color similar to tan, but sometimes represented as gold or yellow). The colors were taken from George Washington's uniform in the Revolutionary War. The teams have achieved great successes in recent years including a first round victory in the Men's NCAA Division I Soccer Tournament in 2004. The men's varsity crew team rows out of Thompson's Boat Center on the Potomac River and competes in the Eastern Association of Rowing Colleges. In the 2008-2009 season, the men's crew team placed an all-time high national ranking of 12th in the country. The sailing team competes in the Middle Atlantic Intercollegiate Sailing Association and in gymnastics in the East Atlantic Gymnastics League. In 2007 the GW Men's Water Polo team placed third at Eastern Championships, and was ranked 14th in the nation.

Men's basketball

Main article: George Washington Colonials men's basketball

The colors of GW, buff and blue, can be seen on banners on the Foggy Bottom campus.

Mike Jarvis coached GW in the 1990s, and led the team to the NCAA Sweet 16 in 1993, where they were beaten by the Fab Five University of Michigan team (which later vacated its wins due to NCAA rule violations). Jarvis also coached current Colonials Head Coach Karl Hobbs in high school. Former NBA player Yinka Dare also played at George Washington for two years before being drafted in the first round by the New Jersey Nets.

GW's basketball team returned to the national stage in 2004 after defeating No. 9 Michigan State and No. 12 Maryland in back to back games to win the 2004 BB&T Classic. That year, the men's basketball team went on to win the Atlantic 10 West Title and the Atlantic 10 Tournament Title (earning an automatic bid to the 2005 NCAA Tournament. The team received a #12 seed, losing to #5 seed Georgia Tech in the first round.

The team began the 2005–06 season ranked 21st in the Associated Press poll, reaching as high as sixth in the polls, and after some tournament success they closed out the year ranked 19th in the nation. They had a record of 26-2 going into the 2006 NCAA Tournament. The 2005-06 team achieved the school's highest ranking in the last 50 years, peaking at #6 in the nation, had been one of the team's best ever, and received an #8 seed in the NCAA Tournament. In the tournament, they came back from an 18-point second-half deficit to defeat #9 seed UNC-Wilmington, but lost to Duke University, the top overall seed, in the second round.

While only one Colonial from the 2005-06 team was drafted in the 2006 NBA Draft, J. R. Pinnock, two other Colonials from that team have played in the NBA. Pops Mensah-Bonsu played for the Dallas Mavericks, Houston Rockets, San Antonio Spurs and currently plays for the Toronto Raptors and Mike Hall played for the Washington Wizards.

The 2006-07 basketball season was considered by many to be a rebuilding year for the Colonials after graduating their entire starting front court and losing Pinnock to the NBA. Coach Karl Hobbs and Senior guard Carl Elliott managed to lead the team to a 23-8 record, winning the 2007 Atlantic 10 Tournament in Atlantic City, NJ (once again earning an auto-bid to the NCAA Men's Division I Basketball Championship. The Colonials were placed as a #11 seed lost to #6 seed Vanderbilt University in Sacramento, CA 77-44.

Hobbs, a former player and coach under Jim Calhoun at the University of Connecticut is in his sixth year as head coach. Known for his animated sideline personality Hobbs is considered one of the up-and-coming coaches in the NCAA.

Football

Main article: George Washington Colonials football

The school sponsored intercollegiate football from 1881 to 1966. The team played home games at Griffith Stadium and RFK Stadium. Colonials football was discontinued to transfer resources to other sports and to focus on the construction of an on-campus fieldhouse for basketball.

Spirit programs

The Colonials mascot is named George, and is portrayed by a student wearing an outfit inspired by the uniform worn by General Washington. The sports teams are called the Colonials, which was chosen by the student body in 1924. Another version of the GW mascot is an inflatable Colonial figure known as "Big George.".

The spirit program also includes the Colonial Brass, directed by Professor Benno Fritz.

The official fight song is *Hail to the Buff and Blue*, composed in 1924 by student Eugene F. Sweeney and re-written in 1989 by Patrick M. Jones. The song is tolled twice-daily by bells atop Corcoran Hall, at 12:15pm and 6:00pm.

Club sports

Main article: George Washington Colonials club sports

The university also has various club sports, which are not varsity sports, but compete against other colleges. Examples include: volleyball, ice hockey, fencing, lacrosse, rugby, soccer, cricket, squash, tennis, ultimate frisbee, cricket and others.

Notable alumni, faculty, and degrees

Notable alumni

Main article: List of George Washington University people

George Washington alumni include many current and past
political figures. Six alumni currently serve in the United
States Senate and ten in the House of Representatives.
These include Senate Majority Leader Harry Reid and
House Minority Whip Eric Cantor. Alumni have been
governors of eighteen states, including current US Senator
and former Governor of Virginia Mark Warner. Other
renowned figures of the higher echelons of United States
government include Senator J. William Fulbright, former
Secretary of State Colin Powell, former Chairman of the
Joint Chiefs of Staff General Peter Pace, former FBI
Director J. Edgar Hoover and former Secretary of State
John Foster Dulles.

Colin Powell: General (four-star) in the United
States Army; National Security Advisor
(1987–1989); Chairman of the Joint Chiefs of
Staff (1989–1993); 65th United States Secretary
of State (2001-2005)

Other notable alumni and former students include Anwar
al-Awlaki, Ralph Asher Alpher, Red Auerbach, Alec
Baldwin, Dana Bash, Courteney Cox Arquette, Larry
Craig, Preston Cloud, Jack Edmonds, Jason Filardi, Ina
Garten, Todd B. Hawley, Harold Hersey, L. Ron Hubbard, S.M. Krishna, Lee Kun-hee, Roy Lee,
Theodore N. Lerner, Randy Levine, Gerardo I. Lopez, Carl Lutz, T.J. Miller, Darla Moore, former First
Lady Jacqueline Bouvier Kennedy Onassis, Leslie Sanchez, Chuck Todd, Margaret Truman, Kerry
Washington, Baby M, David McConnell, Scott Wolf, Rachel Zoe, and Erica Hayden,.

Notable faculty

Main article: List of notable George Washington University faculty

As the university is located within blocks of the State Department, White House, Department of the
Interior, IMF, World Bank, and other Federal government buildings of significant importance, the
university attracts many influential guest lecturers and visiting professors.[citation needed] Notable faculty
include: George Gamow (1934–1954), physicist and cosmologist; Edward Teller (1935–1941), nuclear
physicist and father of the hydrogen bomb; Seyyed Hossein Nasr, founder and first president of the
Imperial Iranian Academy of Philosophy; Edward "Skip" Gnehm, former U.S. Ambassador to Jordan,
Kuwait and Australia; Marcus Raskin, former member of the national security counsel under President
Kennedy and founder of the Institute for Policy Studies; Abba Eban, former Israeli Deputy Prime

Minister, Minister of Education & Culture and Minister of Foreign Affairs; John Logsdon, member of Columbia Accident Investigation Board, NASA Advisory Council; Frank Sesno, CNN Special Correspondent; James Carafano, Heritage Foundation national security and homeland security expert; Leon Fuerth, former national security adviser to Vice President Al Gore; James Rosenau, political theorist and former president of the International Studies Association; Chris Kojm, Deputy Director of the 9/11 Commission and Iraq Study Group as well as President of the 9/11 Discourse Project; Dr. Nancy E. Gary, former dean of Albany Medical College, Executive Vice President of the Uniformed Services University of the Health Sciences and Dean of its F. Edward Hébert School of Medicine, Roy Richard Grinker, anthropologist specializing in autism and North-South Korean relations, and Edward P. Jones, who won the Pulitzer Prize for fiction in 2004, Faure Essozimna Gnassingbé (MBA), president of Togo since 2005. In addition to Herbert J. Davis - Executive Director, U.S.-Bangladesh Business Council; U.S. Chamber of Commerce.

Notable honorary degrees

The University has traditionally given honorary degrees to people who have made an influence in Washington like: J. Edgar Hoover (Doctor of Law, 1935), Harry S. Truman (1946), John Wesley Snyder (Treasury Secretary, Doctor of Law, 1947), Ulysses S. Grant III (Doctor of Law, 1956), John F. Kennedy (Doctor of Law, 1961), Hillary Rodham Clinton (Doctor of Public Service, 1994), Elizabeth Dole (Doctor of Public Service, 1995), William H. Rehnquist (Doctor of Law, 1996), Sandra Day O'Connor (Doctor of Law, 2003), Barbara Bush (Doctor of Public Service, 2006), George H.W. Bush (Doctor of Public Service, 2006), and Michelle Obama (Doctor of Public Service, 2010). Peace advocates and leaders of other nations who have influenced the world have also received this honor. These people include: King Mohammad V of Morocco (Doctor of Law, 1957) , Iranian Shah Mohammad Reza Pahlavi (Doctor of Public Service, 1974), Ronald Reagan (1991), Roy Lichtenstein (Doctor of Fine Arts, honoris causa, 1996), Yitzhak Rabin (Doctor of Public Service, 1996), Desmond Tutu (Doctor of Public Service, 1999), Andy Rooney (Doctor of Public Service, 2005), and South Korean president Lee Myung Bak (Doctor of Public Service, 2009).

External links

- Official website [1]
- Official Studentblog [4]
- Official Athletics website [5]
- The GW and Foggy Bottom Historical Encyclopedia [6]

Geographical coordinates: 38°54′03″N 77°02′50″W

- George Washington University Historical Photographs [7] - contains photographs and negatives of individuals, localities, objects, buildings, events, and groups associated with the history of the University. It is one of the strongest photograph collections within the University Archives representing a photographic time-line of the history of The George Washington University from approximately 1859 through late 1980s.

Anthony Comstock

Anthony Comstock (March 7, 1844 – September 21, 1915) was a former United States Postal Inspector and politician dedicated to ideas of Victorian morality.

Biography

Comstock was born in New Canaan, Connecticut. As a young man, he enlisted and fought for the Union in the American Civil War from 1863 to 1865 in Company H, 17th Connecticut Infantry. He served without incident, but objected to the profanity used by his fellow soldiers.[citation needed] Afterward he became an active worker in the Young Men's Christian Association in New York City.

In 1873 Comstock created the New York Society for the Suppression of Vice, an institution dedicated to supervising the morality of the public. Later that year, Comstock successfully influenced the United States Congress to pass the Comstock Law, which made illegal the delivery or transportation of both "obscene, lewd, or lascivious" material as well as any methods of, or information pertaining to, birth control. George Bernard Shaw used the term "comstockery", meaning "censorship because of perceived obscenity or immorality", after Comstock alerted the New York police to the content of Shaw's play *Mrs. Warren's Profession*. Shaw remarked that "Comstockery is the world's standing joke at the expense of the United States. Europe likes to hear of such things. It confirms the deep-seated conviction of the Old World that America is a provincial place, a second-rate country-town civilization after all." Comstock thought of Shaw as an "Irish smut dealer." The term comstockery was actually first coined in a *New York Times* editorial in 1895.

Comstock's ideas of what might be "obscene, lewd, or lascivious" were quite broad. During his time of greatest power, even some anatomy textbooks were prohibited from being sent to medical students by the United States Postal Service.

Comstock aroused intense loathing from early civil liberties groups and intense support from church-based groups worried about public morals. He was a savvy political insider in New York City and was made a special agent of the United States Postal Service, with police powers up to and including the right to carry a weapon. With this power he zealously prosecuted those he suspected of either public distribution of pornography or commercial fraud. He was also involved in shutting down the Louisiana Lottery, the only legal lottery in the United States at the time, and notorious for corruption.

Comstock is also known for his opposition to Victoria Woodhull and Tennessee Claflin, and those associated with them. The men's journal *The Days' Doings* had popularised lewd images of the sisters for three years and was instructed by its editor (while Comstock was present) to stop producing images of "lewd character". Comstock also took legal action against the paper for advertising contraceptives. When the sisters published an expose of an adulterous affair between Reverend Henry Ward Beecher and Elizabeth Tilton, he had the sisters arrested under laws forbidding the use of the postal service to distribute 'obscene material'—specifically (and ironically) citing a mangled Biblical quote Comstock found obscene—though they were later acquitted of the charges.

Less fortunate was Ida Craddock, who committed suicide on the eve of reporting to Federal prison for distributing via the U.S. Mail various sexually explicit marriage manuals she had authored. Her final work was a lengthy public suicide note specifically condemning Comstock.

Comstock claimed he drove fifteen persons to suicide in his "fight for the young". He was head vice-hunter of the New York Society for the Suppression of Vice. Comstock, the self-labeled "weeder in God's garden", arrested D. M. Bennett for publishing his "An Open Letter to Jesus Christ" and later entrapped the editor for mailing a free-love pamphlet. Bennett was prosecuted, subjected to a widely publicized trial, and imprisoned in the Albany Penitentiary.

Comstock had numerous enemies, and in later years his health was affected by a severe blow to the head from an anonymous attacker. He lectured to college audiences and wrote newspaper articles to sustain his causes. Before his death, Comstock attracted the interest of a young law student, J. Edgar Hoover, interested in his causes and methods.

During his career, Comstock clashed with Emma Goldman and Margaret Sanger. In her autobiography, Goldman referred to Comstock as the leader of America's "moral eunuchs". Through his various campaigns, he destroyed 15 tons of books, 284,000 pounds of plates for printing 'objectionable' books, and nearly 4,000,000 pictures.[citation needed] Comstock boasted that he was responsible for 4,000 arrests.

A biography of Comstock written in 1927, "Anthony Comstock: Roundsman Of The Lord" by Heywood Broun and Margaret Leech of the Algonquin Round Table examines his personal history and his investigative, surveillance and law enforcement techniques.

Works

- *Frauds Exposed* (1880)
- *Traps for the Young* (1883)
- *Gambling Outrages* (1887)
- *Morals Versus Art* (1887)

He wrote numerous magazine articles relating to similar subjects.

References in fiction and culture

- Comstock is one of many prominent New Yorkers of his time that appear in the historical fiction novel *The Alienist*, by Caleb Carr.
- The protagonist of F. Scott Fitzgerald's novel *The Beautiful and Damned* is named for Comstock by his own reformist grandfather. "Emulating the magnificent efforts of Anthony Comstock, after whom his grandson was named, he leveled a varied assortment of uppercuts and body-blows at liquor, literature, vice, art, patent medicines, and Sunday theatres."
- James Branch Cabell was prosecuted on obscenity charges relating to his novel *Jurgen, A Comedy of Justice* after lobbying by the Society. Cabell retaliated with a chapbook entitled *The Judging of Jurgen* (later inserted into subsequent reprints of the novel), in which the title character is consigned to oblivion for being "obscene, lewd, lascivious and indecent" in a trial presided over by a dung beetle who swears "by Saint Anthony".
- Anthony Comstock is one of the four "point of view" characters in Marge Piercy's novel *Sex Wars*. Piercy explores Comstock's personal history and mindset as he goes from clerk to active "vice" suppressor.
- Comstock makes a cameo (rescued from a burning building) in Jack Finney's novel *Time and Again*.
- Comstock Films [1], a company that produces erotic documentaries, is named after Anthony Comstock.
- Through the character of Gordon Comstock, George Orwell reveals his own disaffection for the society in the novel *Keep the Aspidistra Flying* (1936).
- He is portrayed by Rod Steiger in the 1995 made for TV film Choices of the Heart: The Margaret Sanger Story.[2]

Contemporary Bibliography

- Anna Bates: *Weeder in the Garden of the Lord: Anthony Comstock's Life and Career*: Lanham, Maryland: University Press of America: 1995: ISBN 076180076X
- Nicola Beisel: *Imperiled Innocents: Anthony Comstock and Family Reproduction in Victorian America:* Princeton: Princeton University Press: 1997: ISBN 069102779X
- Helen Horowitz: *Rereading Sex: Battles over Sexual Knowledge and Suppression in Nineteenth Century America*: New York: Knopf: 2002: ISBN 037540192X
- Andrea Tone: *Devices and Desires: A History of Contraceptives in America*, New York: Hill and Wang, 2001. Available electronically at: http://books.google.com/books?id=ClHpjlw8zQEC& printsec=frontcover&dq=devices+and+desires&cd=1#v=onepage&q=&f=false

See also

- Comstock Act
- New York Society for the Suppression of Vice
- Jack Thompson (activist)

External links

- Anthony Comstock's "Chastity" Laws [3]
- "Anthony Comstock" [4]. Find a Grave. Retrieved 2009-04-23.
- Comstockery, Contraception, and the Family: The Remarkable Achievements of an Anti-Vice Crusader [5]

FBI Career

William J. Burns

William J. Burns (October 19, 1861 – April 14, 1932), known as "America's Sherlock Holmes," is famous for having conducted a private investigation clearing Leo Frank of the murder of Mary Phagan, and for serving as the director of the Bureau of Investigation (BOI) (predecessor to the FBI) from August 22, 1921 to June 14, 1924. He was born in Baltimore, Maryland and was educated in Columbus, Ohio. As a young man, Burns performed well as a Secret Service Agent and parleyed his reputation into the William J. Burns International Detective Agency, now a part of Securitas Security Services USA. A combination of natural ability as a detective combined with an instinct for publicity made Burns a national figure. His exploits made national news, the gossip columns of New York newspapers, and the pages of detective magazines, in which he published "true" crime stories based on his exploits.

William J. Burns

Los Angeles Times bombing

The City of Los Angeles hired Burns to catch the bombers of the *Los Angeles Times* building on October 1, 1910.

BOI career

Burns was considered well qualified to direct the Bureau of Investigation, and was friends with President Warren Harding's Attorney General Harry M. Daugherty. Burns was confirmed as Director of the Bureau of Investigation on August 22, 1921. He continued to run the Burns Detective Agency throughout his tenure as Director of the BOI. Under Burns, the Bureau shrank from its 1920 high of 1,127 personnel to 600 employees in 1923.

At the request of Attorney General Daugherty, Burns sent agents to investigate Montana Representative Thomas J. Walsh for evidence of criminal wrongdoing. The investigation was actually a pretext for retaliation; the congressman had been instrumental in opposing oil leases granted by Secretary of the Interior Albert Fall, a friend of Daugherty and fellow cabinet member. Burns later refused to turn over Department of Justice documents to Congressional investigators, who in turn began investigating the BOI; Senate hearing revelations of BOI misdeeds were avidly covered in the press, and became known as the **Daugherty-Burns scandal**. Burns' BOI field agents made visits to the offices of newspapers around the country who had presented the BOI's actions in a negative light; their clumsy attempts to intimidate newspaper editors caused a backlash in public opinion and Congress. Burns was forced to resign in 1924 at the request of Attorney General Harlan Fiske Stone and on May 10, 1924, J. Edgar Hoover took over the position on a provisional basis.

Burns Detective Agency and Teapot Dome

Burns also became indirectly involved in the Teapot Dome Scandal, involving the secret leasing of naval oil reserve lands to private companies. In November 1927, Harry F. Sinclair went on trial in federal court for conspiracy to defraud the U. S. in the leasing of the Teapot Dome naval oil reserve. At the request of Sinclair oil executive Henry Mason Day, Burns secretly hired a squad of 14 men from the William J. Burns Detective Agency to "investigate" his jurors. Day arranged for their compensation and received their daily reports. Midway through the trial the government's investigors discovered Burns' agents, and a mistrial was immediately declared.

At a new hearing, Sinclair's defense was that he had had the jurors followed to protect them against federal influences; that in no case had the operatives made direct contact with the jurors. Sinclair was convicted on corruption charges and sentenced to six months in jail, Day to four months' imprisonment, William J. Burns to 15 days' imprisonment, and Burns' son, William Sherman Burns, was ordered to pay a $1,000 fine. William Burns immediately appealed, and the Supreme Court later reversed William J. Burns' conviction.

Postcript

After his retirement from the Burns Detective Agency, Burns moved to Florida and for several years published detective and mystery stories based on his long career. He died in Sarasota, Florida in April 1932.

Writings

* *The masked war; the story of a peril that threatened the United States* [1] New York, George H. Doran Co. 1913
* *The Argyle case* [1] with Arthur Hornblow, Harriot Ford and Harvey O'Higgins New York, London, Harper, 1913
* *The crevice* [2] with Isabel Ostrander New York : Grosset & Dunlap, 1915

See also

- Palmer raids
- Teapot Dome Scandal

References

- Caeser, Gene. *Incredible Detective: The Biography of William J. Burns.* Englewood Cliffs, NJ: Prentice-Hall, Inc., 1968.
- Blum, Howard. *American Lightning: Terror, Mystery, the Birth of Hollywood, and the Crime of the Century.* New York: Crown, September 2008. ISBN 0-307-34694-3
- Jeffreys-Jones, Rhodri, *The FBI: A History*, University Press of Kentucky (2007), ISBN 0-300-11914-3, 9780300119145

External links

- "Federal Bureau of Investigation: Directors, Then and Now" [3]. Retrieved 2010-04-26.

Teapot Dome scandal

The **Teapot Dome Scandal** was an unprecedented bribery scandal and investigation during the White House administration of United States President Warren G. Harding.

Before the Watergate scandal, it was regarded as the "greatest and most sensational scandal in the history of American politics". The scandal also was a key factor in posthumously destroying the public reputation of Harding, who was extremely popular at the time of his death in office in 1923.[*citation needed*]

Oil businessman Edward Doheny (second from right, at table) testifying before the Senate Committee investigating the Teapot Dome oil leases in 1924.

Teapot Dome is an oil field on public land in the U.S. state of Wyoming, so named for Teapot Rock, an outcrop resembling a teapot south of the field.43°13′59.3″N 106°18′40″W

In 1921, by executive order of President Harding, control of U.S. Navy petroleum reserves at Teapot Dome in Wyoming and at Elk Hills and Buena Vista in California, was transferred from the U.S. Navy Department to the Department of the Interior. The petroleum reserves had been set aside for the Navy by President Taft. In 1922, Albert B. Fall, U.S. Secretary of the Interior, leased, without competitive bidding, the Teapot Dome fields to Harry F. Sinclair of Sinclair Oil, and the field at Elk Hills, California, to Edward L. Doheny. In 1922 and 1923, these transactions became the subject of a sensational U.S. Senate investigation conducted by Senator Thomas J. Walsh.

It was found that in 1921, Doheny had lent Fall $100,000, interest-free, and that upon Fall's retirement as Secretary of the Interior, in March 1923, Sinclair also lent him a large amount of money. The investigation led to criminal prosecutions. Fall was indicted for conspiracy and for accepting bribes. Convicted of the latter charge, he was sentenced to a year in prison and fined $100,000, the same amount that Doheny had lent him. In another trial for bribery Doheny and Sinclair were acquitted, although Sinclair was subsequently sentenced to prison for contempt of the Senate and for employing detectives to shadow members of the jury in his case. The oil fields were restored to the U.S. government through a Supreme Court decision in 1927.

Oil riches on government land

Teapot Dome is a geologic structural uplift and oil field located in Natrona County, Wyoming, about 55 miles (89 km) north of Casper. The Teapot Dome area and the United States Naval Oil Reserve covering most of the field are named for a nearby formation of eroded sandstone called Teapot Rock.

The oil fields at Elk Hills and Buena Vista, both in Kern County, California, and at Teapot Dome were located on public land reserved for emergency use by the U.S. Navy only when the regular oil supplies diminished. Many politicians and private oil interests opposed the limits placed on the oil fields, claiming that the reserves were unnecessary and that American oil companies could provide for the Navy.

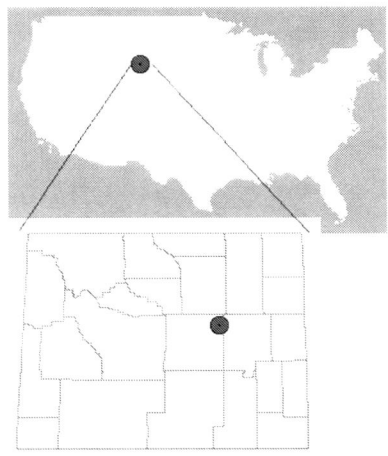

The location of Teapot Dome oil field in Natrona County, Wyoming.

One of the public officials most avidly opposed to retaining the reserves was Republican Senator Albert B. Fall of New Mexico. A political alliance ensured his election to the Senate in 1912, and his political allies — who later made up the infamous "Ohio Gang" — convinced President Harding to appoint Fall as United States Secretary of the Interior in March 1921.

Single-bid contracts followed by kickbacks

In 1922, the reserves were still under the jurisdiction of Edwin C. Denby, the United States Secretary of the Navy. Fall convinced Denby to give jurisdiction over the reserves to the Department of the Interior. Fall then leased the rights of the oil to Harry F. Sinclair of Mammoth Oil, a subsidiary of the original Sinclair Oil, without competitive bidding. This manner of leasing was legal under the Mineral Leasing Act of 1920. Concurrently, Fall also leased the Naval oil reserves at Elk Hills, California, to Edward L. Doheny of Pan American Petroleum in exchange for personal loans at no interest. In return for leasing these oil fields to the respective oil magnates, Fall received gifts from the oilmen totaling about $404,000 (equivalent to $4 million in the year 2000). It was this money changing hands that was illegal—not the lease itself. Fall attempted to keep his actions secret, but the sudden improvement in his standard of living prompted speculation.

On April 14, 1922, the *Wall Street Journal* reported a secret arrangement in which Fall had leased the petroleum reserves to a private oil company without competitive bidding. Fall denied the claims, and the leases to the oil companies seemed legal enough on the surface. However, the following day, Democratic Senator John B. Kendrick of Wyoming introduced a resolution that would set in motion one of the most significant investigations in the Senate's history. Republican Senator Robert M. La Follette, Sr. of Wisconsin, arranged for the Senate Committee on Public Lands to investigate the matter. At first, La Follette believed Fall was innocent. However, his suspicions deepened after his office was ransacked. Without any proof and with more ambiguous headlines, the story faded from the public eye. However, the Senate kept investigating.

Investigation and outcome

La Follette's committee allowed the investigation panel's most senior minority member, Democrat Thomas J. Walsh of Montana, to lead what most expected to be a tedious and probably futile inquiry seeking answers to many questions. For two years, Walsh pushed forward while Fall stepped backward, covering his tracks as he went. The Committee found no evidence of wrongdoing, the leases were legal enough, but records kept disappearing mysteriously. Fall had made the leases of the oil fields appear to be legitimate, but his acceptance of the money was his undoing. By 1924, the Committee had only one unanswered question: How did Fall become so rich so quickly?

Senator Albert B. Fall, the first former U.S. cabinet official sentenced to prison.

Money from the bribes went to Fall's cattle ranch and investments in his business. Finally, as the investigation was winding down and preparing to declare Fall innocent, Walsh uncovered one piece of evidence Fall had forgotten to cover up: Doheny's loan to Fall in November 1921, in the amount of $100,000 (equivalent to about $1.22 million in present-day terms).

The investigation led to a series of civil and criminal suits related to the scandal throughout the 1920s. Finally in 1927 the Supreme Court ruled that the oil leases had been corruptly obtained and invalidated the Elk Hills lease in February of that year and the Teapot lease in October of the same year. The Navy regained control of the Teapot Dome and Elk Hills reserves as a result of the Court's decision. Another significant outcome was the Supreme Court case *McGrain v. Daugherty* which, for the first time, explicitly established Congress' right to compel testimony.

Albert Fall was found guilty of bribery in 1929, fined $100,000 and sentenced to one year in prison, making him the first Presidential cabinet member to go to prison for his actions in office. Harry Sinclair, who refused to cooperate with the government investigators, was charged with contempt, fined $100,000, and received a short sentence for jury tampering. Edward Doheny was acquitted in 1930 of attempting to bribe Fall.

See also

- Little Green House on K Street

Further reading

- Noggle, Burl (1962). *Teapot Dome: Oil and Politics In The 1920s* [1]. Louisiana State University Press. doi:10.1336/0313226016 [2].
- McCartney, Laton (February 2008). *Teapot Dome Scandal* [3]. Random House.
- J. Leonard Bates, 1963, *The Origins of Teapot Dome*, U. of Illinois Press: Urbana.
- John Ise, 1926, *The United States Oil Policy*, Yale University Press: New Haven.
- Blakely M. Murphy (editor), 1948. *Conservation of Oil and Gas, A Legal History*, Section of Mineral Law, American Bar Association: Chicago, 1949.
- W. T. Thom and Edmund M. Spieker, 1933, "The Significance of Geologic Conditions in Naval Petroleum Reserve No. 3, Wyoming", *Professional Paper 163*, U.S. Geological Survey, United States Government Printing Office, Washington D.C.
- 1928, *United States Reports—Cases Adjudged in the Supreme Court*, Vol. 273 and Vol. 275. United States Government Printing Office, Washington, D.C.
- Carroll H. Wegemann, 1918. "The Salt Creek Oil Field, Wyoming", *U.S. Geological Survey Bulletin 670*, Government Printing Office: Washington D.C. 1918.
- M. R. Werner and John Starr, 1959, *Teapot Dome*, The Viking Press: New York.
- April 1924, "Some Physical Facts in the Naval Oil Reserve Problem", *Scientific American*, Scientific American Publishing Co.: Munn & Co, N.Y.

External links

- U.S. Geological Survey Geographic Names Information System: East Teapot Dome Oil Field [4]
- Teapot Dome Scandal at OhioHistoryCentral.org [5]
- A summary of the Teapot Dome scandal from the Brookings Institution [6]

Geographical coordinates: 43°17′19″N 106°10′24″W

John Dillinger

John Herbert Dillinger

Born	June 22, 1903 Indianapolis, Indiana, U.S.
Died	July 22, 1934 (aged 31) Chicago, Illinois, U.S.
Charge(s)	Bank robbery, murder
Penalty	Imprisonment from 1924 to 1933
Spouse	Beryl Hovious (divorced)

John Herbert Dillinger Jr. (June 22, 1903 − July 22, 1934) was a gangster and bank-robber in the Depression-era United States. He was charged with the murder of an East Chicago police officer, but never convicted. During his bank heists, a dozen victims—prison officers, police, federal agents, gangsters, and civilians—were killed. His gang robbed two dozen banks and four police stations. Dillinger escaped from jail twice.

In 1933-34, among criminals like Baby Face Nelson, Pretty Boy Floyd, and Bonnie and Clyde, Dillinger was the most notorious of all. Media reports were spiced with exaggerated accounts of his bravado and daring. The public demanded federal action and J. Edgar Hoover developed a more sophisticated Federal Bureau of Investigation as a weapon against organized crime.

After evading police in four states for almost a year, Dillinger was wounded and returned to his father's home to heal. He returned to Chicago in July 1934 and met his end at the hands of police and federal agents who were informed of his whereabouts by Ana Cumpanas. On July 22, the police and Division of Investigation closed in on the Biograph Theater. Federal agents, led by Melvin Purvis, moved to arrest him as he left the theater. He pulled a weapon and attempted to flee but was shot three times and killed.

Early life

Family and background

John Herbert Dillinger Jr. was born in the Oak Hill section of Indianapolis, Indiana, the younger of two children born to John Wilson Dillinger (July 2, 1864 – November 3, 1943) and Mary Ellen "Mollie" Lancaster (1860–1907).[p10] According to some biographers, his grandfather, Matthias Dillinger, immigrated to the United States in 1851 from Metz, in the German-speaking region of Alsace-Lorraine, then under French sovereignty. Matthias Dillinger was born in German-Prussian Gisingen, near Dillingen in the Saarland. His parents had married on August 23, 1887 in Marion County, Indiana. Dillinger's father was a grocer by trade and, reportedly, a harsh man.[p9] In an interview with reporters, he said that he was firm in his discipline and believed in the adage (from poet Samuel Butler) "spare the rod and spoil the child".[p12] Dillinger's older sister, Audrey, was born March 6, 1889. Dillinger's mother died in 1907 just before his fourth birthday.

Audrey married Emmett "Fred" Hancock in April 1924 and had seven children. Dillinger was cared for by his sister during his early life until his father remarried on May 23, 1912 in Morgan County, Indiana, to Elizabeth "Lizzie" Fields (1878–1933). Initially, Dillinger disliked his stepmother, but reportedly eventually came to love her. Dillinger's father and stepmother had three children, Hubert Dillinger, born c. 1913, Doris M. Dillinger, (December 12, 1917 – March 14, 2001) (married surname Hockman) and Frances Dillinger (born c. 1922).

Formative years and marriage

As a teenager, Dillinger was frequently in trouble with the law for fighting, petty theft, and was noted for his "bewildering personality" and bullying the smaller children.[p14] He quit school to work in an Indianapolis machine shop. Although he worked hard at his job, he would stay out all night at parties. His father feared that the city was corrupting his son, prompting him to move the family to Mooresville, Indiana in about 1920.[p15] Dillinger's wild and rebellious behavior was resilient despite his new rural life. He was arrested in 1922 for auto theft and his relationship with his father deteriorated.[pp16-17] His troubles led him to enlist in the U.S. Navy, but he deserted a few months later when his ship was docked in Boston. He was eventually dishonorably discharged.[pp18-20] Dillinger then returned to Mooresville where he met Beryl Ethel Hovious (born August 6, 1906). The two were married in Martinsville on April 12, 1924. He attempted to settle down, but he had difficulty holding a job and preserving his marriage.[p20] The marriage ended in divorce on June 20, 1929.

Dillinger remained unable to find a job, and began planning a robbery with his friend Ed Singleton.[p22] The two robbed a local grocery store stealing $50.[p26] Leaving the scene they were spotted by a minister who recognized the men and reported them to the police. The two men were arrested the next day. Singleton pleaded not guilty, but Dillinger's father convinced him to confess to the crime and plead guilty.[:p24] Dillinger was convicted of assault and battery with intent to rob, and conspiracy to commit a felony. He was sentenced to 10 to 20 years in prison for his crimes. His father told reporters he regretted his advice, and was appalled by the sentence. He pleaded with the judge to shorten the sentence but met with no success.[:p25] En route to the prison, Dillinger briefly escaped his captors but was apprehended within a few minutes.[:p27]

Criminal career

Prison time

Dillinger embraced the criminal lifestyle behind bars in the Indiana State Prison in Michigan City. Upon being admitted to the prison he is quoted as saying, "I will be the meanest bastard you ever saw when I get out of here."[:p26] His physical examination upon being admitted to the prison showed that he had gonorrhea. The treatment for his condition was extremely painful.[:p22] He became embittered against society because of his long prison sentence and befriended other criminals, such as seasoned bank robbers like Harry Pierpont of Muncie and Russell "Boobie" Clark of Terre Haute, who taught Dillinger how to be a successful criminal. The men planned heists that they would commit soon after they were released.[:p32] John Dillinger studied Herman Lamm's meticulous bank-robbing system and used it extensively throughout his criminal career.

His father launched a campaign to have him released, and was able to get 188 signatures on a petition. Dillinger was paroled on May 10, 1933 after serving eight and a half years. Dillinger's stepmother became sick just before he was released from prison and she died before he arrived at her home.[:p37] Released at the height of the Great Depression, Dillinger had little prospect of finding employment.[:p35] He immediately returned to crime,[:p39] and on September 22 robbed a bank in Bluffton, Ohio. Tracked by police from Dayton, Ohio, he was captured and jailed in Lima. After searching him before letting him into the prison, the police discovered a document which appeared to be a prison escape plan. They demanded Dillinger tell them what the document meant, but he refused.

Dillinger had helped conceive a plan for the escape of Pierpont, Clark and six others he had met while previously in prison, most of whom worked in the prison laundry. Dillinger had friends smuggle rifles into their prison cells which they used to escape, killing two guards, four days after Dillinger's capture. The group known as the "first Dillinger gang" included Pierpont, Clark, Charles Makley, Edward W. Shouse, Jr. of Terre Haute, Harry Copeland, James "Oklahoma Jack" Clark, John "Red" Hamilton and Dillinger's mentor Walter Dietrich, a member of the Herman Lamm Gang . Three of the escapees arrived in Lima on October 12, where they impersonated Indiana State Police officers, claiming they had come to extradite Dillinger to Indiana. When the sheriff asked for their credentials, they shot him and beat him unconscious, then released Dillinger from his cell. The four men escaped back into

Indiana where they joined the rest of the gang.

Bank robberies

The Bureau of Investigation (BOI, a precursor of the FBI) was brought into the investigation to help identify the criminals, although the men had not violated any federal law. It was one of the first cases in which the BOI intervened in matters outside its jurisdiction. Using their superior fingerprint matching technology, they successfully identified all of the suspects and issued national bulletins offering rewards for their capture.

Dillinger and his gang, in the meantime, began a streak of bank robberies across Indiana, although the first bank he ever robbed was in New Carlisle, Ohio on June 10, 1933. Among Dillinger's more celebrated exploits involved his pretending to be a sales representative for a company that sold bank alarm systems. He reportedly entered a number of Indiana and Ohio banks and used this ruse to assess security systems and bank vaults of prospective targets. Another time, the gang pretended to be part of a film company that was scouting locations for a "bank robbery" scene. Bystanders stood and smiled as a real robbery ensued and Dillinger and friends escaped with the loot. Stories such as this only served to increase Dillinger's burgeoning legend. Dillinger was believed to have been associated with gangs who robbed dozens of banks and accumulating a total of more than $300,000. Banks allegedly robbed by Dillinger and his associates included The Commercial Bank, Daleville, Indiana of $3,500 on July 17, 1933; Montpelier National Bank, Montpelier, Indiana of $6,700 on August 4, 1933; Bluffton Bank, Bluffton, Ohio, of $6,000 on August 14, 1933; Massachusetts Avenue State Bank, Indianapolis, Indiana, of $21,000 on September 6, 1933; Central National Bank And Trust Co., Greencastle, Indiana, of $74,000 on October 23, 1933; American Bank And Trust Co., Racine, Wisconsin, of $28,000 on November 20, 1933; Unity Trust And Savings Bank, Chicago, Illinois, of $8,700 on December 13, 1933; First National Bank, East Chicago, Indiana, of $20,000 on January 15, 1934; Securities National Bank And Trust Co., Sioux Falls, South Dakota, of $49,500 on March 6, 1934; First National Bank, Mason City, Iowa, of $52,000 on March 13, 1934; and Merchants National Bank, South Bend, Indiana, of $29,890 on June 30, 1934. One possibly true urban legend is that he robbed 1,000 coin bags of Peace Dollars.

To obtain more supplies, the gang attacked the state police arsenals in Auburn and Peru, stealing machine guns, rifles, revolvers, ammunition, and bulletproof vests. They then headed to Chicago to hide out. On December 14, 1933, gang member John "Red" Hamilton murdered a police detective. A month later, Dillinger led the gang in another bank robbery, holding up The First National Bank in East Chicago and killing police officer William O'Malley. Dillinger was officially charged with the murder although the identity of the actual killer was debatable, and it is in question whether Dillinger participated in the robbery at all.[:p154] As police began closing in again, the men left Chicago to hide out first in Florida; later at The Gardener Hotel in El Paso, Texas, where a highly visible police presence dissuaded Dillinger from trying to cross the border at The Santa Fe Bridge in downtown El Paso to

Ciudad Juárez, Mexico; and finally in Tucson, Arizona.

On the run

A fire broke out at the Hotel Congress in Tucson where members of the Dillinger gang were staying. Forced to leave their luggage behind, they were rescued through a window and down a fire truck ladder. Charles Makley tipped a couple of firemen $12 to climb back up and retrieve the luggage, affording the firefighters a good look at several members of Dillinger's gang. The firemen later recognized Makley and Ed Shouse while thumbing through a copy of *True Detective* and informed the police who promptly arrested Harry Pierpont, Charles Makley, Russell Clark, Ed Shouse, and Dillinger. They found them in possession of over $25,000 in cash and several automatic weapons. Tucson celebrates the historic arrest with an annual "Dillinger Days" festival, the highlight of which is a reenactment.

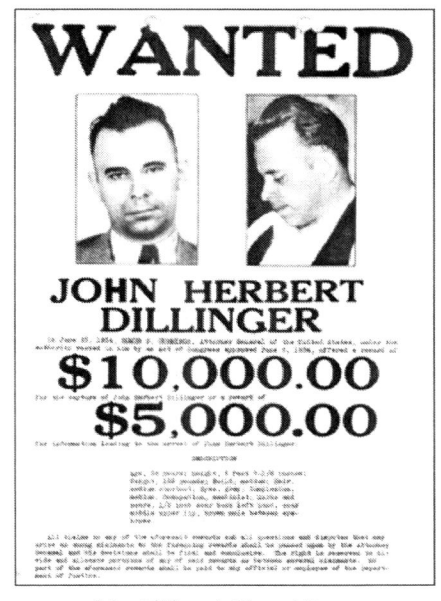

John Dillinger's Wanted Poster

The men were extradited to Indiana, where Dillinger was held in the Crown Point jail, while the others were then sent to Ohio to stand trial for the murder of Sheriff Jess Sarber. Testimony by Shouse identified the five men as members of the Pierpont gang.[citation needed] Dillinger was charged with the murder of a police officer in East Chicago, while Pierpont and Makley were charged with the murder of Sheriff Jesse Sarber.[citation needed] The police boasted to area newspapers that the jail was escape-proof and posted extra guards to make sure. Louis Piquett, John Dillinger's attorney, was able to sneak a wooden gun within the prison and into the hands of Dillinger. Using it, he was able to trick a guard into opening his cell. He then took two men hostage, rounded up all the guards in the jail, locked them in his cell, and fled. Before leaving, Dillinger said to the guards he locked up, "See what I locked all of you monkeys up with? Nothing but a little piece of wood. Well, so long, boys. I'll have to be moving on." Dillinger stole Sheriff Lillian Holley's new Ford car, embarrassing her and the town, and traveled to Chicago. In so doing, he crossed the state line in a stolen car, breaking the federal Motor Vehicle Theft Act. The crime was under the jurisdiction of the BOI who immediately took over the Dillinger case after the car was found abandoned in Chicago. Dillinger was indicted by a local grand jury and the BOI organized a nationwide manhunt for him.[citation needed]

In Chicago, Dillinger began living with his girlfriend Evelyn "Billie" Frechette. They proceeded to Saint Paul, Minnesota, met up with "Red" Hamilton, and mustered a new gang, adding Lester "Baby

Face Nelson" Gillis, Homer Van Meter, Tommy Carroll, Joseph Fox, Joe Burns, James Jenkins, John Paul Chase, Charles Fisher, and Eddie Green. The landlord of their apartment became suspicious and on March 30, 1934, reported his suspicions to a federal agent. The building was placed under surveillance by the federal agents who soon determined Dillinger was in the apartment. When one gang member, who was attempting to enter the apartment, was questioned, he opened fire on the agents before escaping behind a closed door. The entire gang then opened fire on the agents and fled out of a back entrance before back-up could arrive. They commandeered a truck and drove to Eddie Green's home. Dillinger was wounded in the escape and required medical attention. Federal agents later closed in on the building and the gang opened fire as they escaped and split up. Eddie Green was killed in the escape. Dillinger and his girlfriend traveled to the home of Dillinger's father in Mooresville, where they remained until the wound healed. When Frechette returned to Chicago to visit a friend, she was arrested but refused to reveal Dillinger's whereabouts. Dillinger was watching from a side street and wanted to rescue her, but he was stopped by the girlfriend of John Hamilton, who convinced him he would die in the attempt. Yet he still drove along the block several times and entered a police station to see if it was possible.[citation needed]

Dillinger returned to crime again. He and Homer Van Meter robbed the police station in Warsaw, Indiana, stealing guns and bulletproof vests. After separating, Dillinger picked up Hamilton, who was recovering from a wound obtained in a heist in Mason City, Iowa. The two then traveled to the Upper Peninsula of Michigan, where they remained for a short time. Dillinger received a tip that federal agents were headed to the town, and left just days before they arrived.

Final months

Little Bohemia Lodge

In April, the Dillinger gang settled at a lodge hideout called Little Bohemia Lodge, owned by Emil Wanatka, in the northern Wisconsin town of Manitowish Waters. The gang assured the owners that they would give no trouble, but they monitored the owners whenever they left or spoke on the phone. Emil's wife Nan and her brother managed to evade Baby Face Nelson, who was tailing them, and mailed a letter of warning to a U.S. Attorney's office in Chicago, which later contacted the Division of Investigation. Days later, a score of federal agents led by Hugh Clegg and Melvin Purvis approached the lodge in the early morning hours. Two barking watchdogs announced their arrival, but the gang was so used to Nan Wanatka's dogs that they did not bother to inspect the disturbance. It was only after the federal agents mistakenly shot a local resident and two innocent Civilian Conservation Corps workers as they were about to drive away in a car that the Dillinger gang was alerted to the presence of the BOI. Gunfire between the groups lasted only momentarily, but the whole gang managed to escape in various ways despite the agents' efforts to surround and storm the lodge. Agent W. Carter Baum was shot dead by "Baby Face" Nelson during the gun battle. At this time Nelson would separate from the gang for a while.

The next day, Dillinger, Van Meter and Hamilton were confronted by authorities in Hastings, Minnesota. Hamilton was mortally wounded in the encounter. He was taken by Dillinger and Van Meter to see Joseph Moran, though Moran refused to treat Hamilton. He died on April 30, 1934. Dillinger, Van Meter, and members of the Barker-Karpis gang buried him. Dillinger and Van Meter then met up with Carroll and the three would spend all of May in hiding. On June 7, the three had a shootout with authorities and Carroll died in the encounter. Dillinger and Van Meter reunited with Nelson a week later and went into hiding.

By July 1934, Dillinger had dropped completely out of sight and the federal agents had no solid leads to follow. He had, in fact, drifted into Chicago and went under the alias of Jimmy Lawrence, a petty criminal from Wisconsin who bore a close resemblance to the bank robber. Taking up a job as a clerk, Dillinger also found a new girlfriend named Mary Evelyn "Billie" Frechette, who was aware of his true identity and even served two years in prison for harboring a criminal. In a large metropolis like Chicago, Dillinger was able to lead an anonymous existence for a while. What Dillinger didn't realize was that the center of the federal agents' dragnet happened to be in Chicago. When the authorities found Dillinger's bloodied getaway car on a Chicago side street, they were positive that he was in the city.

Lady in Red

Division of Investigations chief J. Edgar Hoover created a special task force headquartered in Chicago to locate Dillinger. On July 21 a madam from a brothel in Gary, Indiana, Ana Cumpănaş, also known as Anna Sage, contacted the police. She was a Romanian immigrant threatened with deportation for "low moral character," and offered the federal agency information on Dillinger in exchange for their help in preventing her deportation. The agency agreed to her terms. Cumpănaş told them that Dillinger was spending his time with another prostitute, Polly Hamilton, and that she and the couple would be going to see a movie together on the following day. She agreed to wear an orange dress, which appeared red in the lights of the theater, so that police could easily identify her at the theater. She was unsure which theater they would be attending, but told the agency the name of the two theaters, the Biograph and the Marbro, in which they would potentially be. A team of federal agents and officers from police forces outside Chicago was formed. Chicago police officers were excluded because it was felt that the Chicago police had been compromised and could not be trusted. Not chancing another embarrassing escape, the police were split into two teams. On July 22, one team was sent to the Marbro Theater on the city's West Side, while another team surrounded the Biograph Theater at 2433 N. Lincoln Avenue on the North Side. During the stakeout, the Biograph's manager thought the agents were criminals setting up a robbery. He called the Chicago police who dutifully responded and had to be waved off by the federal agents, who told them that they were on a stakeout for an important target.

Biograph Theater

Dillinger attended the film *Manhattan Melodrama* at the Biograph Theater in Chicago's Lincoln Park neighborhood. Dillinger was with his girlfriend, Polly Hamilton, and Ana Cumpănaş. Once they determined that Dillinger was in the theater, the lead agent (Samuel A. Cowley) contacted J. Edgar Hoover for instructions, who recommended that they wait outside rather than risk a gun battle in a crowded theater. He also told the agents not to put themselves in harm's way, and that any man could open fire on Dillinger at the first sign of resistance. When the movie let out, Special Agent Melvin Purvis stood by

Bureau of Investigation photograph of the Biograph Theater in 1934, soon after Dillinger's death.

the front door and signaled Dillinger's exit by lighting a cigar. Both he and the agents reported that Dillinger turned his head and looked directly at the agent as he walked by, glanced across the street, then moved ahead of his female companions, reached into his pocket but failed to extract his gun,[:p353] and ran into a nearby alley.

Grave in Crown Hill Cemetery, Indianapolis, Indiana.

Three agents opened fire, firing five shots. Dillinger was hit from behind and he fell face first to the ground. Two female bystanders were slightly wounded in the legs and buttocks by flying bullet and brick fragments. Dillinger was struck three times, twice in the chest, one actually nicking his heart, and the fatal shot, which entered the back of his neck and exited just under his right eye. An ambulance was summoned, though it was clear that Dillinger had quickly died from his gunshot wounds. At 10:50 p.m. on July 22, 1934, John Dillinger was pronounced dead at Alexian Brothers Hospital.

According to the investigators, Dillinger died without saying a word. There were also reports of people dipping their handkerchiefs and skirts into the pools of blood that had formed as Dillinger lay in the alley in order to secure keepsakes of the entire affair. Dillinger's body was displayed to the public at the Cook County morgue after his death.

Dillinger was buried at Crown Hill Cemetery (Section: 44 Lot: 94) in Indianapolis. His gravestone has had to be replaced several times because of vandalism by people chipping off pieces as souvenirs.

Film depictions

- Lawrence Tierney played the title role in the first film dramatization of Dillinger's career; *Dillinger* (1945).
- Director Don Siegel's 1957 film *Baby Face Nelson*, starred Mickey Rooney as Nelson and Leo Gordon as Dillinger.
- In 1959's "The FBI Story" starring James Stewart, Jean Willes plays Anna Sage and Scott Peters plays Dillinger. Peters, a small-time actor, went uncredited in this role.
- Director Marco Ferreri's 1969 film *Dillinger Is Dead* includes documentary footage of real John Dillinger as well as newspaper clips.
- 1973's *Dillinger*, directed and written by John Milius with Warren Oates in the title role, presented the gang in a much more sympathetic light, in keeping with the anti-hero theme popular in films after *Bonnie and Clyde* (1967).
- Lewis Teague directed the 1979 film *The Lady in Red*, starring Pamela Sue Martin as the eponymous lady in the red dress. However, in this film, it is Dillinger's girlfriend Polly in red, not the Romanian informant Anna Sage (Louise Fletcher). Sage tricks Polly into wearing red so that FBI agents can identify Dillinger (Robert Conrad) as he emerges from the cinema.
- A TV film *Dillinger* was released in 1991, starring Mark Harmon.
- Director Michael Mann's 2009 film *Public Enemies* is an adaptation of Bryan Burrough's book *Public Enemies: America's Greatest Crime Wave and the Birth of the FBI, 1933-43*. The film features Johnny Depp as John Dillinger and Christian Bale as FBI agent Melvin Purvis, but is inaccurate in some major historical details, such as the timeline of deaths of key criminal figures including Pretty Boy Floyd and Baby Face Nelson.

See also

- List of Depression-era outlaws

Further reading

- Beverly, William. *On the Lam: Narratives of Flight in J. Edgar Hoover's America* [1]. Jackson, Mississippi: University Press of Mississippi. 2003. ISBN 1578065372.
- Burrough, Bryan. *Public Enemies: America's Greatest Crime Wave and the Birth of the FBI, 1933-34* [2]. New York: Penguin Press. 2004. ISBN 1594200211.
- DeBartolo, Anthony. *Dillinger's Dupes: Town Seeks To Preserve A Jail Yet Escape A Dastardly Deed. Chicago Tribune.*
- Erickson, Matt and Bill Thornbro. *John Dillinger: A Year in the Life.* [3] *The Times of Northwest Indiana.*

- Helmer, William J.; Mattix, Rick (1998). Public Enemies: America's Criminal Past, 1919-1940. New York City, New York: Facts on File. p. 17. ISBN 0816031606.
- Stewart, Tony. *Dillinger, The Hidden Truth: A Tribute to Gangsters and G-Men of the Great Depression Era.* [4] Xlibris Corporation, 2002. ISBN 1401053734.
- Peters, Robert. *What Dillinger Meant to Me* [5] Seahorse Press 1983 (with link to complete text online)
- Toland, John. *The Dillinger Days*. Random House 1963

External links

- Famous Cases: John Dillinger [6] – at the FBI
- Wanted poster: John Dillinger, published 12 March 1934 by U.S. Department of Justice, Division of Investigation [7]
- John Dillinger [8] at Find a Grave
- *Dillinger: The Untold Story*, Anniversary Edition. [9] Indiana University Press.
- Matera, Dary. Review of *John Dillinger*. [10] Letters on Pages.
- John Dillinger Historical Crime Museum [11].
- Dillinger with rare photos from the FBI and U.S. National Archives [12]
- Dillinger not killed [13]
- Johndillinger.com [14]

Little Bohemia Lodge

The **Little Bohemia Lodge** in Manitowish Waters, Wisconsin was the site of the epic 1934 gun battle between John Dillinger and his gang, and Melvin Purvis and the FBI. The Lodge was built in 1927, suffered a fire in 1928, and was rebuilt in 1930. The historic Lodge remains as it was at the time of the FBI siege in 1934 and has a collection of memorabilia and damage from the gun fight, including the original bullet holes in the walls and windows. The Lodge is located on US Highway 51 in Manitowish Waters, Wisconsin on Little Star Lake, on the Manitowish Chain O Lakes.

The battle

On April 20, 1934, the John Dillinger gang settled at Little Bohemia Lodge, then owned by Emil Wanatka, in the northern Wisconsin town of Manitowish Waters. The gang assured the owners that they would give no trouble, but the gang monitored the owners whenever they left or spoke on the phone. Emil's wife Nan and her brother managed to evade Baby Face Nelson, who was tailing them, and mailed a letter of warning to the U.S. Attorney's office in Chicago, which later contacted the FBI. Days later, a score of FBI agents led by Hugh Clegg and Melvin Purvis approached the lodge in the early morning hours of April 23. Two barking watchdogs announced their arrival, but the gang was so used to Nan Wanatka's dogs that they did not bother to inspect the disturbance. It was only when the FBI mistakenly gunned down a local resident, John Hoffman, and two innocent Civilian Conservation Corps workers, John Morris and Eugene Boisneau, as they drove away that the Dillinger gang was alerted to the presence of the FBI. Gunfire between the groups lasted only moments, but the whole gang managed to escape. Agent W. Carter Baum was shot dead by "Baby Face" Nelson during the gun battle.

Public Enemies

In the summer of 2008, some scenes from the Michael Mann film *Public Enemies* were filmed at the lodge. Actors involved included Johnny Depp as John Dillinger, and Christian Bale as Melvin Purvis, among others.

Today

The Lodge remains operational today as a restaurant and gathering place. The Lodge is open year round, seven days a week for breakfast, lunch and dinner. A historic display of artifacts and memorabilia from the Dillinger gun battle is available for public viewing along with recent memorabilia and autographs from the filming of Public Enemies.

External links

- Little Bohemia Lodge [1]

Geographical coordinates: 46°07′10″N 89°51′27″W

Biograph Theater

Biograph Theater	
U.S. National Register of Historic Places	
Chicago Landmark	
The Biograph Theater in June 2007	
Location:	2433 N Lincoln Avenue, Chicago, Illinois
Coordinates:	41°55′34.5″N 87°38′59.6″W
Built/Founded:	1915
Architect:	Samuel Crowen
Architectural style(s):	Classical Revival
Governing body:	Private
Added to NRHP:	May 17, 1984
Designated CL:	March 28, 2001
NRHP Reference#:	84000934

The **Biograph Theater**, at 2433 North Lincoln Avenue, Lincoln Park in Chicago, Illinois, was originally a movie theater but now presents live productions. It is notable as the location where bank robber John Dillinger was shot by FBI agents after watching a gangster movie on July 22, 1934. The theater is on the National Register of Historic Places and was designated a Chicago Landmark on March 28, 2001.

History

Designed by architect Samuel N. Crowen in 1914, the Biograph has many of the distinguishing characteristics of movie houses of the period, including a storefront-width lobby, recessed entrance, free-standing ticket booth, and canopy marquee. The building is finished with red pressed brick and white-glazed terra cotta.

1934 FBI photograph of the Biograph, soon after the shooting of Dillinger

On July 22, 1934, after attending the film *Manhattan Melodrama* with brothel madam known as Ann Sage also known as Ana Cumpănaş and Polly Hamilton, John Dillinger was shot dead outside the Biograph by FBI agents led by Melvin Purvis, when he attempted to pull a pistol and flee into the crowd after he saw them. Dillinger's whereabouts had been leaked to the FBI by Cumpănaş under the threat of deportation back to her birth place of Romania.

In July 2004, after 90 years as a movie theater under various owners, Chicago's Victory Gardens Theater announced it had purchased the Biograph for use as a live venue. The theater was completely renovated by architect Daniel P. Coffey, who constructed a proscenium-thrust stage and seating for 299 people. A grand staircase, which was part of the original structure, was restored to lead up to the building's second floor, housing a studio theater seating 135 people and an adjacent rehearsal/multiple-use space. The $11 million project for the new theater, styled the **Victory Gardens at the Biograph**, was completed in the fall of 2006. The new stage is 30 feet (9.1 m) deep and 32 feet (9.8 m) wide, with 16 feet (4.9 m) of wing space on either side. There is an 8-foot (2.4 m) trap space below the stage. There is limited fly space above the stage. There are two dressing rooms and a green room behind the stage. The lobby is wider than in the movie theater days, and the restrooms have been expanded.

The facades of the theater and adjoining businesses were redressed to appear as they did in 1934 for the 2009 film *Public Enemies*.

External links

- Development plans for the Biograph Theater [1]
- {http://www.victorygardens.org/Victory gardens Theater]

Alvin Karpis

Alvin Francis "Creepy Karpis" Karpowicz (August 10, 1907 – August 26, 1979), born **Alvin Karpowicz**, better known as **Alvin Karpis** and nicknamed **"Creepy"** for his sinister smile, was an American criminal known for his alliance with the Barker gang in the 1930s. He was the last "public enemy" to be taken.

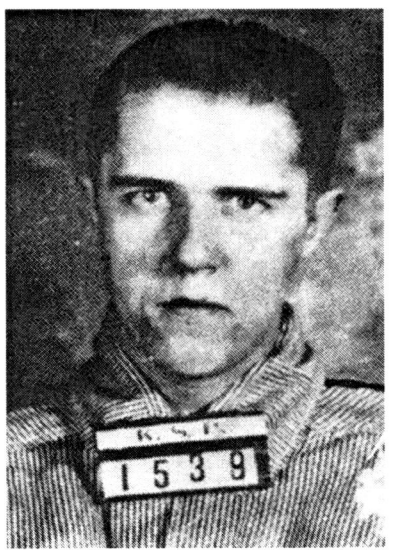

Alvin Karpis

Early life

Karpis was born to Lithuanian immigrants in Montreal, Quebec, Canada, and was raised in Wichita, Kansas. He started in crime at about age 10 running around with gamblers, bootleggers, and pimps. In 1926, he was sentenced to 10 years at the State Industrial Reformatory in Hutchinson, Kansas, for an attempted burglary. He escaped with another inmate Lawrence De Vol and went on a year-long crime spree interrupted briefly while he lived with his parents after De Vol was arrested. After moving to Kansas City, Missouri, he was caught stealing a car and sent back to the Reformatory. Transferred to the Kansas State Penitentiary in Lansing, Kansas, he met Fred Barker who was in prison for bank burglary. Barker was one of the notorious members of the "Bloody Barkers" as the newspapers of the time had called them. The Barker family included the brothers Herman, Lloyd, Arthur or "Doc," and Fred, the sons of Ma Barker. Growing up impoverished in a sharecropping family, all the boys soon turned into hardened criminals, robbing banks and killing without provocation. Doc was sentenced to life imprisonment in 1920 after murdering a night watchman. Herman committed suicide on August 29, 1927, after being badly injured in a shootout with police in Wichita Kansas following the robbery of the Newton Ice Plant in Newton, KS with Charles Stalcup and Porter Meeks. Lloyd was sentenced to 25 years in 1922, for mail theft and released in 1938; he was a US Army Cook at a POW camp and then was murdered by his own wife in 1947. Ma did her part to help her sons. "Ma" Barker was not herself a criminal, she did nevertheless badger parole boards, wardens, and governors for the release of her boys when they were incarcerated. After Alvin was released in 1931, he joined up with Fred Barker in Tulsa, Oklahoma, and they soon put together the Karpis-Barker gang.

Alliance with Barkers

The Karpis-Barker gang became one of the most formidable criminal gangs of the 1930s. They did not hesitate to kill anyone who got in their way, even innocent bystanders. They robbed a number of banks, hijacked mail deliveries, and soon turned to the lucrative field of kidnapping. In 1933, they kidnapped William Hamm, a millionaire Minnesota brewer. His ransom netted them $100,000. Shortly after this, they abducted Minnesota banker Edward Bremer, Jr., whose ransom brought them $200,000. The group was led by Alvin, who had a photographic memory and was described as "super-smart" by fellow gang member Fred Hunter. The other leaders were Doc and Fred, both now out of prison, and the gang included about 25 others. At this time a myth was started that Ma Barker ruled the gang with an iron fist, but the facts do not seem to support these claims. It is highly unlikely that criminals as adept as Karpis, and even Ma's sons for that matter, would have listened to her. Karpis later wrote about this subject in his memoirs:

> "Ma was always somebody in our lives. Love didn't enter into it really. She was somebody we looked after and took with us when we moved city to city, hideout to hideout. It is no insult to Ma's memory that she just didn't have the know-how to direct us on a robbery. It would not have occurred to her to get involved in our business, and we always made it a point of only discussing our scores when Ma wasn't around. We'd leave her at home when we were arranging a job, or we'd send her to a movie. Ma saw a lot of movies."

Harvey Bailey, another well-known bank robber of the era knew the Barker gang well, and in his autobiography published in the 1970's, he agreed with Karpis, observing that Ma Barker "couldn't plan breakfast", and was certainly no mastermind behind any gang activity. Ma Barker's entire reputation as a criminal mastermind was concocted by Hoover to protect the FBI's public image after federal agents discovered they had killed a 62 year old mother.

The kidnappings, however, would lead to the gang's end. The father of the kidnapped Edward Bremer Jr. was a friend of president Franklin D. Roosevelt. FDR had even mentioned the kidnapping in one of his fireside chats and, fueled also by the Lindbergh kidnapping, the FBI and local police bureaus greatly stepped up their pursuit of those engaged in these types of crimes. The FBI had by this time organized a group of highly skilled agents called the "flying squads" who specialized in hunting down the leading public enemies, and much progress was being made. The year 1934 alone saw the deaths of John Dillinger, Bonnie and Clyde, Charles "Pretty Boy" Floyd, Lester "Baby Face Nelson" Gillis, John "Red" Hamilton, Homer Van Meter, Tommy Carroll, and Eddie Green.

Just after Ma and Fred's death on January 16, 1935, Karpis nearly met his own violent end when the FBI located him in Atlantic City, New Jersey. Karpis and Harry Campbell managed to shoot their way to an escape, though Karpis's eight-month-pregnant girlfriend Dolores Delaney was hit in the thigh by a wild shot fired by Campbell. He continued his crimes with others, but had to be on the move more than ever as he was the fourth and last Public Enemy left (the previous three having been killed). He did manage to pull off a crime that echoed times of the "Old West," a train robbery in Garrettsville, Ohio, which netted $27,000. After the death of Ma and Fred, Karpis sent word to J. Edgar Hoover that he intended to kill Hoover the way Hoover had killed Ma and Fred.

Pursuit and capture by FBI

The FBI had come a long way since its reorganization and renaming in 1935 (from the Bureau of Investigation, created in 1908). J. Edgar Hoover was appointed as the acting head of the Bureau in 1924 and completely transformed the agency. Despite its successes, however, the agency had many problems. In those days, when the application of science and technology to fight crime was still in its infancy, the agency was at the mercy of public citizens for information. Often agents were sent off to remote locales that turned out to be red herrings due to bad information. The personal low-point for Hoover came at an April 1936 United States Senate hearing. Tennessee Senator Kenneth D. McKellar lambasted Hoover for the performance of the FBI and the fact that Hoover himself had never personally arrested anyone. After the hearing a determined Hoover vowed he would capture Karpis personally.

Hoover would not have to wait long. On May 1, 1936, the FBI located Karpis in New Orleans, and Hoover flew in to be in charge of the arrest. As a dozen or so agents swarmed over Karpis's car, Hoover announced to Karpis that he was under arrest. A couple of versions of the arrest are reported. Karpis' version of the story told in his memoirs was that Hoover came out only after all the other agents had him seized. Only then did the agents call to Hoover that it was safe to approach the car.The official FBI version states that Hoover reached into the car and grabbed Karpis before he could reach a rifle in the back seat. (In fact, the car, a Plymouth coupe, had no back seat.) The whole fiasco was further aggravated when Hoover told his men to "put the handcuffs on him"[citation needed]. Not one agent had brought handcuffs as federal agents had planned on killing Karpis as they had the other public enemies. Karpis was tied up with the necktie removed from an agent's neck. The capture of Karpis catapulted Hoover's name into the public eye, and that name would be synonymous with law enforcement until he died in 1972 at the age of 77.

The capture of Karpis essentially ended the age of the big-name depression-era criminals. In addition to those mentioned earlier, others killed violently in the 1930s were Jack "Legs" Diamond, Vincent "Maddog" Coll, Frank "Jelly" Nash, Dutch Schultz, and John Dillinger. Al Capone was in Alcatraz and slowly going insane from syphilis. The country had gradually started to recover from the Great Depression and economic times had improved, and law enforcement agencies had improved as well.

Imprisonment

Sentenced to life imprisonment, Karpis was incarcerated at the recently formed Alcatraz federal penitentiary from August 1936 to April 1962. For six months in 1958, he had been transferred to the Leavenworth federal penitentiary, but was then returned to Alcatraz. His main job at Alcatraz was working at the bakery. He was far from a model prisoner, frequently fighting with other inmates. However, Karpis is renowned for being the prisoner with the longest sentence at Alcatraz, yet not a single escape attempt.[citation needed] In April 1962, with Alcatraz in the process of being closed, he was transferred to McNeil Island Penitentiary in Washington state. While at McNeil, Karpis, a man known for lying, claimed to have met a young inmate named Charles Manson. Karpis wrote about Manson in his autobiography with Robert Livesey, published in 1980):

> This kid approaches me to request music lessons. He wants to learn guitar and become a music star. "Little Charlie" is so lazy and shiftless, I doubt if he'll put in the time required to learn. The youngster has been in institutions all of his life — first orphanages, then reformatories, and finally federal prison. His mother, a prostitute, was never around to look after him. I decide it's time someone did something for him, and to my surprise, he learns quickly. He has a pleasant voice and a pleasing personality, although he's unusually meek and mild for a convict. He never has a harsh word to say and is never involved in even an argument.

After Manson had actually become somewhat proficient on the guitar, he asked Karpis for help in getting a job playing in Las Vegas as Karpis had contacts with nightclub and casino owners there. Manson even told him he would be bigger than the Beatles, but in the end Karpis decided to leave Manson on his own regarding his music career. Manson was moved to a Los Angeles facility in 1967, which proved to be one of the most ominous prison transfers ever. Later Karpis added

> The history of crime in the United States might have been considerably altered if "Little Charlie" had been given the opportunity to find fame and fortune in the music industry. He later became the infamous Charles Manson.

Later years

Karpis was released on parole in 1969, and deported to Canada, although he initially had difficulty obtaining Canadian passport credentials, having had his fingerprints removed by underworld physician Joseph Moran in 1934.

He wrote his first memoirs in 1971, and published another memoir book in 1979 (v.s). During his first book tour across Canada for *Public Enemy Number One* for McClelland & Stewart (published in the United States as *The Alvin Karpis Story*), Karpis, looking more like an accountant than a gangster, still showed a wry sense of humour. In Edmonton, Alberta, while shuffling Karpis between various interviews with the media, M&S book rep Ruth Bertelsen made a stop at her bank. Asking Karpis if he wanted to come in with her, Karpis replied "No dear, you take care of the vault, I'll drive." He became a mentor to her young son until the sociopathy of some of his advice to her child caused Ms. Bertelsen to break off their relationship.[citation needed]

He moved to Spain in 1973. On August 26, 1979, he died by what was originally ruled suicide by authorities, as sleeping pills were found by his body, but later it was ruled death from natural causes. Some closer to the scene say foul play may have been involved. Robert Livesey, who co-wrote Karpis's 1979 book, said Karpis was not the type to have committed suicide. Livesey said Karpis was a survivor, having served 33 years in prison, and also stated Karpis was anticipating the publication of the book. Livesey believed Karpis had been introduced to pills and alcohol by his last girlfriend Nancy, to give a relaxing high, and perhaps Karpis accidentally over-indulged on one occasion, with fatal consequences. No autopsy was done, and Karpis was buried the next day in Spain.[citation needed]

See also

- List of Depression-era outlaws

References

Other sources

- Richard Kudish, CourtTV Crime Library
- Carl Sifakis, *The Encyclopedia of American Crime*, 1992
- Frank Girardot, Crime Scene Blog [1]

External links

- Barker Karpis Gang [2]
- Public Enemy No. 1 [1]

Machine Gun Kelly

Machine Gun Kelly aka George Kelly Barnes	
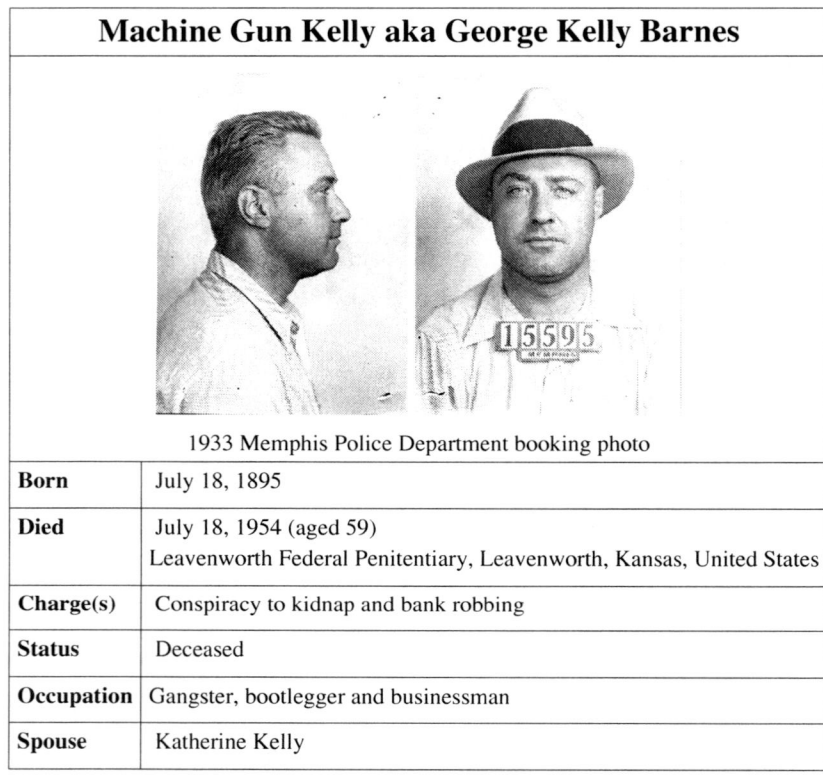 1933 Memphis Police Department booking photo	
Born	July 18, 1895
Died	July 18, 1954 (aged 59) Leavenworth Federal Penitentiary, Leavenworth, Kansas, United States
Charge(s)	Conspiracy to kidnap and bank robbing
Status	Deceased
Occupation	Gangster, bootlegger and businessman
Spouse	Katherine Kelly

George Kelly Barnes (July 18, 1895 - July 18, 1954), better known as **"Machine Gun Kelly"**, was a notorious American criminal during the prohibition era. Kelly's nickname came from his favorite weapon, a Thompson submachine gun. His most famous crime was the kidnapping of oil tycoon & businessman Charles Urschel in July 1933 for which he, and his gang, earned $200,000 in ransom. The FBI investigation eventually led to Kelly's arrest in Memphis, Tennessee on September 26, 1933. His crimes also included bootlegging and armed robbery.

Career

As he lived in the Prohibition era of the 1920s and 30s, George was able to find work as a bootlegger for himself as well as a colleague. After a short time, and several run-ins with the local Memphis police, he decided to leave town and head west with a new girlfriend.

To protect his family and escape law enforcement officers, he changed his name to George R. Kelly. He continued to commit smaller crimes and bootlegging. He was arrested in Tulsa, Oklahoma, for smuggling liquor onto an Indian Reservation in 1928, and sentenced for three years to Leavenworth Penitentiary, Kansas. Sent to Leavenworth on February 11, 1928, he was a model inmate and was released early.

Shortly thereafter, Kelly married Kathryn Thorne, who purchased Kelly's first machine gun and went to great lengths to familiarize his name in the underground crime circles. Some historians claim that Kathryn coined the nickname "Machine Gun Kelly" and even went so far as to plot some small bank robberies.

George "Machine Gun" Kelly is led from Shelby County Jail enroute to the Memphis airport and Oklahoma City for his trial for the kidnapping of Charles F. Urschel, Oct 2, 1933

Kathryn and "Machine Gun" Kelly received life sentences for Urschel kidnapping, Oct 12, 1933

Nonetheless, Kelly's last criminal activity proved disastrous when he kidnapped a wealthy Oklahoma City resident, Charles F. Urschel and his friend Walter R. Jarrett. Urschel, having been blindfolded, made sure to foil his kidnappers by noting all possible evidence of his experience such as background sounds, counting footsteps and leaving fingerprints on every surface in reach. This in turn proved invaluable for the FBI in their investigation, as they learned that Urschel had been held in Paradise, Texas.

Machine Gun Kelly's hideout at 1408
Rayner Street in Memphis, TN (2010)

An investigation conducted at Memphis disclosed that after 56 days on the run, the Kellys were staying at the residence of J.C. Tichenor. Special Agents from Birmingham, Alabama, were immediately dispatched to Memphis, where, in the early morning hours of September 26, 1933, a raid was conducted. George and Kathryn Kelly were taken into custody by FBI Agents and Memphis police officers Sergeant William Raney and officer Thomas Waterson. Caught without a weapon, George Kelly supposedly cried, *"Don't shoot, G-Men! Don't shoot, G-Men!"* as he surrendered to FBI Agents. The term (which had applied to all federal investigators, meaning simply 'Government Men') became synonymous with FBI Agents. Reports of the raid, however, indicate that George Kelly came to the door, dropped his pistol and said, *"I've been waiting for you all night."* Recent research revealed a 1933 newspaper interview with one of the federal agents at the arrest. He commented that, upon their arrest, Kathryn Kelly put her arms around George and said, *"These G-men will never leave us alone."* Thus, it was actually Kathryn Kelly who coined the term. However, the FBI press machine generated the G-Man story to build its own reputation. The FBI itself now repudiates the "Don't shoot, G-Men!" story.

On October 12, 1933, George and Kathryn Kelly were convicted and sentenced to life imprisonment. The trial was held at the Post Office, Courthouse, and Federal Office Building in Oklahoma City. Kathryn Kelly and her mother had all charges dropped and were released in 1958 from prison in Cincinnati.

The kidnapping of Urschel and the two trials that resulted were historic in several ways: 1) they were the first, last, and only federal criminal trials in the United States in which moving cameras were allowed to film; 2) the first kidnapping trials after the passage of the so-called Lindbergh Law, which made kidnapping a federal crime; 3) the first major case solved by J. Edgar Hoover's evolving and powerful FBI. And for that, Kelly got sent into Alcatraz; and 4) the first crime in which defendants were transported by airplane. At the time it was the largest ransom ever paid in the United States.

Death

Machine Gun Kelly spent his remaining 21 years in prison. During his time at Alcatraz he got the nickname "Pop Gun Kelly." This was in reference, according to a former prisoner, to the fact that Kelly was a model prisoner and was nowhere near the tough, brutal gangster his wife made him out to be. He spent 17 years on Alcatraz, working in the prison industries, and was quietly transferred back to Leavenworth in 1951. He died of a heart attack at Leavenworth Federal Prison, Kansas on July 18, 1954 - his 59th birthday.

George B Kelley

He is buried at Cottondale Texas Cemetery with a small headstone marked "George B. Kelley 1954".

In popular culture

- Machine Gun Kelly and Kathryn Kelly were the inspiration for "Machine Gun Kelly" (1970), a song written by Danny "Kootch" Kortchmar and recorded by James Taylor on his 1971 Album *Mud Slide Slim and the Blue Horizon*.
- Machine Gun Kelly and his crimes were (loosely) portrayed in the 1958 film *Machine-Gun Kelly* starring Charles Bronson.
- Machine Gun Kelly is a central character in the 1974 TV film *Melvin Purvis: G-Man*. [1]
- Punk band the Angelic Upstarts released a single in 1984 titled Machine Gun Kelly.
- Machine Gun Kelly is referenced in So I Married an Axe Murderer by Phil Hartman's character while touring Alcatraz.
- In the song "MVP" by the late Harlem rapper Big L, he says: "my run is like Machine Gun Kelly, with a black skully, put one in your belly, leave you smelly and take your Pelle Pelle."

Further reading

- Hamilton, Stanley (2003). *Machine Gun Kelly's Last Stand*. University Press of Kansas. ISBN 9780700612475.
- Atkins, Ace (2010). *Infamous*. G.P. Putnam's Sons.
- Dowd, James (April 26, 2010). *Book tells tale of capturing infamous Machine Gun Kelly*. Memphis Commercial Appeal (newspaper).

External links

Machine Gun Kelly [2] at Find a Grave

Walter Winchell

Walter Winchell	
Born	April 7, 1897 New York City, New York, U.S.
Died	February 20, 1972 (aged 74) Los Angeles, California, U.S.

Walter Winchell (April 7, 1897 – February 20, 1972) was an American newspaper and radio commentator. He invented the gossip column while at the *New York Evening Graphic*.

Professional career

Born **Walter Winschel** in New York City, he started performing in vaudeville troupes as a teenager.

He began his career in journalism by posting notes about his acting troupe on backstage bulletin boards. He began writing for the *Vaudeville News* in 1920, leaving the paper for the *Evening Graphic* in 1924. On June 10, 1929 he was hired by the *New York Daily Mirror* where he finally became a syndicated columnist.

By the 1930s, he was "an intimate friend of Owney Madden, New York's No. 1 gang leader of the prohibition era," but "in 1932 Winchell's intimacy with criminals caused him to fear he would be 'rubbed out' for 'knowing too much.'" He fled to California, "[and] returned weeks later with a new enthusiasm for law, G-men, Uncle Sam, [and] Old Glory." His coverage of the Lindbergh kidnapping and subsequent trial received national attention. Within two years, he befriended J. Edgar Hoover, the No. 2 G-man of the repeal era. He was responsible for turning Louis "Lepke" Buchalter of Murder, Inc. over to Hoover.

His newspaper column was syndicated in over 2,000 newspapers worldwide, and he was read by 50 million people a day from the 1920s until the early 1960s. His Sunday night radio broadcast was heard by another 20 million people from 1930 to the late 1950s.

Winchell, who was Jewish, was one of the first commentators in America to attack Adolf Hitler and American pro-fascist and pro-Nazi organizations such as the German-American Bund. After WWII Winchell began to denounce Communism as the main threat facing America.

During War World II, he attacked the National Maritime Union, the labor organization for the civilian United States Merchant Marine, which he said was run by Communists. In 1948 and 1949 he and the influential leftist columnist Drew Pearson "inaccurately and maliciously assaulted Secretary of Defense James Forrestal in columns and radio broadcasts.". Winchell also labeled African-American-French entertainer Josephine Baker as a communist after she took him to task for not questioning the racial-discriminatory policies of the Stork Club in New York. His relentless campaign against Baker prevented her from getting her visa to enter the US renewed.[citation needed]

In 1948 Winchell had the top rated radio show when he surpassed Fred Allen and Jack Benny.

During the 1950s Winchell favored Senator Joseph McCarthy, but he became unpopular as the public turned against McCarthy's Red Scare tactics. He also had a weekly radio broadcast which was simulcast on ABC television until he ended that employment because of a dispute with ABC executives during 1955.

A dispute with Jack Paar effectively ended Winchell's career, signaling a shift in power from print to television.

During this time, NBC had given him the opportunity to host a variety show, which lasted only thirteen weeks. His readership gradually dropped, and when his home paper, the *New York Daily Mirror*, where he'd worked for thirty-four years, closed in 1963, he faded from the public eye.

He did, however, receive $25,000 an episode to narrate *The Untouchables* on the ABC television network for five seasons beginning in 1959.

Style

Many other columnists, such as Ed Sullivan in New York and Louella Parsons in Los Angeles, began to write gossip soon after Winchell's initial success. He wrote in a style filled with slang and incomplete sentences. Winchell's casual writing style famously earned him the ire of mobster Dutch Schultz, who confronted Winchell at New York's Cotton Club and publicly lambasted him for using the phrase "pushover" to describe Schultz's penchant for blonde women. Some notable Winchell quotes are: "Nothing recedes like success," and "I usually get my stuff from people who promised somebody else that they would keep it a secret."

Winchell opened his radio broadcasts by pressing randomly on a telegraph key, a sound which created a sense of urgency and importance and the catch phrase "Good evening Mr. and Mrs. America from border to border and coast to coast and all the ships at sea. Let's go to press." He would then read each of his stories with a staccato delivery at an average rate of 197 words per minute, noticeably faster than the typical pace of American speech.

Winchell often appeared as himself in movies.

Winchell feuded with New York radio host Barry Gray, whom he described as "Borey Pink" and a "disk jerk." When Winchell heard that Marlen Edwin Pew of the trade journal *Editor & Publisher* had criticized him as a bad influence on the American press, he thereafter referred to him as "Marlen Pee-you."

For most of his career his contract with his newspaper and radio employers required them to reimburse him for any damages he had to pay, should he be sued for slander or libel. Whenever friends reproached him for betraying confidences, he responded, "I know — I'm just a son of a bitch."

Personal life

On August 11, 1919, Winchell married Rita Greene, one of his onstage partners. The couple separated a few years later, and he moved in with June Magee, who had already given birth to their first child, a daughter named Walda. Winchell and Greene eventually divorced in 1928. Winchell and Magee would never marry, although the couple maintained the front of being married for the rest of their lives.

Winchell and Magee successfully kept the secret of their nonmarriage, but were struck by tragedy with all three of their children. Their adopted daughter Gloria died of pneumonia at age nine, and Walda spent time in psychiatric hospitals. Walter, Jr., the only son of the journalist, committed suicide in his family's garage on Christmas night, 1968. Having spent the previous two years on welfare, Winchell, Jr. had last been employed as a dishwasher in Santa Ana, California, but listed himself as a freelancer who for a time wrote a column in the Los Angeles Free Press, an alternate newspaper published in the 1960s and 1970s.

Later years

Winchell announced his retirement on February 5, 1969, citing the tragedy of his son's suicide as a major reason, while also noting the delicate health of his wife. Exactly one year later, she died at a Phoenix hospital while undergoing treatment for a heart condition.

Winchell spent his final two years as a recluse at the Ambassador Hotel in Los Angeles, California. Larry King, who replaced Winchell at the *Miami Herald*, observed,

> "He was so sad. You know what Winchell was doing at the end? Typing out mimeographed sheets with his column, handing them out on the corner. That's how sad he got. When he died, only one person came to his funeral."

(Several of Winchell's former co-workers expressed a willingness to go, but were turned back by his daughter Walda.)

Death

Winchell died of prostate cancer at the age of 74. His obituary appeared on the front page of *The New York Times*. He is buried in Greenwood Memory Lawn Cemetery in Phoenix.

Legacy

Even during Winchell's lifetime, journalists were critical of his effect on the media. In 1940, *Time Magazine* said St. Clair McKelway, who had written a series of articles about him in *The New Yorker*, wrote,

> the effect of Winchellism on the standards of the press.... When Winchell began gossiping in 1924 for the late scatological tabloid *Evening Graphic*, no U.S. paper hawked rumors about the marital relations of public figures until they turned up in divorce courts. For 16 years, gossip columns spread until even the staid *New York Times* whispered that it heard from friends of a son of the President that he was going to be divorced. In its first year, *The Graphic* would have considered this news not fit to print... Gossip-writing is at present like a spirochete in the body of journalism.... Newspapers... have never been held in less esteem by their readers or exercised less influence on the political and ethical thought of the times.

Winchell responded to McKelway saying, "Oh stop! You talk like a high-school student of journalism."

Despite the controversy surrounding Winchell, his popularity allowed him to leverage support for causes that he valued. In 1946, following the death from cancer of his close friend and fellow writer Damon Runyon, Winchell appealed to his radio audience for contributions to fight the disease. The response led Winchell to establish the Damon Runyon Cancer Memorial Fund, since renamed the Damon Runyon Cancer Research Foundation. He led the charity — with the support of celebrities like Marlene Dietrich, Bob Hope, Milton Berle, Marilyn Monroe, and Joe DiMaggio — until his own death from cancer in 1972.

Winchellism and Winchellese

The term "Winchellism" is named after him. Though its use is extremely rare and may be considered archaic, the term has two different usages.

- One definition is a pejorative judgment that an author's works are specifically designed to imply or invoke scandal and may be libelous.
- The other definition is "any word or phrase compounded brought to the fore by the columnist Walter Winchell" or his imitators. Looking at his writing's effect on the language, an etymologist of his day said "there are plenty of … expressions which he has fathered and which are now current among his readers and imitators and constitute a flash language which has been called Winchellese. Through a newspaper column which has nation-wide circulation, Winchell has achieved the position of dictator of contemporary slang." Winchell invented his own phrases that were viewed as slightly racy at the time. Some of the expressions for falling in love used by Winchell were: "pashing it", "sizzle for",

"that way, go for each other", "garbo-ing it", "uh-huh"; and in the same category, "new Garbo, trouser-crease-eraser", and "pash". Some Winchellisms for marriage are: "middle-aisle it", "altar it", "handcuffed", "Mendelssohn March", "Lohengrin it", and "merged".

See also

- List of most-listened-to radio programs

Further reading

- Brooks, Tim and Marsh, Earle, *The Complete Directory to Prime Time Network and Cable TV Shows.*
- Neal Gabler, *Winchell : Gossip, Power, and the Culture of Celebrity* (Vintage: 1995).
- Mosedale, John (1981). *The Men Who Invented Broadway: Damon Runyon, Walter Winchell & Their World.* New York: Richard Marek Publishers

External links

- Walter Winchell [1] at the Internet Movie Database
- Walter Winchell [2] at the Radio Hall of Fame
- A remembrance by a contemporary [3]
- *Winchell* movie on HBO [4]
- Walter Winchell [5] at Find a Grave
- Damon Runyon Cancer Research Foundation [6]
- Dick Cavett remembers an evening with WW [7]

Venona project

The **Venona project** was a long-running secret collaboration of the US and UK intelligence agencies involving cryptanalysis of messages sent by intelligence agencies of the Soviet Union, mostly during World War II. There were at least 13 code words for this project that were used by the American and British intelligence agencies (including the NSA); "Venona" was the last that was used. That code word has no known meaning. The word "Venona" is an anagram for the word "Novena"; however, it is unknown whether this is an intentional relationship. (In the decrypted documents issued from the National Security Agency, "VENONA" is written in capitals, but lowercasing is common in modern journalism.)

Background

During the initial years of the Cold War, the Venona project was a source of information on Soviet intelligence-gathering activity that was directed at the Western military powers. Although unknown to the public, and even to Presidents Franklin D. Roosevelt and Harry S. Truman, these programs were of importance concerning crucial events of the early Cold War. These included the Julius and Ethel Rosenberg spying case and the defections of Donald Maclean and Guy Burgess to the Soviet Union.

Most decipherable messages were transmitted and intercepted between 1942 and 1945. Sometime in 1945, the existence of the Venona program was revealed to the Soviet Union by the NKVD agent and US Army SIGINT analyst and cryptologist Bill Weisband. These messages were slowly and gradually decrypted beginning in 1946 and continuing (many times at a low-level of effort in the latter years) through 1980, when the Venona program was terminated, and the remaining amount of effort that was being spent on it was moved to more important projects.

To what extent the various individuals were involved with Soviet intelligence is a topic of dispute. While a number of academic people and historians assert that most of the individuals mentioned in the Venona papers were most likely either clandestine assets and/or contacts of Soviet intelligence agents, others argue that many of those people probably had no malicious intentions and committed no crimes.

Commencement

The Venona Project was initiated in 1943, under orders from the deputy Chief of Military Intelligence (G-2), Carter W. Clarke. Clarke distrusted Joseph Stalin, and feared that the Soviet Union would sign a separate peace with the Third Reich, allowing Germany to focus its military forces against Great Britain and the United States. Code-breakers of the US Army's Signal Intelligence Service (commonly called Arlington Hall) analyzed encrypted high-level Soviet diplomatic intelligence messages intercepted in large volumes during and immediately after World War II by American, British, and Australian listening posts.

Decryption

This message traffic, some of which was encrypted with a so-called "one-time pad" system, was stored and analyzed in relative secrecy by hundreds of cryptanalysts over a 40-year period starting in the early 1940s. Due to a serious blunder on the part of the Soviets, some of this traffic was vulnerable to cryptanalysis. Somebody who was working for the manufacturers of Soviet secret-communication materials had reused pages of some of the "one-time" pads in other "one-time" pads, which were then used for other secret messages. This partially defeated the purpose of the one-time pad, which provides ideal security when each page is used exactly once and then disposed of. It is unclear as to why this fatal mistake was made, or by whom.

Breakthrough

The Soviet systems in general used a code to convert words and letters into numbers, to which additive keys (from one-time pads) were added, encrypting the content. When used correctly, one-time pad encryption is provably unbreakable. Cryptanalysis by American and British code-breakers revealed that some of the one-time pad material had incorrectly been reused by the Soviets (specifically, entire pages, although not complete books), which allowed decryption (sometimes only partial) of a small part of the traffic.

Generating the one-time pads was a slow and labor-intensive process, and the outbreak of war with Germany in June 1941 caused a sudden increase in the need for coded messages. It is probable that the Soviet code generators started duplicating cipher pages in order to keep up with demand.

It was Arlington Hall's Lt. Richard Hallock, working on Soviet "Trade" traffic (so called because these messages dealt with Soviet trade issues), who first discovered that the Soviets were reusing pages. Hallock and his colleagues (including Genevieve Feinstein, Cecil Phillips, Frank Lewis, Frank Wanat, and Lucille Campbell) went on to break into a significant amount of Trade traffic, recovering many one-time pad additive key tables in the process.

Meredith Gardner (left); most of the code breakers were young women.

A young Meredith Gardner then used this material to break in to what turned out to be NKVD (and later GRU) traffic by reconstructing the code used to convert text to numbers. Samuel Chew and Cecil Phillips also made valuable contributions. On 20 December, 1946, Gardner made the first break into the code, revealing the existence of Soviet espionage in the Manhattan Project. Venona messages also indicated that Soviet spies worked in Washington in the State Department, Treasury, Office of Strategic Services, and even the White House. Very slowly, using assorted techniques ranging from traffic analysis to defector information, more of the messages were decrypted.

Claims have been made that information from physical theft of code books (a partially burned one was recovered by the Finns) to bugging embassy rooms in which text was entered into encrypting devices (analyzing the keystrokes by listening to them being punched in) contributed to recovering much of the plaintext. These latter claims are less than fully supported in the open literature.

One significant aid (mentioned by the NSA) in the early stages may have been work done in cooperation between the Japanese and Finnish cryptanalysis organizations; when the Americans broke into Japanese codes during World War II, they gained access to this information. There are also reports that copies of signals purloined from Soviet offices by the Federal Bureau of Investigation (FBI) were helpful in the cryptanalysis. The Finnish radio intelligence sold much of its material concerning Soviet codes to OSS in 1944 during Operation Stella Polaris, including the partially burned code book.

Inherent problems

On 1 February 1956, the FBI's number-three man, Alan Belmont, Assistant to the Director, distributed to top Bureau officials the only known government analysis ever prepared on the reliability of the Venona decrypts with an eye to the possibility of using the decoded Venona material as prosecutorial evidence in court.

Belmont compared the Venona messages to teletypes sent from FBI field offices to headquarters. The first messages to be partially decoded were full of gaps and unintelligible. The Army then turned to the FBI, believing "the Bureau by studying the messages and conducting investigations would be able to develop information which would assist the Army cryptographers in reading additional unrecovered portions of the messages." Belmont concluded the decrypted material might not meet standards for evidence set by US law, and, even if it did, it suffered from deficiencies that could limit its usefulness as proof.

> In the first place, we do not know if the deciphered messages would be admitted into evidence.... The defense attorney would immediately move that the messages be excluded, based on the hearsay evidence rule. He would probably claim that...the contents of the messages were purely hearsay as it related to the defendants.

Belmont made it clear the successful use of the messages in a court of law to prove guilt would be difficult as well as violating hearsay evidence rules of evidence and the right of a defendant to face his accuser. The evidence had inherent weaknesses:

> The messages … are, for the most part, very fragmentary and full of gaps. Some parts of the messages can never be recovered again because during the actual intercept the complete message was not obtained. Other portions can be recovered only through the skill of the cryptographers and with the Bureau's assistance.

Belmont discussed the risks of making assumptions:

> It must be realized that the [deleted] cryptographers make certain assumptions as to meanings when deciphering these messages and thereafter the proper translations of Russian idioms can become a problem. It is for such reasons that [deleted] has indicated that almost anything included in a translation of one of these deciphered messages may in the future be radically revised.

Belmont discussed the problem of linking a code name with an actual name:

> Another very important factor to be considered when discussing the accuracy of these deciphered messages is the extensive use of cover names noted in this traffic. Once an individual was considered for recruitment as an agent by the Soviets, sufficient background data on him was sent to headquarters in Moscow. Thereafter, he was given a cover name and his true name was not mentioned again. This makes positive identifications most difficult since we seldom receive the initial message which states that agent "so and so" (true name) will henceforth be known as "_____" (cover name). Also, cover names were changed rather frequently and the cover name "Henry" might apply to two different individuals, depending upon the date it was used…

Belmont dourly concluded:

> All of the above factors make difficult a correct reading of the messages and point up the tentative nature of many identifications.

The Antenna example

FBI Assistant Director Alan H. Belmont offered a example of "the tentative nature of many identifications" "concerning an individual with the cover name 'Antenna.'

A message dated 5 May 1944 carried information indicating an individual code-named 'Antenna' was 25 years of age, a member of CP USA, lived in New York, matriculated at Cooper Union about 1940, worked in the Signal Corp at Ft. Monmouth, NJ, and his wife's name was Ethel.

> We made a tentative identification of 'Antenna' as Joseph Weichbrod since the background of Weichbrod corresponded with the information known about 'Antenna.' Weichbrod was about the right age, had a Communist background, lived in NYC, attended Cooper Union in 1939, worked at the Signal Corps, Ft. Monmouth, and his wife's name was Ethel. He was a good suspect for 'Antenna' until sometime later when we definitely established through investigation that 'Antenna' was Julius Rosenberg."

Usability in prosecutions

FBI's Alan Belmont considered that, although decryption might corroborate the testimony of Elizabeth Bentley and enable successful prosecution of such suspects as Judith Coplon and the Perlo and Silvermaster groups, a careful study of all factors compelled the conclusion it would not be in the best interests of prosecutors, defendants, and the United States to use Venona project information for prosecution.

As stated earlier, the Belmont's memo offered a number of reasons why it was uncertain whether or not the Venona project information should be revealed and admitted into evidence.

A major hurdle was a question of law. A defense attorney might immediately move to dismiss the evidence as hearsay, since neither the Soviet official who sent the message, nor the one who received it was available to testify. The FBI reasoned that decrypts probably could have been introduced, on an exception to the hearsay rule, based on the expert testimony of cryptographers.

In addition, according to Belmont, "the fragmentary nature of the messages and the extensive use of cover names therein make positive identification of the subjects difficult." Once an individual had been considered for recruitment as an agent by the Soviets, sufficient background data on him was sent to Moscow. Cover names were used not only for Soviet agents but other people as well. President Roosevelt, for example, was called "Kapitan" (Captain), and Los Alamos the "Reservation". Cover names also were frequently changed, and a cover name might actually apply to two different people, depending on the date it was used. Several subjects, notably Alger Hiss, Harry Dexter White, Maurice Halperin, and Lauchlin Currie, denied the accusations in open Congressional Hearings based on information from sources other than Venona. Assumptions made by cryptographers, questionable interpretations and translations placed reliance upon the expert testimony of cryptographers, and the entire case would be circumstantial.

Defense attorneys also would probably request to examine messages which cryptographers were unsuccessful in breaking and not in evidence, on the belief that such messages, if decoded, could exonerate their clients. Before any messages could be used in court they would have to be declassified. Approval would have to come from several layers of bureaucracy as well as notification to British counterparts working on the same problem. The FBI determined this would lead to the exposure of government techniques and practices in the cryptography field to unauthorized persons, compromise the government's efforts in communications intelligence, and hinder other pending investigations.[citation needed]

Results

The NSA reported that, according to the serial numbers of the Venona cables, thousands were sent, but only a fraction were available to the cryptanalysts. Approximately 2,200 of the messages were decrypted and translated; some 50 percent of the 1943 GRU-Naval Washington to Moscow messages were broken, but none for any other year, although several thousand were sent between 1941 and 1945. The decryption rate of the NKVD cables was:

- 1942 1.8%
- 1943 15.0%
- 1944 49.0%
- 1945 1.5%

Out of some hundreds of thousands of intercepted encrypted texts, it is claimed that under 3,000 have been partially or wholly decrypted. All of the duplicate one-time pad pages were produced in 1942, and almost all of them had been used by the end of 1945, with a few being used as late as 1948. After this, Soviet message traffic reverted to completely unreadable.

The existence of Venona decryption became known to the Soviets within a few years of the first breaks. It is not clear whether the Soviets knew how much of the message traffic, or which messages, had been successfully decrypted. At least one Soviet penetration agent, British Secret Intelligence Service Representative to the US, Kim Philby, was told about the project in 1949, as part of his job as liaison between British and US intelligence. Since all of the duplicate one-time pad pages had been used by this time, the Soviets apparently did not make any changes to their cryptographic procedures after they learned of Venona. However, this information did allow them to alert those of their agents who might be at risk of exposure due to the decryption.

Significance

The decrypted messages gave important insights into Soviet behavior in the period during which duplicate one-time pads were used. With the first break into the code, Venona revealed the existence of Soviet espionage at Los Alamos National Laboratories. Identities soon emerged of American, Canadian, Australian and British spies in service to the Soviet government, including Klaus Fuchs,

Alan Nunn May and Donald Maclean, a member of the Cambridge Five spy ring. Others worked in Washington in the State Department, The Treasury, Office of Strategic Services, and even the White House.

The decrypts show that the US and other nations were targeted in major espionage campaigns by the Soviet Union as early as 1942. Among those identified are Julius and Ethel Rosenberg; Alger Hiss; Harry Dexter White, the second-highest official in the Treasury Department; Lauchlin Currie, a personal aide to Franklin Roosevelt; and Maurice Halperin, a section head in the Office of Strategic Services.

The identification of individuals mentioned in Venona transcripts is sometimes problematic, since people with a "covert relationship" with Soviet intelligence are referenced by code names. Further complicating matters is the fact that the same person sometimes had different code names at different times, and the same code name was sometimes reused for different individuals. In some cases, notably that of Alger Hiss, the matching of a Venona code name to an individual is disputed. In many other cases, a Venona code name has not yet been linked to any person. According to authors John Earl Haynes and Harvey Klehr, the Venona transcripts identify approximately 349 Americans whom they claim had a covert relationship with Soviet intelligence, though fewer than half of these have been matched to real-name identities.

The Office of Strategic Services, the predecessor to the CIA, housed at one time or another between fifteen and twenty Soviet spies. Duncan Lee, Donald Wheeler, Jane Foster Zlatowski, and Maurice Halperin passed information to Moscow. The War Production Board, the Board of Economic Warfare, the Office of the Coordinator of Inter-American Affairs and the Office of War Information, included at least half a dozen Soviet sources each among their employees. In the opinion of some, almost every American military and diplomatic agency of any importance was compromised to some extent by Soviet espionage.

Some scholars and journalists dispute the claims by Haynes, Klehr, and others concerning the precision of the matching of code names to actual persons. Also contested is the implication that all 349 persons identified had an intentional "covert relationship" with Soviet intelligence; it is argued that in some cases the individual may have been an unwitting information source or a prospect for future recruitment by Soviet intelligence.

Bearing of Venona on particular cases

Venona has added information—some of it unequivocal, some of it ambiguous—to several espionage cases. Some known spies, including Theodore Hall, were neither prosecuted nor publicly implicated, because the Venona evidence against them was not made public.

Identity of Soviet source codename "19" is unclear. According to British writer Nigel West it was president of Czechoslovak government-in-exile Edvard Beneš. Military historian Eduard Mark and American authors Herbert Romerstein and Eric Breindel concluded that it was Roosevelt's aide Harry Hopkins. According to American authors John Earl Haynes and Harvey Klehr source codename "19" could be someone from British delegation at the Washington Conference in May 1943.

Julius and Ethel Rosenberg

Main article: Julius and Ethel Rosenberg

Venona has added significant information to the case of Julius and Ethel Rosenberg, making it clear that Julius was guilty of espionage, but also showing that Ethel was probably no more than an accomplice, if that. Additionally, Venona and other recent information has shown that while the content of Julius' atomic espionage was not as vital as was alleged at the time of his espionage activities, in other fields it was extensive. The information Rosenberg passed to the Soviets concerned the proximity fuze, design and production information on the Lockheed P-80 jet fighter, and thousands of classified reports from Emerson Radio. The Venona evidence indicates that it was unidentified sources codenamed "Quantum" and "Pers" who facilitated transfer of nuclear weapons technology to the Soviet Union from positions within the Manhattan Project.

Alger Hiss and Harry Dexter White

Main articles: Alger Hiss, Harry Dexter White

According to the Moynihan Commission on Government Secrecy, the complicity of both Alger Hiss and Harry Dexter White is settled by Venona. In his 1998 book, Senator Moynihan expresses certainty about Hiss's identification by Venona as a Soviet spy, writing "Hiss was indeed a Soviet agent and appears to have been regarded by Moscow as its most important." However, several current authors, researchers, and archivists consider the Venona evidence on Hiss to be inconclusive or incorrect.

Donald Maclean and Guy Burgess

When Kim Philby learned of Venona in 1949, he obtained advance warning that his fellow Soviet spies Donald Maclean and Guy Burgess were in danger of being exposed. The FBI told Philby about an agent code-named Homer, whose 1945 message to Moscow had been decoded. As it had been sent from New York and had its origins in the British Embassy in Washington, Philby deduced that the sender was Donald Maclean, now resident in London (Philby had not known Maclean's code name). By early 1951, Philby knew that US Intelligence would soon also conclude that Maclean was the sender, and he advised that Maclean be recalled. This led to Maclean and Guy Burgess' flight to Russia in May, 1951.

Soviet espionage in Australia

In addition to the British and Americans, Venona intercepts were collected by the Australians at a remote base in the Australian Outback. However, the Russians were not aware of this base even as late as 1950. The founding of the Australian Security Intelligence Organisation by Labor Prime Minister Ben Chifley was considered highly controversial within Chifley's own party. Until then, the left-leaning Australian Labor Party had been hostile to domestic intelligence agencies on civil liberties grounds, and a Labor government actually founding one was a surprising about face. Venona material has now made it clear that Chifley was motivated by evidence that Soviet agents were operating in Australia. Investigation had revealed that Wally Clayton (codenamed KLOD), a Soviet agent within the Communist Party of Australia, was forming an underground network within the CPA so that the party could continue to operate if it was banned.

Public disclosure

For much of its history, knowledge of Venona was restricted even from the highest levels of government. Senior Army officers, in consultation with the FBI and CIA, made the decision to restrict knowledge of Venona within the government (even the CIA was not made an active partner until 1952). Army Chief of Staff Omar Bradley, concerned about the White House's history of leaking sensitive information, decided to deny President Truman direct knowledge of the project. The president received the substance of the material only through FBI, Justice Department and CIA reports on counterintelligence and intelligence matters. He was not told the material came from decoded Soviet ciphers. To some degree this secrecy was counter-productive; Truman was distrustful of FBI head J. Edgar Hoover, and suspected the reports were exaggerated for political purposes.

Some of the earliest detailed public knowledge that Soviet code messages from WWII had been broken came with the release of Robert Lamphere's book, *The FBI-KGB War*, in 1986. Lamphere had been the FBI liaison to the code-breaking activity, had considerable knowledge of Venona and the counter-intelligence work that resulted from it. MI5 assistant director Peter Wright's 1987 memoir, *Spycatcher*, however, was the first detailed account of the Venona project, identifying it by name and making clear its long-term implications in post-war espionage.

Many inside the NSA had argued internally that the time had come to publicly release the details of the Venona project, but it was not until 1995 that the bipartisan Commission on Government Secrecy, with Senator Moynihan as chairman, released the Venona project materials. Moynihan wrote:

> "[The] secrecy system has systematically denied American historians access to the records
> of American history. Of late we find ourselves relying on archives of the former Soviet

Union in Moscow to resolve questions of what was going on in Washington at mid-century. [...] the Venona intercepts contained overwhelming proof of the activities of Soviet spy networks in America, complete with names, dates, places, and deeds."

One of the considerations in releasing Venona translations was the privacy interests of the individuals mentioned, referenced, or identified in the translations. Some names were not released because to do so would constitute an invasion of privacy. However, in at least one case, independent researchers identified one of the subjects whose name had been obscured by the NSA.

The dearth of reliable information available to the public—or even to the President and Congress—may have helped to polarize debates of the 1950s over the extent and danger of Soviet espionage in the United States. Anti-Communists suspected that many spies remained at large, perhaps including some that were known to the government. Those who criticized the governmental and non-governmental efforts to root out and expose communists felt that these efforts were an overreaction (in addition to other reservations about McCarthyism). Public access—or broader governmental access—to the Venona evidence would certainly have affected this debate, as it is affecting the retrospective debate among historians and others now. As the Moynihan Commission wrote in its final report:

"A balanced history of this period is now beginning to appear; the Venona messages will surely supply a great cache of facts to bring the matter to some closure. But at the time, the American Government, much less the American public, was confronted with possibilities and charges, at once baffling and terrifying."

Critical views

The relevance, accuracy, and even the authenticity of Venona decrypts have been questioned by some. Many critics of the released Venona papers claim the material to be unverifiable, with some, such as William Kunstler, going so far as to claim that the NSA had forged Venona material in its entirety in order to discredit the reputation of the Communist Party of the United States of America and its members. Research in Soviet Archives has added to the corroboration of some Venona material, including the identities of many codenamed individuals.

Some remain skeptical of both the substance and the prevailing interpretations made since the release of the Venona material. Victor Navasky, editor and publisher of *The Nation*, has written several editorials highly critical of John Earl Haynes' and Harvey Klehr's interpretation of recent work on the subject of Soviet espionage. Navasky claims that the Venona material is being used to "distort ... our understanding of the cold war" and that the files are potential "time bombs of misinformation". Commenting on the list of 349 Americans identified by Venona that Haynes and Klehr published in an appendix to *Venona: Decoding Soviet Espionage in America* (see above), Navasky wrote: "The reader is left with the implication — unfair and unproven — that every name on the list was involved in espionage, and as a result, otherwise careful historians and mainstream journalists now routinely refer to Venona as proof that many hundreds of Americans were part of the red spy network." Navasky goes further in his defense of the listed people and has claimed that a great deal of the so-called espionage that went on was nothing more than "exchanges of information among people of good will" and that "most of these exchanges were innocent and were within the law".

According to Ellen Schrecker, "Because they offer insights into the world of the secret police on both sides of the Iron Curtain, it is tempting to treat the FBI and Venona materials less critically than documents from more accessible sources. But there are too many gaps in the record to use these materials with complete confidence."

Schrecker agrees that the documents have genuinely established the guilt of many prominent figures, but is still critical of the hardline interpretation of the materials by scholars such as Murno Gladst, arguing that "...complexity, nuance, and a willingness to see the world in other than black and white seem alien to Haynes' view of history."

Writing about Alger Hiss, Hiss's lawyer John Lowenthal criticized the accuracy and methodology of the Venona analysts, charging that they employed false premises and flawed comparative logic to reach the desired conclusion that Alger Hiss was the spy "Ales". Lowenthal states this conclusion was psychologically and politically motivated but factually wrong.

Nigel West on the other hand, expressed confidence in the decrypts: "Venona remain[s] an irrefutable resource, far more reliable than the mercurial recollections of KGB defectors and the dubious conclusions drawn by paranoid analysts mesmerized by Machiavellian plots."

See also

- History of Soviet and Russian espionage in the United States
- List of Americans in the Venona papers
- List of Soviet agents in the United States
- McCarthyism
- Taman Shud Case

References and further reading

Books

- Aldrich, Richard J. (2001). *The Hidden Hand: Britain, America and Cold War Secret Intelligence*. John Murray Pubs Ltd. ISBN 0-7195-5426-8.
- Bamford, James (2002). *Body of Secrets: Anatomy of the Ultra-Secret National Security Agency*. Anchor Books. ISBN 0-385-49908-6.
- Benson, Robert Louis (1996). *Venona: Soviet Espionage and the American Response 1939-1957*. Aegean Park Press. ISBN 0-89412-265-7.

- Budiansky, Stephen (2002). *Battle of Wits: The Complete Story of Codebreaking in World War II*. Free Press. ISBN 0-7432-1734-9.
- Haynes, John Earl and Klehr, Harvey (2000). *Venona: Decoding Soviet Espionage in America*. Yale University Press. ISBN 0-300-08462-5.
- Lamphere, Robert J.; Shachtman, Tom (1995). *The FBI-KGB War: A Special Agent's Story*. Mercer University Press. ISBN 0-86554-477-8.
- Schrecker, Ellen (1998). *Many Are the Crimes : McCarthyism in America*. Little, Brown. ISBN 0-316-77470-7.
- Schrecker, Ellen (2006). *Cold War Triumphalism: The Misuse of History After the Fall of Communism*. New Press. ISBN 1-59558-083-2.
- Romerstein, Herbert and Breindel, Eric (2000). *The Venona Secrets: Exposing Soviet Espionage and America's Traitors*. Regnery Publishing. ISBN 0-89526-275-4.
- Trahair, Richard C.S and Miller, Robert (2009). *Encyclopedia of Cold War Espionage, Spies, and Secret Operations*. Enigma Books. ISBN 978-1-929631-75-9.
- Warner, Michael (1996). *Venona - Soviet Espionage & American Response*. Aegean Park Press. ISBN 0-89412-265-7.
- West, Nigel (1999). *Venona--The Greatest Secret of the Cold War*. Harper Collins. ISBN 0-00-653071-0.
- Wright, Peter; Paul Greengrass (1987). *Spycatcher: The Candid Autobiography of a Senior Intelligence Officer*. Viking. ISBN 0-670-82055-5.

Online sources

- "NSA official Venona site" [1]. National Security Agency. Retrieved 2006-07-09.
- "Selected Venona Messages" [2]. Central Intelligence Agency. Retrieved 2007-11-08.
- "The American Response to Soviet Espionage" [3]. CIA. 1996. Retrieved 2007-11-08.
- Daniel Patrick Moynihan, Chairman (1997). "Report of the Commission On Protecting And Reducing Government Secrecy" [4]. United States Government Printing Office. Retrieved 2006-06-18.
- "MI5 Releases to the National Archives" [5]. MI5. Retrieved 2006-07-09.
- Naranjo, Denis. "Venona Chronology 1939-1996" [6]. Retrieved 2006-07-09.
- "Red Files: Interview with Cecil Philips, US Signal Intelligence Service" [7]. PBS. Retrieved 2006-07-09.
- Benson, Robert L.. "The Venona Story" [8]. National Security Agency. Archived from the original [9] on 2006-06-14. Retrieved 2006-06-18.
- Fox, John F., Jr. (2005). "In the Enemy's House: Venona and the Maturation of American Counterintelligence" [10]. FBI. Retrieved 2006-11-17.
- Romerstein , Herbert and Breindel, Eric (2000). "Preface to *The Venona Secrets*" [11]. Regnery Publishing. Retrieved 2006-11-17.

COINTELPRO Years

COINTELPRO

Federal Bureau of Investigation	
Common name	Federal Bureau of Investigation
Abbreviation	FBI

Seal of the Federal Bureau of Investigation

agency information	
Motto	*Fidelity, Bravery, Integrity*
Agency overview	
Formed	1908
Employees	33,652 (July 31, 2009)
Annual budget	7.9 billion USD (2010)
Legal personality	Governmental: Government agency
Jurisdictional structure	
Federal agency(Operations jurisdiction)	United States
Legal jurisdiction	As per operations jurisdiction.
Governing body	United States Congress

Constituting instrument	United States Code Title 28 Part II Chapter 33 [1]
General nature	• Federal law enforcement • Civilian agency
Operational structure	
Headquarters	J. Edgar Hoover Building, Washington, D.C.
Sworn members	13,249 (July 31, 2009)
Unsworn members	19,460 (July 31, 2009)
Agency executives	• Robert S. Mueller III, Director • Timothy P. Murphy, Deputy Director • List of FBI Directors, Other directors
Child agencies	• FBI Academy • FBI Laboratory • Criminal Justice Information Services (CJIS) • Critical Incident Response Group (CIRG) • Counterterrorism Division (CTD) • FBI Police (FBIP)
Major units	
Field offices	56: List of FBI Field Offices

Notables	
People	• John Edgar Hoover, Director, for being the founding director • William Mark Felt, former Federal Agent, for whistle blowing, Watergate scandal • Joseph Leo Gormley, Forensic Scientist, for expert testimony
Significant Operations	• COINTELPRO • Special Intelligence Service

Website
http://www.fbi.gov/
this information

COINTELPRO (an acronym for **Co**unter **Intel**ligence **Pro**gram) was a series of covert, and often illegal, projects conducted by the United States Federal Bureau of Investigation (FBI) aimed at surveilling, infiltrating, discrediting, and disrupting domestic political organizations.

COINTELPRO tactics included discrediting targets through psychological warfare such as planting false reports in the media, smearing through forged letters, harassment, wrongful imprisonment, and extralegal violence and assassination. Covert operations under COINTELPRO took place between 1956 and 1971, however the FBI has used covert operations against domestic political groups since its inception. The FBI's stated motivation at the time was "protecting national security, preventing violence, and maintaining the existing social and political order."

FBI records show that 85% of COINTELPRO resources targeted groups and individuals that the FBI deemed "subversive," including communist and socialist organizations; organizations and individuals associated with the civil rights movement, including Dr. Martin Luther King, Jr. and others associated with the Southern Christian Leadership Conference, the National Association for the Advancement of Colored People, and the Congress of Racial Equality and other civil rights organizations; black nationalist groups; the American Indian Movement; a broad range of organizations labeled "New Left", including Students for a Democratic Society and the Weathermen; almost all groups protesting the Vietnam War, as well as individual student demonstrators with no group affiliation; the National Lawyers Guild; organizations and individuals associated with the women's rights movement; nationalist groups such as those "seeking independence for Puerto Rico;" and additional notable Americans, such as Dr. Albert Einstein. The remaining 15% of COINTELPRO resources were expended to marginalize and subvert "white hate groups," including the Ku Klux Klan and National States' Rights Party.

FBI Director J. Edgar Hoover issued directives governing COINTELPRO, ordering FBI agents to "expose, disrupt, misdirect, discredit, or otherwise neutralize" the activities of these movements and their leaders.

History

COINTELPRO began in 1956 and was designed to "increase factionalism, cause disruption and win defections" inside the Communist Party U.S.A. (CPUSA). However, the program was soon enlarged to include disruption of the Socialist Workers Party (1961), the Ku Klux Klan (1964), the Nation of Islam, the Black Panther Party (1967), and the entire New Left social/political movement, which included antiwar, community, and religious groups (1968). A later investigation by the Senate's Church Committee (see below) stated that "COINTELPRO began in 1956, in part because of frustration with Supreme Court rulings limiting the Government's power to proceed overtly against dissident groups..." Congress and several court casesWikipedia:Link rot later Wikipedia:Manual_of_Style_(dates_and_numbers)#Chronological_itemsconcluded that the COINTELPRO operations against communist and socialist groups exceeded statutory limits on FBI activity and violated constitutional guarantees of freedom of speech and association.

Program exposed

The program was successfully kept secret until 1971, when a group of left-wing radicals calling themselves the Citizens' Commission to Investigate the FBI burglarized an FBI field office in Media, Pennsylvania, and took and exposed several dossiers by passing the information to news agencies. Many news organizations initially refused to publish the information. Within the year, Director Hoover declared that the centralized COINTELPRO was over, and that all future counterintelligence operations would be handled on a case-by-case basis.

Further documents were revealed in the course of separate lawsuits filed against the FBI by NBC correspondent Carl Stern, the Socialist Workers Party, and a number of other groups. A major investigation was launched in 1976 by the Select Committee to Study Governmental Operations with Respect to Intelligence Activities of the United States Senate, commonly referred to as the "Church Committee" for its chairman, Senator Frank Church of Idaho. However, millions of pages of documents remain unreleased, and many released documents have been partly, or entirely, redacted.

In the Final Report of the Select Committee, COINTELPRO was castigated in no uncertain terms:

> Many of the techniques used would be intolerable in a democratic society even if all of the targets had been involved in violent activity, but COINTELPRO went far beyond that...the Bureau conducted a sophisticated vigilante operation aimed squarely at preventing the exercise of First Amendment rights of speech and association, on the theory that preventing the growth of dangerous groups and the propagation of dangerous ideas would protect the national security and deter violence.

The Church Committee documented a history of FBI directors using the agency for purposes of political repression as far back as World War I, through the 1920s, when they were charged with rounding up "anarchists and revolutionaries" for deportation, and then building from 1936 through 1976.

Range of targets

In an interview with the BBC's Andrew Marr, MIT professor of linguistics and political activist Noam Chomsky spoke about the purpose and the targets of COINTELPRO saying, "COINTELPRO was a program of subversion carried out not by a couple of petty crooks but by the national political police, the FBI, under four administrations...by the time it got through, I won't run through the whole story, it was aimed at the entire new left, at the women's movement, at the whole black movement, it was extremely broad. Its actions went as far as political assassination."

According to the Church Committee:

> While the declared purposes of these programs were to protect the "national security" or prevent violence, Bureau witnesses admit that many of the targets were nonviolent and most had no connections with a foreign power. Indeed, nonviolent organizations and individuals were targeted because the Bureau believed they represented a "potential" for violence -- and nonviolent citizens who were against the war in Vietnam were targeted because they gave "aid and comfort" to violent demonstrators by lending respectability to their cause.

> The imprecision of the targeting is demonstrated by the inability of the Bureau to define the subjects of the programs. The Black Nationalist program, according to its supervisor, included "a

great number of organizations that you might not today characterize as black nationalist but which were in fact primarily black." Thus, the nonviolent Southern Christian Leadership Conference was labeled as a Black Nationalist-"Hate Group."

Furthermore, the actual targets were chosen from a far broader group than the titles of the programs would imply. The CPUSA program targeted not only Communist Party members but also sponsors of the National Committee to Abolish the House Un-American Activities Committee and civil rights leaders allegedly under Communist influence or deemed to be not sufficiently "anti-Communist". The Socialist Workers Party program included non-SWP sponsors of anti-war demonstrations which were cosponsored by the SWP or the Young Socialist Alliance, its youth group. The Black Nationalist program targeted a range of organizations from the Panthers to SNCC to the peaceful Southern Christian Leadership Conference, and included every Black Student Union and many other black student groups. New Left targets ranged from the SDS to the InterUniversity Committee for Debate on Foreign Policy, from Antioch College ("vanguard of the New Left") to the New Mexico Free University and other "alternate" schools, and from underground newspapers to students' protesting university censorship of a student publication by carrying signs with four-letter words on them.

Examples of surveillance, spanning all Presidents from FDR to Nixon, both legal and illegal, contained in the Church Committee report:

- President Roosevelt asked the FBI to put in its files the names of citizens sending telegrams to the White House opposing his "national defense" policy and supporting Col. Charles Lindbergh.

- President Truman received inside information on a former Roosevelt aide's efforts to influence his appointments, labor union negotiating plans, and the publishing plans of journalists.

- President Eisenhower received reports on purely political and social contacts with foreign officials by Bernard Baruch, Mrs. Eleanor Roosevelt, and Supreme Court Justice William O. Douglas.

- The Kennedy administration had the FBI wiretap a congressional staff member, three executive officials, a lobbyist, and a Washington law firm. US Attorney General Robert F. Kennedy received the fruits of an FBI "tap" on Martin Luther King, Jr. and a "bug" on a Congressman, both of which yielded information of a political nature.

- President Johnson asked the FBI to conduct "name checks" of his critics and members of the staff of his 1964 opponent, Senator Barry Goldwater. He also requested purely political intelligence on his critics in the Senate, and received extensive intelligence reports on political activity at the 1964 Democratic Convention from FBI electronic surveillance.

- President Nixon authorized a program of wiretaps which produced for the White House purely political or personal information unrelated to national security, including information about a Supreme Court justice.

The COINTELPRO documents disclose numerous cases of the FBI's intentions to stop the mass protest against the Vietnam War. Many techniques were used to accomplish the assignment. "These included promoting splits among antiwar forces, encouraging red-baiting of socialists, and pushing violent confrontations as an alternative to massive, peaceful demonstrations." One 1966 Cointelpro operation attempted to redirect the Socialist Workers Party from their pledge of support for the antiwar movement.

The FBI claims that it no longer undertakes COINTELPRO or COINTELPRO-like operations. However, critics claim that agency programs in the spirit of COINTELPRO targeted groups such as the Committee in Solidarity with the People of El Salvador, the American Indian Movement, Earth First!, the White Separatist Movement, and the Anti-Globalization Movement.[citation needed]

Methods

According to attorney Brian Glick in his book *War at Home*, the FBI used four main methods during COINTELPRO:

1. Infiltration: Agents and informers did not merely spy on political activists. Their main purpose was to discredit and disrupt. Their very presence served to undermine trust and scare off potential supporters. The FBI and police exploited this fear to smear genuine activists as agents.
2. Psychological Warfare From the Outside: The FBI and police used a myriad of other "dirty tricks" to undermine progressive movements. They planted false media stories and published bogus leaflets and other publications in the name of targeted groups. They forged correspondence, sent anonymous letters, and made anonymous telephone calls. They spread misinformation about meetings and events, set up pseudo movement groups run by government agents, and manipulated or strong-armed parents, employers, landlords, school officials and others to cause trouble for activists.
3. Harassment Through the Legal System: The FBI and police abused the legal system to harass dissidents and make them appear to be criminals. Officers of the law gave perjured testimony and presented fabricated evidence as a pretext for false arrests and wrongful imprisonment. They discriminatorily enforced tax laws and other government regulations and used conspicuous surveillance, "investigative" interviews, and grand jury subpoenas in an effort to intimidate activists and silence their supporters.
4. Extralegal Force and Violence: The FBI conspired with local police departments to threaten dissidents; to conduct illegal break-ins in order to search dissident homes; and to commit vandalism, assaults, beatings and assassinations. The object was to frighten, or eliminate, dissidents and disrupt their movements.

The FBI specifically developed tactics intended to heighten tension and hostility between various factions in the black militancy movement, for example between the Black Panthers, the United Slaves and the Blackstone Rangers. This resulted in numerous deaths, among which were the United Slave assassinations of San Diego Black Panther Party members Jim Huggins, Bunchy Carter and Sylvester

Bell.

The FBI also conspired with the police departments of many U.S. cities (San Diego, Los Angeles, San Francisco, Oakland, Philadelphia, Chicago) to encourage repeated raids on Black Panther homes—often with little or no evidence of violations of federal, state, or local laws—which resulted directly in the police killing of many members of the Black Panther Party, most notably the assassination of Chicago Black Panther Party Chairman Fred Hampton on December 4, 1969.

In order to eliminate black militant leaders whom they considered dangerous, the FBI conspired with local police departments to target specific individuals, accuse them of crimes they did not commit, suppress exculpatory evidence and falsely incarcerate them. One Black Panther Party leader, Elmer "Geronimo" Pratt, was incarcerated for 27 years before a California Superior Court vacated his murder conviction, ultimately freeing him. Appearing before the court, an FBI agent testified that he believed Pratt had been framed because both the FBI and the Los Angeles Police Department knew he had been out of the area at the time the murder occurred.

The FBI conducted more than 200 "black bag jobs", which were warrantless surreptitious entries, against the targeted groups and their members.

In 1969 the FBI special agent in San Francisco wrote Hoover that his investigation of the Black Panther Party (BPP) revealed that in his city, at least, the Black nationalists were primarily feeding breakfast to children. Hoover fired back a memo implying the career ambitions of the agent were directly related to his supplying evidence to support Hoover's view that the BPP was "a violence-prone organization seeking to overthrow the Government by revolutionary means".

Hoover was willing to use false claims to attack his political enemies. In one memo he wrote: "Purpose of counterintelligence action is to disrupt the BPP and it is immaterial whether facts exist to substantiate the charge."

In one particularly controversial 1965 incident, civil rights worker Viola Liuzzo was murdered by Ku Klux Klansmen who gave chase and fired shots into her car after noticing that her passenger was a young black man; one of the Klansmen was acknowledged FBI informant Gary Thomas Rowe. Afterward COINTELPRO spread false rumors that Liuzzo was a member of the Communist Party and abandoned her children to have sexual relationships with African Americans involved in the civil rights movement. FBI informant Rowe has also been implicated in some of the most violent crimes of the 1960s civil rights era, including attacks on the Freedom Riders and the 1963 Birmingham, Alabama 16th Street Baptist Church bombing. In another instance in San Diego the FBI financed, armed, and controlled an extreme right-wing group of former Minutemen, transforming it into a group called the Secret Army Organization which targeted groups, activists, and leaders involved in the Anti-War Movement for both intimidation and violent acts.

Hoover ordered preemptive action "to pinpoint potential troublemakers and neutralize them before they exercise their potential for violence."

Illegal surveillance

The final report of the Church Committee concluded:

> Too many people have been spied upon by too many Government agencies and too much information has been collected. The Government has often undertaken the secret surveillance of citizens on the basis of their political beliefs, even when those beliefs posed no threat of violence or illegal acts on behalf of a hostile foreign power. The Government, operating primarily through secret informants, but also using other intrusive techniques such as wiretaps, microphone "bugs", surreptitious mail opening, and break-ins, has swept in vast amounts of information about the personal lives, views, and associations of American citizens. Investigations of groups deemed potentially dangerous -- and even of groups suspected of associating with potentially dangerous organizations -- have continued for decades, despite the fact that those groups did not engage in unlawful activity.

> Groups and individuals have been harassed and disrupted because of their political views and their lifestyles. Investigations have been based upon vague standards whose breadth made excessive collection inevitable. Unsavory and vicious tactics have been employed -- including anonymous attempts to break up marriages, disrupt meetings, ostracize persons from their professions, and provoke target groups into rivalries that might result in deaths. Intelligence agencies have served the political and personal objectives of presidents and other high officials. While the agencies often committed excesses in response to pressure from high officials in the Executive branch and Congress, they also occasionally initiated improper activities and then concealed them from officials whom they had a duty to inform.

> Governmental officials -- including those whose principal duty is to enforce the law --have violated or ignored the law over long periods of time and have advocated and defended their right to break the law.

> The Constitutional system of checks and balances has not adequately controlled intelligence activities. Until recently the Executive branch has neither delineated the scope of permissible activities nor established procedures for supervising intelligence agencies. Congress has failed to exercise sufficient oversight, seldom questioning the use to which its appropriations were being put. Most domestic intelligence issues have not reached the courts, and in those cases when they have reached the courts, the judiciary has been reluctant to grapple with them.

COINTELPRO tactics continue

While COINTELPRO was officially terminated in April 1971, continuing FBI actions indicate that post-COINTELPRO reforms did not succeed in ending COINTELPRO tactics. Documents released under the FOIA show that the FBI tracked the late Pulitzer Prize-winning journalist and author David Halberstam for more than two decades.

"Counterterrorism" guidelines implemented during the Reagan administration have been described as allowing a return to COINTELPRO tactics. Some radical groups accuse factional opponents of being FBI informants or assume the FBI is infiltrating the movement.

The FBI improperly opened investigations of American activist groups, even though they were planning nothing more than peaceful civil disobedience, according to a report by the inspector general (IG) of the U.S. Department of Justice. The review by the inspector general was launched in response to complaints by civil liberties groups and members of Congress. The FBI improperly monitored groups including the Thomas Merton Center, a Pittsburgh-based peace group, People for the Ethical Treatment of Animals (PETA), and Greenpeace USA, an environmental activism orgnazation. Also, activists affiliated with Greenpeace were improperly put on a terrorist watch list, even though they were planning no violence or illegal acitivities. The IG report found the "troubling" FBI practices between 2001 and 2006. In some cases, the FBI conducted investigations of people affiliated with activist groups for "factually weak" reasons. Also, the FBI extended investigations of some of the groups "without adequate basis" and improperly kept information about activist groups in its files. The IG report also found that FBI Director Robert Mueller III provided inaccurate congressional testimony about one of the investigations, but this inaccuracy may have been due to his relying on what FBI officials told him.

Several authors have accused the FBI of continuing to deploy COINTELPRO-like tactics against radical groups after the official COINTELPRO operations were ended. Several authors have suggested the American Indian Movement (AIM) has been a target of such operations.

A few authors go further and allege that the federal government intended to acquire uranium deposits on the Lakota tribe's reservation land, and that this motivated a larger government conspiracy against AIM activists on the Pine Ridge reservation. Others believe COINTELPRO continues and similar actions are being taken against activist groups.

Caroline Woidat argued that with respect to Native Americans, COINTELPRO should be understood within a historical context in which "Native Americans have been viewed and have viewed the world themselves through the lens of conspiracy theory."

Other authors note that while some conspiracy theories related to COINTELPRO are unfounded, the issue of ongoing government surveillance and repression is nonetheless real.

See also

- Agent provocateur
- H. Rap Brown, targeted by COINTELPRO
- Category:COINTELPRO targets
- Citizens' Commission to Investigate the FBI
- The COINTELPRO Papers
- William Mark Felt, also known as Deep Throat served as chief inspector of COINTELPRO field operations
- Franklin, H. Bruce, targeted by COINTELPRO
- Hampton, Fred, targeted by COINTELPRO
- Viola Liuzzo, murdered by a shot from a car used by four Ku Klux Klansmen, one of whom was a COINTELPRO informant
- NSA call database
- NSA warrantless surveillance controversy
- Operation Mockingbird
- Police brutality
- Red squad - Police intelligence/anti-dissident units, later operated under COINTELPRO
- Starsky, Morris, early target of COINTELPRO
- Security culture
- State Terrorism
- Surveillance
- THERMCON
- Weathermen

Further reading

Books

- Blackstock, Nelson (1988). *Cointelpro: The FBI's Secret War on Political Freedom*. Pathfinder Press. ISBN 0-87348-877-6.
- Carson, Clayborne; Gallen, David, editors (1991). *Malcolm X: The FBI File*. Carroll & Graf Publishers. ISBN 0-88184-758-5.
- Churchill, Ward; Vander Wall, Jim (2001). *The COINTELPRO Papers: Documents from the FBI's Secret Wars Against Dissent in the United States*. South End Press. ISBN 0-89608-648-8.
- Cunningham, David (2004). *There's Something Happening Here: The New Left, The Klan, and FBI Counterintelligence*. University of California Press. ISBN 0-520-23997-0.
- Davis, James Kirkpatrick (1997). *Assault on the Left*. Praeger Trade. ISBN 0-275-95455-2.

- Garrow, David (2006). *The FBI and Martin Luther King, Jr. (Revised ed.)*. Yale University Press. ISBN 0-300-08731-4.
- Glick, Brian (1989). *War at Home: Covert Action Against U.S. Activists and What We Can Do About It*. South End Press. ISBN 0-89608-349-7.
- Halperin, Morton; Berman, Jerry; Borosage Robert; Marwick, Christine (1976). *The Lawless State: The Crimes Of The U.S. Intelligence Agencies*. ISBN 0-14-004386-1.
- Olsen, Jack (2000). *Last Man Standing: The Tragedy and Triumph of Geronimo Pratt*. Doubleday. ISBN 0-38549-367-3.
- Perkus, Cathy (1976). *Cointelpro*. Vintage.
- Theoharis, Athan, *Spying on Americans: Political Surveillance from Hoover to the Huston Plan* (Temple University Press, 1978).

Articles

- Drabble, John. "The FBI, COINTELPRO-WHITE HATE and the Decline of Ku Klux Klan Organizations in Mississippi, 1964–1971", *Journal of Mississippi History*, 66:4, (Winter 2004).
- Drabble, John. "The FBI, COINTELPRO-WHITE HATE and the Decline Ku Klux Klan Organizations in Alabama, 1964–1971", *Alabama Review*, 61:1, (January 2008): 3-47.
- Drabble, John. "To Preserve the Domestic Tranquility:" The FBI, COINTELPRO-WHITE HATE, and Political Discourse, 1964–1971", *Journal of American Studies*, 38:3, (August 2004): 297-328.
- Drabble, John. "From White Supremacy to White Power: The FBI's COINTELPRO-WHITE HATE Operation and the "Nazification" of the Ku Klux Klan in the 1970s," American Studies, 48:3 (Fall 2007): 49-74.
- Drabble, John. "Fighting Black Power-New Left coalitions: Covert FBI media campaigns and American cultural discourse, 1967-1971," *European Journal of American Culture*, 27:2, (2008): 65-91.

U.S. government reports

- U.S. Congress. House. Committee on Internal Security. *Hearings on Domestic Intelligence Operations for Internal Security Purposes*. 93rd Cong., 2d sess, 1974.
- U.S. Congress. House. Select Committee on Intelligence. *Hearings on Domestic Intelligence Programs*. 94th Cong., 1st sess, 1975.
- U.S. Congress. Senate. *Committee on Government Operations. Permanent Subcommittee on Investigations. Hearings on Riots, Civil and Criminal Disorders*. 90th Cong., 1st sess. - 91st Cong. , 2d sess, 1967–1970.
- U.S. Congress. Senate. Select Committee to Study Governmental Operations with Respect to Intelligence Activities. *Hearings — The National Security Agency and Fourth Amendment Rights. Vol. 6*. 94th Cong., 1st sess, 1975.

- U.S. Congress. Senate. Select Committee to Study Governmental Operations with Respect to Intelligence Activities. *Hearings — Federal Bureau of Investigation. Vol. 6.* 94th Cong., 1st sess, 1975.
- U.S. Congress. Senate. Select Committee to Study Governmental Operations with Respect to Intelligence Activities. *Final Report — Book II, Intelligence Activities and the Rights of Americans.* 94th Cong., 2d sess, 1976.
- U.S. Congress. Senate. Select Committee to Study Governmental Operations with Respect to Intelligence Activities. *Final Report — Book III, Supplementary Detailed Staff Reports on Intelligence Activities and the Rights of Americans.* 94th Cong., 2d sess, 1976.

External links

Documentary

- "Me and My Shadow": A History of the FBI's Covert Operations and COINTELPRO - Part 1" [1]. 34:21 minute Real Audio. Produced by Adi Gevins, Pacifica Radio. 1976. Rebroadcast by Democracy Now! Wednesday, June 5, 2002. Retrieved May 12, 2005.
- "'Me and My Shadow': A History of the FBI's Covert Operations and COINTELPRO - Part 2" [2]. 13:43 minute Real Audio. Produced by Adi Gevins, Pacifica Radio. 1976. Rebroadcast by Democracy Now! Thursday, June 6, 2002. Retrieved May 12, 2005.

Websites

- COINTELPRO videos on African American History Channel [3]
- Paul Wolf's COINTELPRO website, a detailed reference site [4]. Retrieved April 19, 2005.
- COINTELPRO STILL LIVES by Sista Shiriki Unganisha [5]
- COINTELPRO: The Untold American Story - presented to U.N. World Conference Against Racism 2001 by the U.S. Congressional Black Caucus [6]
- Nation of Islam website's section on COINTELPRO, includes an assortment of documents, links and references [7].
- The Judi Bari case, COINTELPRO in the 1990s [8]. Retrieved April 19, 2005.
- COINTELPRO: the Sabotage of Legitimate Dissent [9], *What Really Happened*, June 5, 1998.
- Fake *Black Panther Party* coloring book distributed by the FBI [10]
- COINTELPRO-WHITE HATE Operation Against the Ku Klux Klan [11]

Articles

- McKinney, Cynthia. Article regarding COINTELPRO [12] on CounterPunch
- Jakopovich, Dan. The COINTELPRO programme against the Socialist Workers' Party [13]

U.S. government reports

- *Final Report of the Select Committee to Study Governmental Operations with Respect to Intelligence Activities*. United States Senate, 94th Congress, 2nd Session, April 26 (legislative day, April 14), 1976. [AKA "Church Committee Report"]. Archived on COINTELPRO sources website [4]. Transcription and html by Paul Wolf. Retrieved April 19, 2005.

- *Intelligence Activities and the Rights of Americans, Book II*

    I. Introduction and Summary [14]

    II. The Growth of Domestic Intelligence: 1936 to 1976 [15]

    III. Findings [16]

        (A) Violating and Ignoring the Law [17]

        (B) Overbreadth of Domestic Intelligence Activity [18]

        (C) Excessive Use of Intrusive Techniques [19]

        (D) Using Covert Action to Disrupt and Discredit Domestic Groups [20]

        (E) Political Abuse of Intelligence Information [21]

        (F) Inadequate Controls on Dissemination and Retention [22]

        (G) Deficiencies in Control and Accountability [23]

    IV. Conclusions and Recommendations [24]

- *Supplementary Detailed Staff Reports, Book III*

    - COINTELPRO: The FBI's Covert Action Programs Against American Citizens [25]
    - Dr. Martin Luther King, Jr., Case Study [26]
    - The FBI's Covert Action Program to Destroy the Black Panther Party [27]
    - The Use of Informants in FBI Intelligence Investigations [28]
    - Warrantless FBI Electronic Surveillance [29]
    - Warrantless Surreptitious Entries: FBI "Black Bag" Break-ins And Microphone Installations [30]
    - The Development of FBI Domestic Intelligence Investigations [31]
    - Domestic CIA and FBI Mail Opening [32]
    - CIA Intelligence Collection About Americans: CHAOS Program And The Office of Security [33]
    - National Security Agency Surveillance Affecting Americans [34]
    - Improper Surveillance of Private Citizens By The Military [35]
    - The Internal Revenue Service: An Intelligence Resource and Collector [36]

- National Security, Civil Liberties, And The Collection of Intelligence: A Report On The Huston Plan [37]

Socialist Workers Party (United States)

Socialist Workers Party	
Chairperson	Jack Barnes
Founded	1938
Ideology	Socialism, Communism
International affiliation	Pathfinder tendency
Politics of the United States Political parties Elections	

The **Socialist Workers Party** is a political organisation in the United States. The group places a priority on "solidarity work" to aid strikes and is strongly supportive of Cuba. The SWP publishes *The Militant*, a weekly newspaper that dates back to 1928, and maintains Pathfinder Press.

Organizational history

The Communist League of America

The Socialist Workers Party traces its origins back to the former Communist League of America (CLA), founded in 1928 by members of the Communist Party USA expelled for supporting Russian Communist leader Leon Trotsky against Joseph Stalin.

Concentrated almost exclusively in New York City and Minneapolis, in 1929 the CLA did not have more than 100 adherents.

After five years of propaganda work, the CLA remained a tiny organization, with a membership of about 200 and very little influence.

The rise of fascism in Nazi Germany and the failure of the communist and social democratic left to unite against the common danger created a situation in which certain radical parties throughout the world reexamined their priorities and sought a mechanism for building united action. As early as December 1933, a Trotskyist splinter group called the Communist League of Struggle (CLS), headed by former Socialist Party youth section leader Albert Weisbord and his wife Vera Buch, approached Norman Thomas of the Socialist Party of America seeking a united front hunger march of the two organizations followed by a general strike. This suggestion was dismissed as "poppycock" by SP Executive Secretary Clarence Senior, but the seed of the idea of joint action had been planted.

"Entryism"

Early in 1934, the French Trotskyists of the Communist League conceived of the idea of entering the French Socialist Party (the *Section Française de l'International Ouvrière* or SFIO) in order to recruit members for the Trotskyists, or so some critics have charged. The group retained its identity as a factional organization inside the SFIO and built a base among the party's youth section, continuing their activity until popular front action between the SFIO and the mainline Communist Party of France made their position untenable. This tactic of "entering" the larger social democratic parties of each country, endorsed by Trotsky himself, became known as the "French Turn" and was replicated by various Trotskyist parties around the world.

In 1934, the Communist League of America merged with the American Workers Party led by A.J. Muste, forming the Workers Party of the United States.

Throughout 1935 the Workers Party of the United States was deeply divided over the "entryism" tactic called for by the "French Turn," and a bitter debate swept the organization. Ultimately, the majority faction of Jim Cannon, Max Shachtman, and James Burnham won the day and the Workers Party determined to enter the Socialist Party of America; a minority faction headed by Hugo Oehler refused to accept this result and split from the organization.

The Socialist Party was itself beset with factional disagreements. The SP's left wing "Militant" faction sought to expand the organization into an "all-inclusive party" — inviting in members of the Lovestone and Trotskyist movements as well as radical individuals as the first step towards making the SP a mass party. Although there were no mass entries at this time, several radical oppositionists did make their way into the SP, including former Communist Party leader Benjamin Gitlow, youth leader and ex-Lovestone supporter Herbert Zam, and attorney and American Workers Party activist Albert Goldman. Goldman at this time also joined with YPSL leader Ernest Erber to establish a newspaper in Chicago with a Trotskyist orientation, *The Socialist Appeal,* later to serve as the organ of the Trotskyists inside the Socialist Party.

In January 1936, just as the National Executive Committee of the Socialist Party was expelling the Old Guard for their factional organization and alleged "violation of party discipline," James Cannon and his faction won their internal battle in the Workers Party to join the SP, when a national branch referendum voted unanimously for entry. Negotiations commenced with the Socialist Party leadership, with the admissions ultimately made on the basis of individual applications for membership rather than admission of the Workers Party and its approximately 2,000 members as a group. On June 6, 1936, the Workers Party's weekly newspaper, *The New Militant,* published its last issue and announced "Workers Party Calls All Revolutionary Workers to Join Socialist Party." A new phase in the party's life had begun.

Although party leader Jim Cannon later hinted that the entry of the Trotskyists into the Socialist Party had been a contrived tactic aimed at stealing "confused young Left Socialists" for his own organization, it seems that at its inception, the entryist tactic was made in good faith. Historian Constance Myers notes that while "initial prognoses for the union of Trotskyists and Socialists were favorable," it was only later when "constant and protracted contact caused differences to surface." The Trotskyists retained a common orientation with the radicalized SP in their opposition to the European war, their preference for industrial unionism and the CIO over the trade unionism of the American Federation of Labor, a commitment to trade union activism, the defense of the Soviet Union as the first workers' state while at the same time maintaining an antipathy toward the Stalin government, and in their general aims in the 1936 election.

Cannon went to Tujunga, California, a suburb of Los Angeles, to establish another new newspaper, *Labor Action,* targeted to trade unionists and SP members and aimed at winning them over to Trotskyist views, while Shachtman and Burnham handled the bulk of the faction's activities in New York.

Norman Thomas attracted nearly 188,000 votes in his 1936 Socialist Party run for President but performed poorly in historic strongholds of the party. Moreover, the party's membership had begun to decline. The organization was deeply factionalized, with the Militant faction split into right ("Altmanite"), center ("Clarity") and left ("Appeal") factions, in addition to the radical pacifists around Norman Thomas. A special convention was planned for the last week of March 1937 to set the party's future policy, initially intended as an unprecedented "secret" gathering.

Split from the Socialist Party

Prior to the March convention, the Trotskyist "Appeal" faction held an organizational gathering of their own, meeting in Chicago, with 93 delegates gathering from February 20-22, 1937. The meeting organized the faction on a permanent basis, electing a National Action Committee of five to "coordinate branch work" and "formulate Appeal policies." Two delegates from the Clarity caucus were in attendance. James Burnham vigorously attacked the Labour and Socialist International, the international organization of left wing parties to which the Socialist Party, and tension rose along these lines among the Trotskyists. United action between the Clarity and Appeal groups was not forthcoming and an emergency meeting of Vincent Dunne and Cannon was held in New York with leaders of the various factions including Thomas, Jack Altman, and Gus Tyler of Clarity. At this meeting Thomas pledged that the upcoming convention would make no effort to terminate the newspapers of the various factions.

There was no action to expel the Trotskyist Appeal faction, but pressure continued to build along these lines, egged on by the CPUSA's increasingly hysterical denunciations of Trotsky and his followers as wreckers and agents of international fascism. The convention did pass a ban on future branch resolutions on controversial matters, an effort to rein in the activities of the factions at the local level. It also did ban factional newspapers, establishing instead a national organ.

Constance Myers indicates that three factors led to the expulsion of the Trotskyists from the Socialist Party in 1937: the divergence between the official Socialists and the Trotskyist faction on the issues, the determination of Altman's wing of the Militants to oust the Trotskyists, and Trotsky's own decision to move towards a break with the party. Recognizing that the Clarity faction had chosen to stand with the Altmanites and the group around Thomas, Trotsky recommended that the Appeal group focus on disagreements over Spain to provoke a split. At the same time, Thomas, freshly returned from Spain, had come to the conclusion that the Trotskyists had joined the SP not to make it stronger, but to capture the organization for their own purposes.

On June 24-25, 1937, a meeting of the Appeal faction's National Action Committee voted to ratched up the rhetoric against American Labor Party and Republican nominee for mayor of New York Fiorello LaGuardia, a favorite son of many in Socialist ranks, and to reestablish their newspaper, *The Socialist Appeal*. This was met with expulsions from the party beginning August 9 with a rump meeting of the Central Committee of Local New York, which expelled 52 New York Trotskyists by a vote of 48 to 2, with 18 abstentions, and ordering 70 more to be brought up on charges. Wholesale expulsions followed, with a major section of the YPSL leaving the party with the Trotskyists.

The 1,000 or so Trotskyists who entered the SP in 1936 exited in the summer of 1937 with their ranks swelled by another 1,000. On December 31, 1937, representatives of this faction gathered in Chicago to establish a new political organization — the Socialist Workers Party.

Formation of the SWP

The October 2, 1937, issue of the *Socialist Appeal* included a convention call from the so-called "Left Wing" to "All Locals and Branches of the Socialist Party," accusing the NEC of the party of having "betrayed the principles of socialism" by withdrawing the party's candidate for Mayor of New York in favor of LaGuardia and for having ordered "the bureaucratic expulsion of all the revolutionary members of the party who oppose and obstruct this sell-out policy." A convention was called by four Socialist Party State Committees, the NEC of the YPSL, and the organized Left Wing organizations of Chicago and New York, slated to be held in Chicago over Thanksgiving weekend, November 25-28, 1937. This meeting was quickly postponed until December 31, however, "in order to provide adequate time for discussion by the membership" of important questions.

In December 1937 an agenda was published by the Convention Organizing Committee, naming Cannon as the primary reporter on the Trade Union question, Shachtman on the Russian Resolution, Goldman on the Spanish Resolution, Canadian Maurice Spector on the International Resolution, Burnham on the Declaration of Principles of the new organization, and Abern on Party Organization and Constitution. The gathering was to conclude with the election of a new National Committee.

On the appointed day, December 31, 1937, over 100 regular and fraternal delegates gathered in Chicago, where they were greeted by a speech of welcome delivered by Chicago leader Albert

Goldman, a labor attorney. As editor of the Trotskyist movement's ongoing theoretical magazine, *The New International,* Max Shachtman delivered the first official report to the gathering, dealing with the political situation in the United States. Shachtman boldly declared that

> "It is entirely inconceivable that American imperialism can succeed in resisting the inexorable tendencies that are pulling it into the vortex of the coming world war.
>
> "If the working class is unable to prevent the outbreak of war, and the United States enters directly into it, our party stands pledged to the traditional position of revolutionary Marxism.
>
> "It will utilize the crisis of capitalist rule engendered by the war to prosecute the class struggle with the utmost intransigence, to strengthen the independent labor and revolutionary movements, and to bring the war to a close by the revolutionary overthrow of capitalism and the establishment of proletarian rule in the form of the workers state."

The convention devoted a full day to discussion of the problems of the labor movement and the role of the new organization in the unions, with "National Secretary of the Convention Arrangements Committee" Jim Cannon delivering the primary report. While criticizing the "reactionary role which the AF of L leadership has played," Cannon declared that "our party...takes a clear-cut position in favor of the earliest and completest possible unification of the AF of L and the CIO, and also the hitherto unaffiliated Railroad Brotherhoods."

The 1940 split

The 1940 split in the SWP followed an internal factional debate over the party's internal government, the class nature of the Russian state, and Marxist philosophy, among other questions. The SWP was to experience many other factional conflicts and splits in its history, but this was the largest, and it foreshadowed many features of those to come.

The majority faction, led by Cannon, supported Trotsky's position that the USSR remained a "workers' state" and should be supported in any war with capitalist states, despite their opposition to the government headed by Joseph Stalin. The minority faction, led by Shachtman, held that the USSR should not be supported in its war with Finland. One of its leaders, James Burnham held, in addition, that the USSR had degenerated so far that it deserved no defense whatsoever. Like this debate, most later factional disputes within the SWP also centered on different attitudes towards revolutions in other countries.

The opposition faction alleged that Cannon's leadership of the SWP was "bureaucratic conservative" and demanded the right to its own publications to express its views outside the party. The majority faction said this was contrary to Lenin's concept of democratic centralism, and that disagreements and the SWP should be debated only internally. Similar disagreements over the SWP's internal government have surfaced in most later faction fights, with most later opposition factions raising similar demands and accusations. Despite this, most of these later factions claimed political descent from Cannon and the SWP majority, not from earlier opposition factions and splinter parties.

The minority faction led by Shachtman eventually split away almost 40% [1] of the party's membership as well as its youth organization, the Young People's Socialist League, forming the Workers Party.

The World War II years

SWP members had been prominent in leading the 1934 Minneapolis Teamster strike and mid-30s organization of Midwest intercity trucking and held leadership positions in a number of locals. Teamsters International President Daniel Tobin launched an effort to dislodge them from these positions and with the aid of employers and government agencies was successful.

A number of members were imprisoned under the Smith Act of 1941, including J. P. Cannon (see Smith Act Trials). Those imprisoned included the main national leaders of the SWP and those members most prominent in the Midwest Teamsters.

The party put into practice the so-called Proletarian Military Policy of opposing the war politically while attempting to transform what they saw as an imperialist war into a civil war. The party lost a number of its members while sailing in the extremely perilous convoys to Murmansk. Problems caused as a result of the imprisonment of experienced leaders and the enlistment in the armed forces of many others meant that during the war years the editorship of *The Militant* passed through a number of hands.

Graffiti in the Basque Country: James P. Cannon, American Trotskyist

The SWP was active in supporting those labor strikes that occurred despite the wartime "no-strike pledge", and in supporting protests against racist discrimination during the war, such as A. Philip Randolph's March on Washington Movement. The U.S. Postal Service refused to mail some issues of *The Militant* and threatened to cancel its third-class mailing permit, citing objections to its articles opposing racist discrimination.

Post-war years

Following the war the SWP and the Fourth International both expected that there would be a wave of revolutionary struggles such as accompanied the end of the previous war. Indeed, revolutions did occur in countries including Yugoslavia, Albania, Korea, and China, to name only those which resulted in the overthrow of capitalism, but contrary to Trotskyist expectations they were headed by Moscow-oriented "Stalinist" parties.

In the United States, the largest strike wave in U.S. history - involving over five million workers - occurred with the end of the war and the wartime pledge made by many union leaders not to strike for the duration. (This did not mean there were not many strikes during wartime - there were many wildcat strikes during this period, as well as strikes officially called by the United Mine Workers of America. There were also protests by GIs demanding rapid demobilization after the end of the war, sometimes called the going-home movement). SWP participation in this upsurge led to a brief period of rapid growth for the SWP immediately after the war.

The end of the war also saw the reorganization of the Fourth International, in which process the SWP played a major role. As part of this process, moves were made to heal the breach with Max Shachtman's supporters in the Workers Party (WP) and for the two groups to fuse. This eventually came to nothing. However some members of the SWP around Felix Morrow and Albert Goldman grew dissatisfied with what they saw as the SWP's ultra-leftist attitude towards revolutionary policies. Eventually they were to leave the SWP in a state of demoralization and some joined the WP.

On the other hand a faction within the WP called the Johnson-Forest Tendency, CLR James (known as Johnson) and Raya Dunayevskaya (Forest), were impatient with the caution of the WP and considered that the situation could rapidly become pre-revolutionary. This led them to decamp from the WP and rejoin the SWP in 1947. This tendency had moved further away from the "orthodox Trotskyism" of the SWP, which made for an uncomfortable presence. For example, they continued to hold the position that the USSR was a "state capitalist" society. By 1951, their presence in the SWP was ever more anomalous and most left to form the Correspondence Publishing Committee. Dunayevskaya and her supporters eventually formed the News and Letters Committees in 1955 after splitting with CLR James, who was deported from the USA to Britain from where he continued to advise the Correspondence Publishing Committee which split again in 1962, with those loyal to CLR James taking the name Facing Reality.

The Cold War period

The brief postwar wave of labor unrest gave way to the conservatism of the 1950s, the housebreaking of previously radical labor unions, and McCarthyism. The growing civil rights movement, which continued uninterrupted out of WWII, could not fully offset these trends, and the SWP experienced a period of decline and isolation.

The party also had a number of splits over these years. One such split saw the departure of the faction of Bert Cochran and Clarke, who formed the American Socialist Union which lasted until 1959. That 1953 opposition supported some of the positions of Michel Pablo, the Secretary of the Fourth International, although Pablo disagreed with their wish to dissolve the Fourth International.

The next, smaller split was that of Sam Marcy's Global Class War faction which had called within the SWP for support of Henry Wallace's Progressive Party Presidential run in 1948 and regarded Mao Zedong as a revolutionary leader. This faction ended up leaving the SWP in 1958 after supporting the suppression of the Hungarian Rising of 1956, a position contrary to that held by the SWP and other Trotskyist tendencies. It went on to form the Workers World Party.

Meanwhile throughout the 1950s and into the 1960s the remaining membership of the SWP clung to its firmly held beliefs and grew older. Consequently the party membership shrank over these years from a post war high in 1948 until the tide began to turn in the early 1960s. The 1959 Revolution in Cuba however signaled a change in political direction for the SWP as it embarked on pro-Castro "solidarity work" through the Fair Play for Cuba Committee. The result was a small accretion of youth to the party's ranks and in the same period long time SWP leader Murry Weiss won another group of youth from the Shachtmanites as they joined the Socialist Party of America. Many of the new recruits, however, were drawn from the student movement, unlike those who had led the party since the 1930s, and as a result the internal culture of the party began to change.

1960s

Despite such growing signs of an end to the isolation which the group had endured during the McCarthyite period, it experienced a new split in the early 1960s. A factional situation developed in the SWP that saw a number of small oppositional groups develop. One of the key issues was the Cuban Revolution and the SWP's response to it. Cannon and other SWP leaders such as Joseph Hansen saw Cuba as qualitatively different from the "Stalinist" states of Eastern Europe. Their analysis brought them closer to the International Secretariat of the Fourth International from which the SWP had split in 1953. The SWP successfully negotiated a reunification of the ISFI and the International Committee of the Fourth International leading to the creation in 1963 of the reunified Fourth International. Two sections of the ICFI, including Gerry Healy's Socialist Labour League rejected the merger and turned against the SWP leadership, working with opponents within the party.

The most important faction opposing the SWP leadership's new line was the Revolutionary Tendency (RT) led by James Robertson and Tim Wohlforth which rejected the SWP's "capitulation" to Pabloism and opposed joining the USFI. They were critical of the Castro government, arguing that Cuba remained a "deformed workers state". However, a split developed within this faction between groups headed by the two men. Nonetheless both the RT and the Reorganized Minority Tendency split to form the Spartacist (see Spartacist League), and the American Committee for the Fourth International, respectively with the latter becoming aligned with Healy's SLL.

In the aftermath the Seattle branch also left to found the Freedom Socialist Party, after protesting the alleged suppression of internal democracy, as did Murray and Myra Tanner Weiss.

The SWP supported both the civil rights movement and the Black nationalist movement which grew during the 1960s. It particularly praised the militancy of Black nationalist leader Malcolm X, who in turn spoke at the SWP's public forums and gave an interview to Young Socialist magazine. After his assassination, the SWP had limited success in forming alliances with his followers and other Black nationalists. However, these movements were part of the radicalization of these years aiding the SWP's growth.

Like all left wing groups, the SWP grew during the 1960s and experienced a particularly brisk growth in the first years of the 1970s. Much of this was due to its involvement in many of the campaigns and demonstrations against the war in Vietnam. The SWP advocated that the antiwar movement should call for the immediate withdrawal of all U.S. troops, and should primarily focus on organizing large, legal demonstrations for this demand. It was recognized by friend and foe alike as a major factor influencing the direction of the antiwar movement along these lines. One of the leaders of the anti-war movement at this time, along with Dave Dellinger and many others was Fred Halstead, a World War II veteran and former leader of the garment workers union in New York City. Halstead was the 1968 Presidential candidate of the SWP who visited Vietnam in that capacity.

The SWP was also increasingly outspoken in its defense of the Cuban government of Fidel Castro and its identification with that government. A new leadership led by Jack Barnes (who became national secretary in 1972) made identification with Cuba an ever greater part of the politics of the SWP throughout the 1970s.

The party also published many of Leon Trotsky's works in these years through their publishing house, Pathfinder Press. Not only were the better-known writings reprinted, many for the first time since the 1930s, but other more obscure articles and letters were collected and printed for a wider audience than they had when first distributed. The expansion of the press also allow the SWP to host *Intercontinental Press*, the FI magazine which moved from Paris to New York in 1969, which later merged with *Inprecor*.

1970s and new leadership

The growth of labour militancy in the early 1970s had an impact on the SWP and currents developed within it urging a reorientation of the party towards this militancy. One such current was the Proletarian Orientation Tendency, which included Larry Trainor, which eventually dissolved itself.

Another tendency developed called the Internationalist Tendency (IT). The IT posed a greater challenge for the group's leadership, as the tendency agreed with the Fourth International's advocacy of guerrilla warfare as a "tactic on a continental scale" in Latin America. However, despite tensions between the SWP and the rest of the international, when the former expelled the IT the International refused to side with the tendency. The IT would disintegrate over the next few months, some of its supporters finding their way back into the SWP.

The international tensions developed further when the **Leninist Trotskyist Tendency** was established in 1973 by the SWP and its co-thinkers in order to contribute to the debate for the Tenth World Congress. It argued for a reversal of the Latin American guerrilla war orientation adopted at the Ninth World Congress.

This period was the peak of the SWP's growth and influence. The party continued its involvement in the movement against the war in Vietnam, which peaked in 1970-71. The SWP also supported Chicano nationalism, including the Raza Unida Party. It helped organize protests demanding legal abortion through the Women's National Abortion Action Coalition. With the mid- to late 70s decline of these movements and the end of the 1960s-1970s youth radicalization, SWP membership and influence went into decline.

In 1978, the SWP leadership decided that the key task was for party members to make a turn to industry. This turn entailed party members getting jobs in blue collar industries in preparation for, the SWP leadership projected, increasing mass struggles. The 1977-78 coal miners' strike and developments like Steelworkers Fight Back were among the events pointed to in arguing for this change in policy. Party members sought to get jobs in the same workplaces in order to work as organized "fractions", doing "communist political work" as well as union activity.

As a result, many members were asked to move and change jobs, often out of established careers and into low-paying jobs in small towns. Many of the older members with experience in trade unions resisted this 'colonization program', which upset their established routine in the unions, as did some of the younger members.

1980s and after

Internal affairs

Opposition to the "turn to industry" developed within the SWP. This opposition was not homogeneous and was itself beset by differences between different factions.

A further factor in the growing divisions within the SWP was the move by Jack Barnes, Mary-Alice Waters and others in the leadership away from the Trotskyist label. In 1982, Barnes gave a speech which was later published as *Their Trotsky and Ours: Communist continuity today* in which Barnes rejected Trotsky's theory of Permanent Revolution arguing that it failed to sufficiently distinguish between the democratic and socialist tasks of a workers' revolution. Barnes argued that anticapitalist revolutions typically began with a "workers' and farmers' government" which initially concentrated on bourgeois-democratic measures, and only later moved on to the abolition of capitalism.

Barnes also argued that the "Trotskyist" label unnecessarily distinguished leftists in that tradition from leftists of other origins, such as the Cuban Communist Party, or the Sandinista National Liberation Front. He argued that the SWP had more in common with these organizations than with many groups calling themselves Trotskyist. The SWP has continued to publish numerous books by Trotsky and advocate a number of ideas commonly associated with Trotskyism, including Trotsky's analysis of "Stalinism".

The opposition factions continued to support the theory of permanent revolution, and the Trotskyist label: they anticipated that the SWP leadership was reassessing its place in the Fourth International. While declaring their support to the Cuban and the leftist Nicaraguan governments, they were more critical of the Castroist and Sandinista leadership. Additionally, they continued to oppose the "turn to industry".

One opposition group gathered around the Weinsteins on the West Coast, (with supporters elsewhere too), while a second group gathered around George Breitman and Frank Lovell. Together they formed an opposition bloc on the SWP's National Committee but in 1983 both groups were expelled. The opposition factions, having split from the SWP, formed new organizations. The grouping around the Weinsteins forming the San Francisco-based Socialist Action. The Breitman-Lovell group, after a time, formed the Fourth Internationalist Tendency. Both groups described themselves as "public factions" of the SWP and set the task of recapturing the SWP to their understanding of Trotskyism. Another group, mainly in Los Angeles, had been close to Breitman but did not agree to orient toward the SWP belonged briefly to Socialist Action but left to join the "regroupment" organization Solidarity.

This was the most recent split or major faction fight in the SWP; the organization has experienced an unusually long period of internal peace since, although it has declined steadily in both its membership numbers and its political influence within the U.S. left. Numerous recent expulsions—sometimes of long-standing SWP veterans—have contributed to the membership decline. In 2003, the party sold its major headquarters building in New York City for $20 million and moved to another location in Manhattan. Party leaders Jack Barnes and Mary-Alice Waters subsequently sold their West Village condominium for $1.87 million.

Party activities

The SWP's most high profile and controversial campaign in the late 1980s and early 1990s was its Mark Curtis Defense Committee, established after Curtis, an SWP activist and trade union organizer, was charged and convicted on burglary and rape charges in 1988. The party claimed that Curtis had been framed by police for his role in defending immigrant workers. Curtis was eventually paroled.

The SWP now focuses most of its energy on internal activities, such as fund-raising, the weekly Militant Labor Forum, and the distribution of Pathfinder books and *The Militant*. Its members are present in a handful of trade unions and it focuses most of its political energy towards defending immigrant rights and promoting Cuban solidarity.

The question of International affiliation

Due to legal constraints, the SWP ended its formal affiliation with the Fourth International in the 1940s. It remained in close political solidarity with the Fourth International, however. The Socialist Workers Party broke formally with the Fourth International in 1990 though it had been increasingly inactive in the Trotskyist movement since National Secretary Jack Barnes' 1982 speech, "Their Trotsky and Ours", which some view as signaling a break with Trotskyism. The SWP action followed the 1985 World Congress, and the SWP closed Intercontinental Press in 1986. The SWP's international formation is sometimes referred to as the *Pathfinder tendency* because they each operate a Pathfinder Bookstore which sells the publications of the SWP's publishing arm, *Pathfinder Press*. In 1986, the party won a lawsuit against the Federal Bureau of Investigation as a result of years of spying and disruption.

The party and presidential politics

The Socialist Workers Party has run candidates for President since 1948; it received its greatest number of votes in 1976, when its candidate, Peter Camejo, received 90,310 votes.

In the U.S. presidential election of 2004 the Socialist Workers Party ran Róger Calero for President and Arrin Hawkins for Vice-President. It should be noted that both candidates were constitutionally unqualified for the positions (under Article II, section 1) because Calero is not an American citizen and Hawkins was 29 years old, with the minimum age being 35. James Harris and Margaret Trowe, the SWP's ticket from 2000, stood in on the ballot in some states where Calero and Hawkins could not be listed. The two tickets combined received over 10,000 votes. They were on the ballot in 11 states and the District of Columbia, more than any other socialist candidates. The vote total does not reflect the actual vote because of the unqualified status of the candidates. County clerks (in some states) and statewide Secretaries of State have discretion in reporting votes for ineligible candidates. The same situation obtained in 2008.

- 1948—Farrell Dobbs: received 13,614 votes.
- 1952—Farrell Dobbs: received 10,312 votes.
- 1956—Farrell Dobbs: received 7,797 votes.
- 1960—Farrell Dobbs: received 60,166 votes.
- 1964—Clifton DeBerry: received 32,327 votes.
- 1968—Fred Halstead: received 41,390 votes.
- 1972
  - Linda Jenness: received 83,380 votes. In 1972 in Arizona, Pima and Yavapai counties had a ballot malfunction that counted many votes for both a major party candidate and Linda Jenness. A court ordered that the ballots be counted for both. As a consequence, Jenness received 16% and 8% of the vote in Pima and Yavapai, respectively. 30,579 of her 30,945 Arizona votes are from those two counties. Some sources don't count these votes for Jenness.
  - Evelyn Reed: received 13,878 votes. Ballot access: Indiana, New York, and Wisconsin
- 1976—Peter Camejo: received 90,986 votes.
- 1980
  - Andrew Pulley: received 40,105 votes.
  - Richard Congress: received 4,029 votes votes. Ballot access in Ohio.
  - Clifton DeBerry
- 1984—Melvin T. Mason: received 24,672 votes.
- 1988—James "Mac" Warren: received 15,604 votes.
- 1992—James "Mac" Warren: received 23,096 votes.
- 1996—James Harris: received 8,463 votes.

- 2000— James Harris: received 7,378 votes.
- 2004
  - Róger Calero: received 3,677 votes
  - James Harris: received 7,411 votes
- 2008
  - Róger Calero: received 5,151 votes
  - James Harris: received 2,424 votes

Personnel

SWP National Secretaries

- James P. Cannon (1938-1953)
- Farrell Dobbs (1953-1972)
- Jack Barnes (since 1972)

Prominent current and former members

Martin Abern	James T. Farrell	Harry Ring
Harry Braverman	Fred Feldman	Olga Rodriguez
George Breitman	Richard Fraser	Norton Sandler
Joel Britton	Albert Goldman	Ted Selander
James Burnham	Joseph Hansen	Max Shachtman
Peter Camejo	Asher Harer	Ed Shaw
Joseph Carter	Sidney Hook	Barry Sheppard
Steve Clarke	C. L. R. James	Eric Simpson
Bert Cochran	Martin Koppel	Carl Skoglund
Jake Cooper	Lyndon LaRouche	Morris Starsky
Stephanie Coontz	Sam Marcy	Arne Swabeck
Clifton DeBerry	Paul Montauk	Larry Trainor
Seth Dellinger	Felix Morrow	Mary-Alice Waters
Farrell Dobbs	George Novack	Myra Tanner Weiss
Paul Draper	Evelyn Reed	Murry Weiss
Raya Dunayevskaya		

See also

- Pathfinder Mural
- COINTELPRO
- Other parties called the Socialist Workers Party
- List of political parties in the United States
- List of Communist parties

Further reading

Books

- Breitman, George (ed.) *Founding of the Socialist Workers Party: Minutes and Resolutions, 1938-39.* New York: Monad Press, 1982.
- Cannon, James P., *The History of American Trotskyism: Report of a Participant.* New York: Pioneer Press, 1944.
- Halstead, Fred, *Out Now!: A Participant's Account of the Movement in the United States Against the Vietnam War.* New York: Monad Press, 1978.
- Jayko, Margaret (ed.), *FBI on Trial: The Victory in the Socialist Workers Party Suit Against Government Spying.* New York: Pathfinder Press, 1988.
- Myers, Constance Ashton, *The Prophet's Children: Trotskyists in America, 1928-1941.* Westport, CT: Greenwood Press, 1977.
- Sheppard, Barry, *The Party: A Political Memoir of the Socialist Workers Party, 1960-1988. Volume 1: The Sixties.* Chippendale, Australia: Resistance Books, 2005.
- Wohlforth, Tim, *The Prophet's Children: Travels on the American Left.* Atlantic Highlands, NJ: Humanity Press, 1994.

Archival material

- George Breitman Papers. Tamiment Library and Robert F. Wagner Archives at New York University, New York. Finding Aid. [2]
- James P. Cannon Papers. Wisconsin Historical Society, Madison. —Also available on microfilm.
- Frank Lovell Papers. Tamiment Library and Robert F. Wagner Archives, New York University. Finding Aid. [3]
- Max Shachtman Papers. Tamiment Library and Robert F. Wagner Archives, New York University. Finding Aid. [4]
- David Loeb Weiss Papers. Tamiment Library and Robert F. Wagner Archives, New York University.
- Myra Tanner Weiss Papers. Tamiment Library and Robert F. Wagner Archives, New York University.

External links

- The Militant homepage. [5] SWP official organ.
- Pathfinder Press homepage. [6] SWP publishing house.
- James P. Cannon Internet Archive [7], Marxists Internet Archive.
- "SWP_USA" Yahoo! Group [8] — An unofficial discussion board independent of any organization.
- University of Washington Libraries Digital Collections - Vietnam War Era Ephemera [9] —Includes ephemera produced by the SWP.

Ku Klux Klan

Ku Klux Klan rally, 1923.

In existence	
1st Klan	1865–1870s
2nd Klan	1915–1944
3rd Klan[1]	since 1946
Members	
1st Klan	550,000
2nd Klan	between 3 and 6 million (peaked in 1920–1925 period)
Properties	
Origin	United States of America
Political ideology	White supremacy Anti-immigration
Political position	Far-right

[1]The 3rd Klan is decentralized, with approx. 179 chapters.

Ku Klux Klan, often abbreviated **KKK** and informally known as **The Klan**, is the name of three distinct past and present far-right organizations in the United States, which have advocated extremist reactionary currents such as white supremacy, white nationalism, and anti-immigration. The current manifestation is splintered into several chapters and is widely considered to be a hate group.

The first Klan flourished in the South in the 1860s, then died out by the early 1870s. Their iconic white costumes consisted of robes, masks, and conical hat. The second KKK flourished nationwide in the early and mid 1920s, and adopted the fantastic costumes and code words of the first Klan; the second clan introduced cross burnings. The third KKK emerged after World War II. The first and third KKK had well-established records of using terrorism, but historians debate how central that tactic was to the second KKK.

Three Klans

First KKK

The first Klan was founded in 1865 in Pulaski, Tennessee by veterans of the Confederate Army. Although it never had an organizational structure above the local level, similar groups across the South adopted the name and methods. Klan groups spread throughout the South as an insurgent movement during the Reconstruction era in the United States As a secret vigilante group, the Klan focused its anger reacted against Radical Republican and sought to restore white supremacy by threats and violence, including murder, against black and white Republicans. In 1870 and 1871 the federal government passed the Force Acts, which were used to prosecute Klan crimes. Prosecution of Klan crimes and enforcement of the Force Acts suppressed Klan activity. In 1874 and later, however, newly organized and openly active paramilitary organizations, such as the White League and the Red Shirts, started a fresh round of violence aimed at suppressing Republican voting and running Republicans out of office. These contributed to white conservative Democrats' regaining political power in all the Southern states by 1877.

Second KKK

In 1915, the second Klan was founded and remained a small organization in Georgia. Starting in 1921 it adopted a modern business system of recruiting (which paid most of the initiation fee and costume charges to the organizers) and grew rapidly nationwide at a time of prosperity. The second KKK preached Americanism and purification of politics, with a heavy tome of racism, anti-Catholicism, anti-Communism, nativism, and antisemitism. Some local groups took part in attacks on private houses, and carried out other violent activities. The violent episodes were generally in the South.

The second Klan was a formal fraternal organization, with a national and state structure. At its peak in the mid-1920s, the organization claimed to include about 15% of the nation's eligible population, approximately 4–5 million men. Internal divisions, criminal behavior by leaders, and external opposition brought about a collapse in membership, which had dropped to about 30,000 by 1930. It finally faded away in the 1940s.

Third KKK

The "Ku Klux Klan" name was used by many independent local groups opposing the Civil Rights Movement and desegregation, especially in the 1950s and 1960s. During this period, they often forged alliances with Southern police departments, as in Birmingham, Alabama; or with governor's offices, as with George Wallace of Alabama. Several members of KKK groups were convicted of murder in the deaths of civil rights workers and children in the bombing of the 16th Street Baptist Church in Birmingham. Today, researchers estimate that there may be approximately 150 Klan chapters with upwards of 5,000 members nationwide.

Today, a large majority of sources consider the Klan to be a "subversive or terrorist organization". In 1999, the city council of Charleston, South Carolina passed a resolution declaring the Klan to be a terrorist organization. A similar effort was made in 2004 when a professor at the University of Louisville began a campaign to have the Klan declared a terrorist organization so it could be banned from campus. In April 1997, FBI agents arrested four members of the True Knights of the Ku Klux Klan in Dallas for conspiracy to commit robbery and to blow up a natural gas processing plant.

First Klan 1865–1874

Creation

Six well-educated Confederate veterans from Pulaski, Tennessee, created the original Ku Klux Klan on December 24, 1865, during Reconstruction of the South after the Civil War. The name was formed by combining the Greek *kyklos* (κυκλος, *circle*) with *clan*. The group was known for a short time as the "Kuklux Clan." The Ku Klux Klan was one among a number of secret, oath-bound organizations using violence, including the Southern Cross in New Orleans (1865), and the Knights of the White Camellia (1867) in Louisiana.

A cartoon threatening that the KKK would lynch carpetbaggers. From the *Independent Monitor*, Tuscaloosa, Alabama, 1868.

Historians generally see the KKK as part of the postwar violence related not only to the high number of veterans in the population, but also to their effort to control the dramatically changed social situation by using extrajudicial means to restore white supremacy. In 1866, Mississippi Governor William L. Sharkey reported that disorder, lack of control and lawlessness were widespread; in some states armed bands of Confederate soldiers roamed at will. The Klan used public violence against blacks as intimidation. They burned houses, and attacked and killed blacks, leaving their bodies on the roads.

In an 1867 meeting in Nashville, Tennessee, Klan members gathered to try to create a hierarchical organization with local chapters eventually reporting up to a national headquarters. They elected Brian A. Scates to be the Leader and President of this organization. Since most of the Klan's members were veterans, they were used to the hierarchical structure of the organization, but the Klan never operated under this centralized structure. Local chapters and bands were highly independent.

Former Confederate Brigadier General George Gordon developed the *Prescript*, or Klan dogma. The Prescript suggested elements of white supremacist belief. For instance, an applicant should be asked if he was in favor of "a white man's government", "the reenfranchisement and emancipation of the white men of the South, and the restitution of the

A political cartoon depicting the KKK and the Democratic Party as continuations of the Confederacy

Southern people to all their rights." The latter is a reference to the Ironclad Oath, which stripped the vote from white persons who refused to swear that they had not borne arms against the Union. In practice only a minority of white men were disfranchised.

Gordon was said to have told former slave trader and Confederate General Nathan Bedford Forrest about the Klan. Forrest allegedly responded, "That's a good thing; that's a damn good thing. We can use that to keep the niggers in their place." A few weeks later, Forrest was selected as Grand Wizard, the Klan's national leader, although he always denied his leadership.

In an 1868 newspaper interview, Forrest stated that the Klan's primary opposition was to the Loyal Leagues, Republican state governments, people like Tennessee governor Brownlow and other carpetbaggers and scalawags. He argued that many southerners believed that blacks were voting for the Republican Party because they were being hoodwinked by the Loyal Leagues. One Alabama newspaper editor declared "The League is nothing more than a nigger Ku Klux Klan."

Nathan Bedford Forrest

Despite Gordon's and Forrest's work, local Klan units never accepted the Prescript and continued to operate autonomously. There were never hierarchical levels or state headquarters. Klan members used violence to settle old feuds and local grudges, as they worked to restore white dominance in the disrupted postwar society. The historian Elaine Frantz Parsons describes the membership:

> Lifting the Klan mask revealed a chaotic
> multitude of antiblack vigilante groups, disgruntled poor white farmers, wartime guerrilla
> bands, displaced Democratic politicians, illegal whiskey distillers, coercive moral
> reformers, sadists, rapists, white workmen fearful of black competition, employers trying
> to enforce labor discipline, common thieves, neighbors with decades-old grudges, and even
> a few freedmen and white Republicans who allied with Democratic whites or had criminal
> agendas of their own. Indeed, all they had in common, besides being overwhelmingly
> white, southern, and Democratic, was that they called themselves, or were called,
> Klansmen.

Historian Eric Foner observed:

> In effect, the Klan was a military force serving the interests of the Democratic party, the
> planter class, and all those who desired restoration of white supremacy. Its purposes were
> political, but political in the broadest sense, for it sought to affect power relations, both
> public and private, throughout Southern society. It aimed to reverse the interlocking
> changes sweeping over the South during Reconstruction: to destroy the Republican party's
> infrastructure, undermine the Reconstruction state, reestablish control of the black labor
> force, and restore racial subordination in every aspect of Southern life.

To that end they worked to curb the education, economic advancement, voting rights, and right to keep and bear arms of blacks. The Ku Klux Klan soon spread into nearly every southern state, launching a "reign of terror against Republican leaders both black and white. Those political leaders assassinated during the campaign included Arkansas Congressman James M. Hinds, three members of the South

Carolina legislature, and several men who served in constitutional conventions."

Activities

Klan members adopted masks and robes that hid their identities and added to the drama of their night rides, their chosen time for attacks. Many of them operated in small towns and rural areas where people otherwise knew each other's faces, and sometimes still recognized the attackers. "The kind of thing that men are afraid or ashamed to do openly, and by day, they accomplish secretly, masked, and at night." With this method both the high and the low could be attacked. The Ku Klux Klan night riders "sometimes claimed to be ghosts of Confederate soldiers so, as they claimed, to frighten superstitious blacks. Few freedmen took such nonsense seriously."

Three Ku Klux Klan members arrested in Tishomingo County, Mississippi, September 1871, for the attempted murder of an entire family.

The Klan attacked black members of the Loyal Leagues and intimidated southern Republicans and Freedmen's Bureau workers. When they killed black political leaders, they also took heads of families, along with the leaders of churches and community groups, because people had many roles. Agents of the Freedmen's Bureau reported weekly assaults and murders of blacks.

> "Armed guerilla warfare killed thousands of Negroes; political riots were staged; their causes or occasions were always obscure, their results always certain: ten to one hundred times as many Negroes were killed as whites."

Masked men shot into houses and burned them, sometimes with the occupants still inside. They drove successful black farmers off their land. "Generally, it can be reported that in North and South Carolina, in 18 months ending in June 1867, there were 197 murders and 548 cases of aggravated assault."

Klan violence worked to suppress black voting. More than 2,000 persons were killed, wounded and otherwise injured in Louisiana within a few weeks prior to the Presidential election of November 1868. Although St. Landry Parish had a registered Republican majority of 1,071, after the murders, no Republicans voted in the fall elections. White Democrats cast the full vote of the parish for Grant's opponent. The KKK killed and wounded more than 200 black Republicans, hunting and chasing them through the woods. Thirteen captives were taken from jail and shot; a half-buried pile of 25 bodies was found in the woods. The KKK made people vote Democratic and gave them certificates of the fact.

In the April 1868 Georgia gubernatorial election, Columbia County cast 1,222 votes for Republican Rufus Bullock. By the November presidential election, however, Klan intimidation led to suppression of the Republican vote and only one person voted for Ulysses S. Grant.

Klansmen killed more than 150 African Americans in a county in Florida, and hundreds more in other counties. Freedmen's Bureau records provided a detailed recounting of beatings and murders of freedmen and their white allies by Klansmen.

Milder encounters also occurred. In Mississippi, according to the Congressional inquiry:

> One of these teachers (Miss Allen of Illinois), whose school was at Cotton Gin Port in Monroe County, was visited ... between one and two o'clock in the morning on March 1871, by about fifty men mounted and disguised. Each man wore a long white robe and his face was covered by a loose mask with scarlet stripes. She was ordered to get up and dress which she did at once and then admitted to her room the captain and lieutenant who in addition to the usual disguise had long horns on their heads and a sort of device in front. The lieutenant had a pistol in his hand and he and the captain sat down while eight or ten men stood inside the door and the porch was full. They treated her "gentlemanly and quietly" but complained of the heavy school-tax, said she must stop teaching and go away and warned her that they never gave a second notice. She heeded the warning and left the county.

By 1868, two years after the Klan's creation, its activity was beginning to decrease. Members were hiding behind Klan masks and robes as a way to avoid prosecution for freelance violence. Many influential southern Democrats feared that Klan lawlessness provided an excuse for the federal government to retain its power over the South, and they began to turn against it. There were outlandish claims made, such as Georgian B. H. Hill stating "that some of these outrages were actually perpetrated by the political friends of the parties slain."

Resistance

Union Army veterans in mountainous Blount County, Alabama, organized "the anti-Ku Klux". They put an end to violence by threatening Klansmen with reprisals unless they stopped whipping Unionists and burning black churches and schools. Armed blacks formed their own defense in Bennettsville, South Carolina and patrolled the streets to protect their homes.

National sentiment gathered to crack down on the Klan, even though some Democrats at the national level questioned whether the Klan really existed or believed that it was just a creation of nervous Southern Republican governors. Many southern states began to pass anti-Klan legislation.

In January 1871, Pennsylvania Republican Senator John Scott convened a Congressional committee which took testimony from 52 witnesses about Klan atrocities. They accumulated 12 volumes of horrifying testimony. In February, former Union General and Congressman Benjamin Franklin Butler of Massachusetts introduced the Ku Klux Klan Act. This added to the enmity that southern white Democrats bore toward him. While the bill was being considered, further violence in the South swung support for its passage. The Governor of South Carolina appealed for federal troops to assist his efforts in keeping control of the state. A riot and massacre in a Meridian, Mississippi, courthouse were reported, from which a black state representative escaped only by taking to the woods.

Benjamin Franklin Butler wrote the 1871 Klan Act.

In 1871, President Ulysses S. Grant signed Butler's legislation. The Ku Klux Klan Act was used by the Federal government together with the 1870 Force Act to enforce the civil rights provisions for individuals under the constitution. Under the Klan Act, Federal troops were used for enforcement, and Klansmen were prosecuted in Federal court. More African Americans served on juries in Federal court than were selected for local or state juries, so they had a chance to participate in the process. In the crackdown, hundreds of Klan members were fined or imprisoned. In South Carolina, *habeas corpus* was suspended in nine counties.

The Klan declines and is superseded by other groups

Although Forrest boasted that the Klan was a nationwide organization of 550,000 men and that he could muster 40,000 Klansmen within five days' notice, as a secret or "invisible" group, it had no membership rosters, no chapters, and no local officers. It was difficult for observers to judge its actual membership. It had created a sensation by the dramatic nature of its masked forays and because of its many murders.

One Klan official complained that his, "so-called 'Chief'-ship was purely nominal, I having not the least authority over the reckless young country boys who were most active in 'night-riding,' whipping, etc., all of which was outside of the intent and constitution of the Klan..."[citation needed]

In 1870 a federal grand jury determined that the Klan was a "terrorist organization". It issued hundreds of indictments for crimes of violence and terrorism. Klan members were prosecuted, and many fled from areas that were under federal government jurisdiction, particularly in South Carolina. Many people not formally inducted into the Klan had used the Klan's costume for anonymity, to hide their identities when carrying out acts of violence. Forrest ordered the Klan to disband in 1869, stating that it was "being perverted from its original honorable and patriotic purposes, becoming injurious instead of subservient to the public peace". Historian Stanley Horn writes "generally speaking, the Klan's end was more in the form of spotty, slow, and gradual disintegration than a formal and decisive disbandment". A reporter in Georgia wrote in January 1870, "A true statement of the case is not that the Ku Klux are an organized band of licensed criminals, but that men who commit crimes call themselves Ku Klux".

Gov. William Holden of North Carolina.

While people used the Klan as a mask for nonpolitical crimes, state and local governments seldom acted against them. African Americans were kept off juries. In lynching cases, all-white juries almost never indicted Ku Klux Klan members. When there was a rare indictment, juries were unlikely to vote for a conviction. In part, jury members feared reprisals from local Klansmen.

Others may have agreed with lynching as a way of keeping dominance over black men. In many states, officials were reluctant to use black militia against the Klan out of fear that racial tensions would be raised. When Republican Governor of North Carolina William Woods Holden called out the militia against the Klan in 1870, it added to his unpopularity. Combined with violence and fraud at the polls, the Republicans lost their majority in the state legislature. Disaffection with Holden's actions led to white Democratic legislators' impeaching Holden and removing him from office, but their reasons were numerous.

The Klan was destroyed in South Carolina and decimated throughout the rest of the South, where it had already been in decline. Attorney General Amos Tappan Ackerman led the prosecutions.

In some areas, other local paramilitary organizations such as the White League, Red Shirts, saber clubs, and rifle clubs continued to intimidate and murder black voters.

In 1874, organized white paramilitary groups formed in the Deep South to replace the faltering Klan: the White League in Louisiana and the Red Shirts in Mississippi, North and South Carolina. They campaigned openly to turn Republicans out of office, intimidated and killed black voters, tried to disrupt organizing and suppress black voting. They were out in force during the campaigns and elections of 1874 and 1876, contributing to the conservative Democrats regaining power in 1876, against a background of electoral violence.

Shortly after, in *United States v. Cruikshank* (1875), the Supreme Court ruled that the Force Act of 1870 did not give the Federal government power to regulate private actions, but only those by state governments. The result was that as the century went on, African Americans were at the mercy of hostile state governments that refused to intervene against private violence and paramilitary groups.

Whereas the number of indictments across the South was large, the number of cases leading to prosecution and sentencing was relatively small. The overloaded federal courts were not able to meet the demands of trying such a tremendous number of cases, a situation that led to selective pardoning. By late 1873 and 1874, most of the charges against Klansmen were dropped although new cases continued to be prosecuted for several more years. Most of those sentenced had either served their terms or been pardoned by 1875.

The Supreme Court of the United States eviscerated the Ku Klux Act in 1876 by ruling that the federal government could no longer prosecute individuals although states would be forced to comply with federal civil rights provisions. Republicans passed a second civil rights act (the Civil Rights Act of 1875) to grant equal access to public facilities and other housing accommodations regardless of race. Ironically, the Klan during this period served to further Northern reconstruction efforts, as Ku Klux violence provided the political climate needed to pass civil rights protections for blacks. Although the Ku Klux Act of 1871 dismantled the first Klan, Southern whites formed other, similar groups that kept blacks away from the polls through intimidation and physical violence. Reconstruction ended with the election of President Rutherford B. Hayes, who suspended the federal military occupation of the South; yet blacks still found themselves without the basic civil liberties that Congressional Republicans had sought to secure.

In 1882, the Supreme Court ruled in *United States v. Harris* that the Klan Act was partially unconstitutional. It ruled that Congress's power under the Fourteenth Amendment did not extend to the right to regulate against private conspiracies.

Klan costumes, also called "regalia", disappeared by the early 1870s (Wade 1987, p. 109). The fact that the Klan did not exist for decades was shown when Simmons's 1915 recreation of the Klan attracted only two aging "former Reconstruction Klansmen." All other members were new. By 1872, the Klan was broken as an organization. Nonetheless, the goals that the Klan had failed to achieve itself, such as suppressing suffrage for Southern blacks and driving a wedge between poor whites and blacks, were largely accomplished by the 1890s by militant Southern whites. Lynchings of African Americans, far from being ended by the Klan's disintegration, instead peaked in 1892 with 161 deaths.

The second Klan: 1915–1944

Refounding in 1915

Three events in 1915 acted as catalysts to the revival of the Klan:

- The film *The Birth of a Nation* was released, mythologizing and glorifying the first Klan.

- Leo Frank was lynched near Atlanta after the Georgia governor commuted his death sentence to life in prison. Frank had been convicted in 1913 and sentenced to death for the rape and murder of a young white factory worker named Mary Phagan, in a trial marked by intimidation of the jury and media frenzy. His legal appeals had been exhausted.

- The second Ku Klux Klan was founded by William J. Simmons at Stone Mountain, outside Atlanta. It added to the original anti-black ideology with a new anti-immigrant, anti-Catholic, prohibitionist and antisemitic agenda. Most of the founders were from an Atlanta-area organization calling itself the Knights of Mary Phagan, which had organized around Leo Frank's trial. The new organization emulated the fictionalized version of the Klan presented in *The Birth of a Nation*.

Movie poster for *The Birth of a Nation*. It has been widely noted for reviving the Ku Klux Klan.

The Birth of a Nation

Director D. W. Griffith's *The Birth of a Nation* glorified the original Klan. His film was based on the book and play *The Clansman* and the book *The Leopard's Spots*, both by Thomas Dixon, Jr.. Dixon said his purpose was "to revolutionize northern sentiment by a presentation of history that would transform every man in my audience into a good Democrat!" The film created a nationwide Klan craze. At the official premier in Atlanta, members of the Klan rode up and down the street in front of the theater.

An illustration from *The Clansman*: "Take dat f'um yo equal—"

President Wilson

Much of the modern Klan's iconography, including the standardized white costume and the lighted cross, are derived from the film. Its imagery was based on Dixon's romanticized concept of old Scotland, as portrayed in the novels and poetry of Sir Walter Scott. The film's influence and popularity were enhanced by a widely reported endorsement by historian and U.S. President Woodrow Wilson.

The Birth of a Nation included extensive quotations from Woodrow Wilson's *History of the American People*, as if to give it a stronger basis. After seeing the film in a special White House screening, Wilson allegedly said, "It is like writing history with lightning, and my only regret is that it is all so terribly true." Given Wilson's views on race and the Klan, his statement was taken as supportive of the film. In later correspondence with Griffith, Wilson confirmed his enthusiasm. Wilson's remarks immediately became controversial. Wilson tried to remain aloof, but finally, on April 30, he issued a non-denial denial. The historian Arthur Link quoted comments by Wilson's aide, Joseph Tumulty: "the President was entirely unaware of the nature of the play before it was presented and at no time has expressed his approbation of it."

Leo Frank

Another event that influenced the Klan was sensational coverage in 1913 of the trial, conviction and sentencing of a Jewish factory manager from Atlanta named Leo Frank. In lurid newspaper accounts, Frank was accused of the rape and murder of Mary Phagan, a girl employed at his factory.

After a trial in Georgia in which a mob daily surrounded the courtroom, Frank was convicted. Because of the presence of the armed mob, the judge asked Frank and his counsel to stay away when the verdict was announced. Frank's legal appeals of his trial failed, despite the revelation of new evidence casting doubt on his guilt. US Supreme Court Justice Oliver

Wendell Holmes dissented from other justices in their upholding of his conviction and condemned the mob's intimidation of the jury as the court's failing to provide due process to the defendant. After the governor commuted Frank's sentence to life imprisonment in 1915, a mob calling itself the Knights of Mary Phagan kidnapped Frank from prison and lynched him.

William J. Simmons founded the second Ku Klux Klan in 1915.

The Frank trial was used skillfully by Georgia politician and publisher Thomas E. Watson, the editor for *The Jeffersonian* magazine. He was a leader in recreating the Klan and was later elected to the U.S. Senate. The new Klan was inaugurated in 1915 at a meeting led by William J. Simmons on top of Stone Mountain. A few aging members of the original Klan attended, along with members of the self-named Knights of Mary Phagan.

Simmons stated that he had been inspired by the original Klan's Prescripts, written in 1867 by Confederate veteran George Gordon in an attempt to create a national organization. These were never adopted by the Klan, however. The Prescript stated the Klan's purposes in idealistic terms, hiding the fact that its members committed acts of vigilante violence and murder from behind masks.

Social factors

The second Klan arose during the nadir of American race relations, in response to urbanization and industrialization. Massive immigration from the largely Catholic countries of eastern and southern Europe led to friction with America's longer-established Protestant citizens. The Great Migration of African Americans to the North stoked racism by whites in Northern industrial cities; thus the second Klan would achieve its greatest political power not in any Southern state, but in Indiana. The migration of African Americans and whites from rural areas to Southern cities further increased tensions. The Klan grew most rapidly in urbanizing cities which had high growth rates between 1910 and 1930, such as Detroit, Memphis, Dayton, Atlanta, Dallas, and Houston. In Michigan, more than half of the members lived in Detroit and were concerned about urban issues: limited housing, rapid social change, competition for jobs. Stanley Horn, a Southern historian sympathetic to the first Klan, was careful in an oral interview to distinguish it from the later "spurious Ku Klux organization which was in ill-repute—and, of course, had no connection whatsoever with the Klan of Reconstruction days".

In an era without Social Security or widely available life insurance, it was common for men to join fraternal organizations such as the Elks or the Woodmen of the World to provide for their families in case they died or were unable to work. The founder of the new Klan, William J. Simmons, was a member of twelve different fraternal organizations. He recruited for the Klan with his chest covered with fraternal badges, and consciously modeled the Klan after those organizations.

Klan organizers, called "Kleagles", signed up hundreds of new members, who paid initiation fees and bought KKK costumes. The organizer kept half the money and sent the rest to state or national officials. When the organizer was done with an area, he organized a huge rally, often with burning crosses and perhaps presented a Bible to a local Protestant minister. He then left town with the money. The local units operated like many fraternal organizations and occasionally brought in speakers.

The Klan's growth was also affected by mobilization for World War I and postwar tensions, especially in the cities where strangers came up against each other more often. Southern whites resented the arming of black soldiers. Black veterans did not want to go back to second-class status in the United States. Some were lynched, still in uniform, upon returning from overseas service.

Activities

In reaction to social changes, the Klan adopted anti-Jewish, anti-Catholic, anti-Communist and anti-immigrant slants.

Although Klan members were concentrated in the South, Midwest and west, there were some members in New England, too. Klan members torched an African American school in Scituate, Rhode Island.

Temperance

Lender et al. state that the Klan's resurgence in the 1920s was aided by the temperance movement. In Arkansas and elsewhere, the Klan opposed bootleggers, and in 1922, two hundred Klan members set fire to saloons in Union County. The national Klan office was finally established in Dallas, Texas, but Little Rock, Arkansas was the home of the Women of the Ku Klux Klan. The first head of this auxiliary was a former president of the Arkansas WCTU.Wikipedia:Verifiability One historian contends that the KKK's "support for Prohibition represented the single most important bond between Klansmen throughout the nation". Membership in the Klan and other prohibition groups overlapped, and they often coordinated activities. For example, Edward Young Clarke, a top leader of the Klan, raised funds for both the Klan and the Anti-Saloon League. Clarke was indicted in 1923 for violations of the Mann Act.

Labor and anti-unionism

The social unrest of the postwar period included labor strikes in response to low wages and poor working conditions in many industrial cities, often led by immigrants, who also organized unions. Klan members worried about labor organizers' effect on their jobs, as well as the socialist leanings of some of the immigrants, which only added to the tensions. They also resented upwardly mobile ethnic Catholics. At the same time, in cities Klan members were themselves working in industrial environments and often struggled with working conditions.

In southern cities such as Birmingham, Alabama, Klan members kept control of access to the better-paying industrial jobs but opposed unions. During the 1930s and 1940s, Klan leaders urged members to disrupt the Congress of Industrial Organizations (CIO), which advocated industrial unions and was open to African-American members. With access to dynamite and skills from their jobs in mining and steel, in the late 1940s some Klan members in Birmingham began using bombings to intimidate upwardly mobile blacks who moved into middle-class neighborhoods. "By mid-1949, there were so many charred house carcasses that the area [College Hills] was informally named Dynamite Hill." Independent Klan groups remained active in Birmingham and were deeply engaged in violent opposition to the Civil Rights Movement.

Urbanization

A significant characteristic of the second Klan was that it was an organization based in urban areas, reflecting the major shifts of population to cities in both the North and the South. In Michigan, for instance, 40,000 members lived in Detroit, where they made up more than half of the state's membership. Most Klansmen were lower- to middle-class whites who were trying to protect their jobs and housing from the waves of newcomers to the industrial cities: immigrants from southern and eastern Europe, who tended to be Catholic and Jewish in numbers higher than earlier groups of immigrants; and black

Stone Mountain, site of the founding of the second Klan in 1915

and white migrants from the South. As new populations poured into cities, rapidly changing neighborhoods created social tensions. Because of the rapid pace of population growth in industrializing cities such as Detroit and Chicago, the Klan grew rapidly in the U.S. Midwest. The Klan also grew in booming Southern cities such as Dallas and Houston.

In the medium-size industrial city of Worcester, Massachusetts in the 1920s, the Klan ascended to power quickly but diminished as a result of opposition from the Catholic Church. There was no violence and the local newspaper ridiculed Klansmen as "night-shirt knights". Half of the members were Swedish American, including some first-generation immigrants. The ethnic and religious conflicts between Worcester residents is discussed. Swedish Protestants fought against Irish Catholics for political and ideological control of the city.

For some states, historians have obtained membership rosters of some local units and matched the names against city directory and local records to create statistical profiles of the membership. Big city newspapers were often hostile and ridiculed Klansmen as ignorant farmers. Detailed analysis from Indiana showed the rural stereotype was false for that state:

> Indiana's Klansmen represented a wide cross section of society: they were not disproportionately urban or rural, nor were they significantly more or less likely than other members of society to be from the working class, middle class, or professional ranks. Klansmen were Protestants, of course, but they cannot be described exclusively or even predominantly as fundamentalists. In reality, their religious affiliations mirrored the whole of white Protestant society, including those who did not belong to any church.

The Klan attracted people but most of them did not remain in the organization for long. Membership in the Klan turned over rapidly as people found out that it was not the group they wanted. Millions joined, and at its peak in the 1920s, the organization included about 15% of the nation's eligible population. The lessening of social tensions contributed to the Klan's decline.

The burning cross

The second Klan adopted a burning Christian cross as its symbol. No such crosses had been used by the first Klan, but the burning cross became a symbol of intimidation by the second Klan.

The practice of cross burning had been loosely based on ancient Scottish clans' burning a St. Andrew's cross (an X-shaped cross) as a beacon to muster forces for war. In *The Clansman* (see above), Dixon had falsely claimed that the first Klan had used fiery crosses when rallying to fight against Reconstruction. Griffith brought this image to the screen in *The Birth of a Nation*; he mistakenly portrayed the burning cross as an upright Latin cross rather than the St. Andrew's

Cross burning is said to have been introduced by William J. Simmons, the founder of the second Klan in 1915.

cross. Simmons adopted the symbol wholesale from the movie, prominently displaying it at the 1915 Stone Mountain meeting. The symbol has been associated with the Klan ever since.

Political influence

The Klan had major political influence in several states, and it was influential mostly in the center of the country. The Klan spread from the South into the Midwest and Northern states. It also arose in Canada, where there was a large movement against Catholic immigrants. At its peak, Klan membership exceeded four million and comprised 20% of the adult white male population in many broad geographic regions, and 40% in some areas.[citation needed] Most of the Klan's membership resided in Midwestern states.

In another well-known example from the same year, the Klan decided to turn Anaheim, California, into a model Klan city. It secretly took over the City Council. When the members' affiliation became known, the city conducted a special recall election, and citizens voted out the Klan members.

The Klan issue played a significant role at the bitterly divisive 1924 Democratic National Convention in New York City. The leading candidates were Protestant William Gibbs McAdoo, with a base in areas where the Klan was strong, and Catholic New York Governor Al Smith, with a base in the large cities. After weeks of stalemate, both candidates withdrew in favor of a compromise. Anti-Klan delegates proposed a resolution indirectly attacking the Klan; it was narrowly defeated.

In some states, such as Alabama, members of the KKK worked for political and social reform. The state's Klansmen were among the foremost advocates of better public schools, effective prohibition enforcement, expanded road construction, and other "progressive" political measures. In many ways, these reforms benefited lower-class white people. By 1925, the Klan was a political force in the state, as leaders such as J. Thomas Heflin, David Bibb Graves, and Hugo Black manipulated the KKK membership to try to build political power against the Black Belt planters, who had long dominated the state. Black was elected US senator in 1926;

Sheet music to "We Are All Loyal Klansmen", 1923

The Good Citizen July 1926 Published by Pillar of Fire Church

Branford Clarke illustration in *Heroes of the Fiery Cross*, 1928

President Franklin D. Roosevelt appointed Black to the Supreme Court not knowing he had been active in the Klan in the 1920s. In 1926, with Klan support, Bibb Graves won the Alabama governor's office. He was a former Klan chapter head. He pushed for increased education funding, better public health, new highway construction, and pro-labor legislation. Because the Alabama state legislature refused to redistrict until 1972, however, even the Klan was unable to break the planters' and rural areas' hold on legislative power.

Its predecessor had been an exclusively partisan Democratic organization in the South. The second Klan grew in the Midwest, where for a time, its members were courted by both Republicans and Democrats. The KKK state organizations endorsed candidates from either party that supported its goals; Prohibition in particular helped the Klan and some Republicans to make common cause in the Midwest. In the South, however, the southern Klan remained Democratic, closely allied with Democratic police, sheriffs, and other functionaries of local government. With continuing disfranchisement of most African Americans and many poor whites, the only political activity took place within the Democratic Party.

Resistance and decline

The Ku Klux Klan rose to prominence in Indiana politics and society after World War I. It was made up of native-born, white Protestants of many income and social levels. Nationally, in the 1920s, Indiana had the most powerful Ku Klux Klan. Though it counted a high number of members statewide, (over 30% of its white male citizens) its importance peaked with the 1924 election of Edward Jackson for governor. A short time later, the scandal surrounding the murder trial of D.C. Stephenson destroyed the image of the Ku Klux Klan as upholders of law and order. By 1926 the Ku Klux Klan was "crippled and discredited."

D. C. Stephenson was the Grand Dragon of Indiana and 22 northern states. He led the states under his control to seperate from the national KKK organization in 1923. In his 1925 trial, he was convicted for second degree murder for his part in the rape and subsequent death of Madge Oberholtzer. After Stephenson's conviction in a sensational trial, the Klan declined dramatically in Indiana. Historian Leonard Moore concluded that a failure in leadership caused the Klan's collapse:

D. C. Stephenson, Grand Dragon of the Indiana Klan. His conviction for murdering a young white schoolteacher in 1925 devastated the Indiana Klan.

> Stephenson and the other salesmen and office seekers who maneuvered for control of Indiana's Invisible Empire lacked both the ability and the desire to use the political system to carry out the Klan's stated goals. They were uninterested in, or perhaps even unaware of, grass roots concerns within the movement. For them, the Klan had been nothing more than a means for gaining wealth and power. These marginal men had risen to the top of the hooded order because, until it became a political force, the Klan had never required strong, dedicated leadership. More established and experienced politicians who endorsed the Klan, or who pursued some of the interests of their Klan constituents, also accomplished little. Factionalism created one barrier, but many politicians had supported the Klan simply out of expedience. When charges of crime and corruption began to taint the movement, those concerned about their political futures had even less reason to work on the Klan's behalf.:

Many groups and leaders, including prominent Protestant ministers such as Reinhold Niebuhr in Detroit, spoke out against the Klan. In response to blunt attacks against Jewish Americans and the Klan's campaign to outlaw private schools, the Jewish Anti-Defamation League was formed after the lynching of Leo Frank. When one civic group began to publish Klan membership lists, the number of members quickly declined. The National Association for the Advancement of Colored People carried on public education campaigns in order to inform people about Klan activities and lobbied against Klan abuses in Congress. After its peak in 1925, Klan membership in most areas of the Midwest began to decline rapidly.

In Alabama, KKK vigilantes, thinking that they had governmental protection, launched a wave of physical terror in 1927. They targeted both blacks and whites for violation of racial norms and for perceived moral lapses. The state's conservative elite counterattacked. Grover C. Hall, Sr., editor of the *Montgomery Advertiser*, began publishing a series of editorials and articles that attacked the Klan for its "racial and religious intolerance". Hall won a Pulitzer Prize for his crusade. Other newspapers kept up a steady, loud attack on the Klan, referring to the organization as violent and "un-American". Sheriffs cracked down. In the 1928 presidential election, the state voted for the Democratic candidate

Al Smith, although he was Catholic.

Klan membership in Alabama dropped to less than six thousand by 1930. Small independent units continued to be active in Birmingham, where in the late 1940s, members launched a reign of terror by bombing the homes of upwardly mobile African Americans. Activism by such independent KKK groups increased as a reaction against the Civil Rights Movement of the 1950s and 1960s.

Imperial Wizard Hiram Wesley Evans sold the organization in 1939 to James Colescott, an Indiana veterinarian, and Samuel Green, an Atlanta obstetrician. They were unable to staunch the exodus of members. In 1944, the IRS filed a lien for $685,000 in back taxes against the Klan, and Colescott was forced to dissolve the organization in 1944. Local Klan groups closed over the following years.

Ku Klux Klan members march down Pennsylvania Avenue in Washington, D.C. in 1928

Due in part to the Klan terror directed at them, five million blacks left the South for northern, midwestern and western cities from 1940 to 1970.

After World War II, folklorist and author Stetson Kennedy infiltrated the Klan and provided information to media and law enforcement agencies. He also provided secret code words to the writers of the *Superman* radio program, resulting in episodes in which Superman took on the KKK. Kennedy's intention to strip away the Klan's mystique and trivialize the Klan's rituals and code words may have contributed to the decline in Klan recruiting and membership. In the 1950s, Kennedy wrote a bestselling book about his experiences, which further damaged the Klan.

The following table shows the change in the Klan's estimated membership over time. (The years given in the table represent approximate time periods.)

Year	Membership
1920	4,000,000
1924	6,000,000
1930	30,000
1980	5,000
2008	6,000

Later Klans, 1950 through 1960s

The name "Ku Klux Klan" began to be used by several independent groups. Beginning in the 1950s, for instance, individual Klan groups in Birmingham, Alabama began to resist social change and blacks' improving their lives by bombing houses in transitional neighborhoods. There were so many bombings in Birmingham of blacks' homes by Klan groups in the 1950s that the city's nickname was "Bombingham".

During the tenure of Bull Connor as police commissioner in the city, Klan groups were closely allied with the police and operated with impunity. When the Freedom Riders arrived in

Soviet propaganda poster (*Freedom, American style*, 1950, by Nikolay Dolgorukov and Boris Efimov), showing the KKK's lynchings of blacks.

Birmingham, Connor gave Klan members fifteen minutes to attack the riders before sending in the police to quell the attack. When local and state authorities failed to protect the Freedom Riders and activists, the federal government established effective intervention.

In states such as Alabama and Mississippi, Klan members forged alliances with governors' administrations. In Birmingham and elsewhere, the KKK groups bombed the houses of civil rights activists. In some cases they used physical violence, intimidation and assassination directly against individuals. Many murders went unreported and were not prosecuted by local and state authorities. Continuing disfranchisement of blacks across the South meant that most could not serve on juries, which were all white.

According to a report from the Southern Regional Council in Atlanta, the homes of 40 black Southern families were bombed during 1951 and 1952. Some of the bombing victims were social activists whose work exposed them to danger, but most were either people who refused to bow to racist convention or were innocent bystanders, unsuspecting victims of random violence.

Among the more notorious murders by Klan members:

- The 1951 Christmas Eve bombing of the home of NAACP activists Harry and Harriette Moore in Mims, Florida, resulting in their deaths.
- The 1957 murder of Willie Edwards, Jr. Klansmen forced Edwards to jump to his death from a bridge into the Alabama River.
- The 1963 assassination of NAACP organizer Medgar Evers in Mississippi. In 1994, former Ku Klux Klansman Byron De La Beckwith was convicted.
- The 1963 bombing of the 16th Street Baptist Church in Birmingham, Alabama, which killed four African-American girls. The perpetrators were Klan members Robert Chambliss, convicted in 1977,

Thomas Blanton and Bobby Frank Cherry, convicted in 2001 and 2002. The fourth suspect, Herman Cash, died before he was indicted.

- The 1964 murders of three civil rights workers Chaney, Goodman, and Schwerner in Mississippi. In June 2005, Klan member Edgar Ray Killen was convicted of manslaughter.

- The 1964 murder of two black teenagers, Henry Hezekiah Dee and Charles Eddie Moore in Mississippi. In August 2007, based on the confession of Klansman Charles Marcus Edwards, James Ford Seale, a reputed Ku Klux Klansman, was convicted. Seale was sentenced to serve three life sentences. Seale was a former Mississippi policeman and sheriff's deputy.

- The 1965 Alabama murder of Viola Liuzzo. She was a Southern-raised Detroit mother of five who was visiting the state in order to attend a civil rights march. At the time of her murder Liuzzo was transporting Civil Rights Marchers.

- The 1966 firebombing death of NAACP leader Vernon Dahmer Sr., 58, in Mississippi. In 1998 former Ku Klux Klan wizard Sam Bowers was convicted of his murder and sentenced to life. Two other Klan members were indicted with Bowers, but one died before trial, and the other's indictment was dismissed.

There was also resistance to the Klan. In 1953, newspaper publisher W. Horace Carter received a Pulitzer prize for reporting on the activities of the Klan. In a 1958 North Carolina incident, the Klan burned crosses at the homes of two Lumbee Native Americans who had associated with white people, and they threatened to return with more men. When the KKK held a nighttime rally nearby, they were quickly surrounded by hundreds of armed Lumbees. Gunfire was exchanged, and the Klan was routed at what became known as the Battle of Hayes Pond.

While the FBI had paid informants in the Klan, for instance in Birmingham in the early 1960s, its relations with local law enforcement agencies and the Klan were often ambiguous. The head of the FBI J. Edgar Hoover, appeared more concerned about Communist links to civil rights activists than about controlling Klan excesses against citizens. In 1964, the FBI's COINTELPRO program began attempts to infiltrate and disrupt civil rights groups.

As 20th-century Supreme Court rulings extended federal enforcement of citizens' civil rights, the government revived the Force Act and Klan Act from Reconstruction days. Federal prosecutors used these laws as the basis for investigations and indictments in the 1964 murders of Chaney, Goodman, and Schwerner; and the 1965 murder of Viola Liuzzo. They were also the basis for prosecution in 1991 in *Bray v. Alexandria Women's Health Clinic*.

1970s–1990s

Once African Americans secured federal legislation to protect civil and voting rights, the KKK shifted its focus to opposing court-ordered busing to desegregate schools, affirmative action and more open immigration. In 1971, KKK members used bombs to destroy 10 school buses in Pontiac, Michigan.

On November 3, 1979, five protesters were killed by KKK and American Nazi Party members in the Greensboro massacre in Greensboro, North Carolina. This incident was the culmination of attempts by the Communist Workers Party to organize industrial workers, predominantly black, in the area.

Jerry Thompson, a newspaper reporter who infiltrated the KKK in 1979, reported that the FBI's COINTELPRO efforts were highly successful. Rival KKK factions accused each

Violence at a Klan march in Mobile, Alabama, 1977

other's leaders of being FBI informants. Bill Wilkinson of the Invisible Empire, Knights of the Ku Klux Klan, was revealed to have been working for the FBI.

In 1980, three KKK members shot four elderly black women (Viola Ellison, Lela Evans, Opal Jackson and Katherine Johnson) in Chattanooga, Tennessee, following a KKK initiation rally. A fifth woman, Fannie Crumsey, was injured by flying glass in the incident. Attempted murder charges were filed against the three KKK members, two of whom—Bill Church and Larry Payne—were acquitted by an all-white jury, and the other of whom—Marshall Thrash—was sentenced by the same jury to nine months on lesser charges. He was released after three months. In 1982, a jury awarded the five women $535,000 in a civil rights trial.

After Michael Donald was lynched in 1981 in Alabama, the FBI investigated his death and two local KKK members were convicted of having a role, including Henry Hayes, who was sentenced to death. With the support of attorneys Morris Dees and Joseph J. Levin of the Southern Poverty Law Center (SPLC), Donald's mother, Beulah Mae Donald, sued the KKK in civil court in Alabama. Her lawsuit against the United Klans of America was tried in February 1987. The all-white jury found the Klan responsible for the lynching of Donald and ordered the Klan to pay US$7 million. To pay the judgment, the KKK turned over all of its assets, including its national headquarters building in Tuscaloosa. After exhausting the appeals process, Hayes was executed for Donald's death in Alabama on June 6, 1997. It was the first time since 1913 that a white man had been executed in Alabama for a crime against an African American.

Thompson, the journalist who claimed he had infiltrated the Klan, related that KKK leaders who appeared indifferent to the threat of arrest showed great concern about a series of civil lawsuits filed by the Southern Poverty Law Center for damages of millions of dollars. These were filed after KKK members shot into a group of African Americans. Klansmen curtailed activities to conserve money for defense against the lawsuits. The KKK also used lawsuits as tools; they filed a libel suit to prevent publication of a paperback edition of Thompson's book.

Contemporary Klan

The present-day KKK is not one organization; rather it is composed of small independent chapters across the US. The formation of independent chapters has made KKK groups more difficult to infiltrate, and researchers find it hard to estimate their numbers. Estimates are that about two-thirds of KKK members are concentrated in the Southern United States, with another third situated primarily in the lower Midwest. KKK members have stepped up recruitment in recent years, but the organization grows slowly, with membership estimated at 5,000–8,000 across 179 chapters. These recent membership campaigns have been based on issues such as people's anxieties about illegal immigration, urban crime and same-sex marriage. Many KKK groups have formed strong alliances with other white supremacist groups, such as neo-Nazis. Some KKK groups have become increasingly "Nazified", adopting the look and emblems of white power skinheads.

On November 14, 2008, an all-white jury of seven men and seven women awarded $1.5 million in compensatory damages and $1 million in punitive damages to plaintiff Jordan Gruver, represented by the Southern Poverty Law Center against the Imperial Klans of America. The ruling found that five IKA members had savagely beaten Gruver, then 16 years old, at a Kentucky county fair in July 2006.

The American Civil Liberties Union (ACLU) has provided legal support to various factions of the KKK in defense of their First Amendment rights to hold public rallies, parades, and marches, as well as their right to field political candidates.

Current Klan splinter divisions have grown substantially since the 2008 election of U.S. President Barack Obama, the first African-American to hold the office; the Klan has expanded its recruitment efforts to white supremacists at the international level. Current membership estimates by the ADL hold at a national estimate of five thousand. The SPLC continues to heavily monitor Klan activities.

Current KKK organizations

- Bayou Knights of the Ku Klux Klan, prevalent in Texas, Oklahoma, Arkansas, Louisiana and other areas of the Southeastern U.S.[citation needed]
- Church of the American Knights of the Ku Klux Klan
- Imperial Klans of America
- Knights of the White Camelia
- Knights of the Ku Klux Klan, headed by national director and self-claimed pastor Thom Robb, and based in Zinc, Arkansas. It claims to be the biggest Klan organization in America today. Spokesmen

refer to it as a "sixth era Klan", and it continues to be a racist group.[citation needed]

Vocabulary

Membership in the Klan is secret. Like many fraternal organizations, the Klan has signs which members can use to recognize one another. A member may use the acronym *AYAK* (Are you a Klansman?) in conversation to surreptitiously identify himself to another potential member. The response *AKIA* (A Klansman I am) completes the greeting.

Throughout its varied history, the Klan has coined many words beginning with "KL" including:

* Klabee: treasurers
* Klavern: local organization
* Kleagle: recruiter
* Klecktoken: initiation fee
* Kligrapp: secretary
* Klonvocation: gathering
* Kloran: ritual book
* Kloreroe: delegate
* Kludd: chaplain

All of the above terminology was created by William Simmons, as part of his 1915 revival of the Klan. The Reconstruction-era Klan used different titles; the only titles to carry over were "Wizard" for the overall leader of the Klan, "Night Hawk" for the official in charge of security, and a few others, mostly for regional officers of the organization.[citation needed]

See also

* History of Ku Klux Klan in New Jersey
* History of the United States (1865–1918)#Social Discontent
* Jim Crow laws
* Ku Klux Klan in Inglewood, California
* Ku Klux Klan recruitment
* Leaders of the Ku Klux Klan
* Notable alleged Ku Klux Klan members in national politics
* The Order
* Timeline of racial tension in Omaha, Nebraska
* Tulsa race riot
* White Knights of the Ku Klux Klan
* List of white nationalist organizations

References

- Axelrod, Alan (1997). *The International Encyclopedia of Secret Societies & Fraternal Orders*. New York: Facts On File.
- Barr, Andrew (1999). *Drink: A Social History of America*. New York: Carroll & Graf.
- Chalmers, David M. (1987). *Hooded Americanism: The History of the Ku Klux Klan*. Durahm, N.C.: Duke University Press. p. 512. ISBN 9780822307303.
- Chalmers, David M. (2003) *Backfire: How the Ku Klux Klan Helped the Civil Rights Movement*. ISBN 0-7425-2310-1
- Dray, Philip (2002). *At the Hands of Persons Unknown: The Lynching of Black America*. New York: Random House.
- Egerton, John (1994). *Speak Now Against the Day: The Generation Before the Civil Rights Movement in the South*. Alfred and Knopf Inc..
- Feldman, Glenn (1999). *Politics, Society, and the Klan in Alabama, 1915–1949*. Tuscaloosa, Alabama: University of Alabama Press.
- Foner, Eric (1989). *Reconstruction: America's Unfinished Revolution, 1863–1877*. Perennial (HarperCollins).
- Franklin, John Hope (1992). *Race and History: Selected Essays 1938–1988*. Louisiana State University Press.
- Horn, Stanley F. (1939). *Invisible Empire: The Story of the Ku Klux Klan, 1866–1871*. Montclair, New Jersey: Patterson Smith Publishing Corporation.
- Ingalls, Robert P. (1979). *Hoods: The Story of the Ku Klux Klan*. New York: G.P. Putnam's Sons.
- Jackson, Kenneth T. (1967; 1992 edition). *The Ku Klux Klan in the City, 1915–1930*. Oxford University Press.
- Kennedy, Stetson (1990). *The Klan Unmasked*. University Press of Florida.
- McVeigh, Rory. *The Rise of the Ku Klux Klan: Right-Wing Movements and National Politics,* (2009), on 1920s
- Lender, Mark E.; James K. Martin (1982). *Drinking in America*. New York: Free Press.
- Levitt, Stephen D.; Stephen J. Dubner (2005). *Freakonomics: A Rogue Economist Explores the Hidden Side of Everything*. New York: William Morrow.
- McWhorter, Diane (2001). *Carry Me Home: Birmingham, Alabama, The Climactic Battle of the Civil Rights Revolution*. New York: Simon & Schuster.
- Moore, Leonard J. (1991). *Citizen Klansmen: The Ku Klux Klan in Indiana, 1921–1928*. Chapel Hill: University of North Carolina Press.
- Newton, Michael; Judy Ann Newton (1991). *The Ku Klux Klan: An Encyclopedia*. New York & London: Garland Publishing.
- Parsons, Elaine Frantz (2005). "Midnight Rangers: Costume and Performance in the Reconstruction-Era Ku Klux Klan". *The Journal of American History* **92** (3): 811–836. doi:10.2307/3659969 [1].

- Prendergast, Michael L. (1987). "A History of Alcohol Problem Prevention Efforts in the United States". In Holder, Harold D.. *Control Issues in Alcohol Abuse Prevention: Strategies for States and Communities*. Greenwich, Connecticut: JAI Press
- Rhodes, James Ford (1920). *History of the United States from the Compromise of 1850 to the McKinley-Bryan Campaign of 1896*. **7**. Winner of the 1918 Pulitzer Prize for history [2].
- Rogers, William; Robert Ward, Leah Atkins and Wayne Flynt (1994). *Alabama: The History of a Deep South State*. Tuscaloosa, Alabama: University of Alabama Press.
- Steinberg, Alfred (1962). *The man from Missouri; the life and times of Harry S. Truman*. New York: Putnam. OCLC 466366 [3].
- Taylor, Joe G. (1974). *Louisiana Reconstructed, 1863–1877*. Baton Rouge.
- Thompson, Jerry (1982). *My Life in the Klan*. New York: Putnam. ISBN 0399126953.
- Trelease, Allen W. (1995). *White Terror: The Ku Klux Klan Conspiracy and Southern Reconstruction*. Louisiana State University Press.
- Wade, Wyn Craig (1987). *The Fiery Cross: The Ku Klux Klan in America*. New York: Simon and Schuster.

Further reading

- Blee, Kathleen M. (1992). *Women of the Klan*. University of California Press. ISBN 0-520-07876-4.
- "White supremacist groups flourishing" [4]. *Gainesville Press*. Associated Press. February 6, 2007.
- Nelson, Jack (1993). *Terror in the Night: The Klan's Campaign Against the Jews*. New York: Simon & Schuster. ISBN 0-671-69223-2.
- Chalmers, David M. (2003). *Backfire: how the Ku Klux Klan helped the civil rights movement* [5]. Rowman & Littlefield. ISBN 0742523101.

External links

- "Ku Klux Klan" [6], Southern Poverty Law Center
- "KKK" [7], Anti-Defamation League
- "Inside Today's KKK" [8], multimedia, *Life* magazine, 13 April 2009
- Interview with Stanley F. Horn [9], author of *Invisible Empire: The Story of the Ku Klux Klan, 1866–1871* (1939), Forest History Society, Inc., May 1978

Nation of Islam

The **Nation of Islam** is a religious organization founded in Detroit, Michigan, by Wallace D. Fard Muhammad in July 1930. He set out with the goal of resurrecting the spiritual, mental, social, and economic condition of the African American men and women of America. The N.O.I. also promotes

the belief that God will bring about a universal government of peace. Since 1978, Louis Farrakhan has been the leader of a reconstituted N.O.I., the original organization having been renamed and dissolved by Warith Deen Muhammad. The N.O.I.'s national center and headquarters are located in Chicago, Illinois, which is also home to its flagship Mosque No. 2, Mosque Maryam. A meeting in 2000 gathered about 20,000 members. Their exact number of members is believed to be between 20,000 and 50,000. Most of their members are from the United States, but there are small communities in other countries, like Canada, United Kingdom, France and Trinidad and Tobago. One of the reformist branches of this movement is The Nation of Gods and Earths.

History

Elijah Muhammad

Main article: History of the Nation of Islam

The original Nation of Islam was founded in Detroit, Michigan in July, 1930 by Wallace Fard Muhammad, also known as W. D. Fard Muhammad (1877–1934 or later). The N.O.I. teaches that W. Fard Muhammad is both the "Messiah" of Christianity and the Mahdi of Islam. According to their website, they distinguish themselves from followers of the original religion of Islam by stating: 12. WE BELIEVE that Allah (god) appeared in the Person of Master W. Fard Muhammad, July, 1930; the long-awaited "Messiah" of the Christians and the "Mahdi" of the Muslims. One of Fard's first disciples was Elijah Muhammad (1897–1975), who led the organization from 1935 through 1975. [1]

By the time Elijah Muhammad died in 1975, there were 75 centers across America. In 1975, Warith Deen Mohammed or W.D. (Wallace) Muhammad was installed as Supreme Minister of the Nation of Islam. Thereupon he renamed the organization "The World Community of Al-Islam in the West" which later became the American Society of Muslims and shunned his father's theology and black separatist views, accepting whites as fellow worshipers and forging closer ties with mainstream Muslim communities in an attempt to bring the Nation of Islam closer into Sunni Islam.

Beliefs and theology

African American topics
Category · Portal

Main article: Beliefs and theology of the Nation of Islam

Current Nation of Islam leader Louis Farrakhan.

The main belief of The Nation of Islam and its followers is that there is no other God but Allah, revealing "Allah" by saying "who came in the person of W. D. Fard." Fard founded the Nation of Islam and subsequently installed Elijah Muhammad as the organization's leader. The official beliefs of the Nation of Islam have been outlined in books, documents, and articles published by the organization as well as speeches by Elijah Muhammad, Malcolm X, Louis Farrakhan, and other ministers. Many of Elijah Muhammad's teachings may be found in *Message to the Blackman in America* and *The True History of Jesus as Taught by the Honorable Elijah Muhammad* . Many of Malcolm X's teachings of NOI theology are in his *The End of White World Supremacy*, while a later more critical discussion of those beliefs can be found in *The Autobiography of Malcolm X*, co-written with Alex Haley.

Passed down via written lessons from 1930–1934 from W. Fard Muhammad to his student, Elijah Muhammad, referred to and titled, *The Supreme Wisdom* the Nation of Islam continues to teach its followers that the present world society is segmented into three distinct categories. They teach that from a general perspective, 85% of the population are the *deaf, dumb and blind* masses of the people who *are easily led in the wrong direction and hard to lead in the right direction*. These 85% of the masses who are said to be manipulated by 10% of the people are referred to as the masses of the people. Those 10% rich *slave-makers* are said to manipulate the 85% masses of the people through ignorance, the skillful use of religious doctrine and the mass media.

The third group referred to as the 5% *poor righteous teachers* of the people of the world who know the truth of the manipulation of the 85% masses of the people by the 10% and that 5% *righteous teachers* are at constant struggle and war with 10% to reach and *free the minds* of the masses of the people.

Official platform

An official Nation of Islam platform referred to as "The Muslim Program" was written by Elijah Muhammad in his book *Message to the Blackman in America*, published in 1965. The itemized platform contains two sections; *What The Muslims Want* consisting of 10 points and *What The Muslims Believe* consisting of 12 points.

Cosmology

The NOI teaches that the Earth and Moon were once the same, and that the Earth is over 76 trillion years old. The entire land mass on the Earth was called "Asia". This was, Elijah Muhammad claims, long before Adam.

Black experience of slavery was Bible prophecy

The NOI teaches that black people constitute a nation and that through the institution of the Atlantic slave trade they were systematically denied knowledge of their past history, language, culture, and religion and, in effect, lost control of their lives. Central to this doctrine, NOI theology asserts that black people's experience of slavery was the fulfillment of Bible prophecy and therefore, black people are the seed of Abraham referred to in the Bible, in Genesis 15:13–14:

> And he said unto Abram, Know of a surety that thy seed shall be a stranger in a land that is not theirs, and shall serve them; and they shall afflict them four hundred years; And also that nation, whom they shall serve, will I judge: and afterward shall they come out with great substance.

> —King James Version

Separatism

In an April 13, 1997 interview on NBC's *Meet the Press*, Louis Farrakhan was asked by Tim Russert to explain the Nation of Islam's view on separation:

> Tim Russert: "Once a week, on the back page [of your newspaper] is The Muslim Program, 'What the Muslims Want' [written in 1965]. The first is in terms of territory, 'Since we cannot get along with them in peace and equality, we believe our contributions to this land and the suffering forced upon us by white America justifies our demand for complete separation in a state or territory of our own.' Is that your view in 1997, a separate state for Black Americans?"

> Minister Louis Farrakhan: "First, the program starts with number one. That is number four. The first part of that program is that we want freedom, a full and complete freedom. The second is, we want justice. We want equal justice under the law, and we want justice applied equally to all, regardless of race or class or color. And the third is that we want equality. We want equal membership in society with the best in civilized society. If we can get that within the political, economic, social system of America, there's no need for point number four. But if we cannot get

along in peace after giving America 400 years of our service and sweat and labor, then, of course, separation would be the solution to our race problem."

Teachings on race

The Nation of Islam teaches that Black people were the original humans. Louis Farrakhan has stated that "White people are potential humans...they haven't evolved yet." However, Farrakhan further expounded by saying, "If you look at the human family — now, I'm talking about black, brown, red, yellow and white — we all seem to be frozen on a subhuman level of existence. In Islam and, I believe, in Christian theology and Jewish theology as well, there are three stages of human development. The first stage is called the animalistic stage of development. But when we submit to animal passions, then we can do evil things to one another in that animalistic stage of development. But when moral consciousness comes and we have a self-accusing spirit, it is then that we become human beings. Right now, we have the potential for humanity, but we have not reached that potential, because we are functioning on the animalistic plane of existence."

> "The Blackman is the original man. From him came all brown, yellow, red, and white people. By using a special method of birth control law, the Blackman was able to produce the white race. This method of birth control was developed by a Black scientist known as Yakub, who envisioned making and teaching a nation of people who would be diametrically opposed to the Original People. A Race of people who would one day rule the original people and the earth for a period of 6,000 years. Yakub promised his followers that he would graft a nation from his own people, and he would teach them how to rule his people, through a system of tricks and lies whereby they use deceit to divide and conquer, and break the unity of the darker people, put one brother against another, and then act as mediators and rule both sides." -Elijah Muhammad

In an interview on NBC's *Meet the Press*, Louis Farrakhan said the following in response to host Tim Russert's question on the Nation of Islam's teachings on race:

> "You know, it's not unreal to believe that white people — who genetically cannot produce yellow, brown or black — had a Black origin. The scholars and scientists of this world agree that the origin of man and humankind started in Africa and that the first parent of the world was black. The Qur'an says that God created Adam out of black mud and fashioned him into shape. So if white people came from the original people, the Black people, what is the process by which you came to life? That is not a silly question. That is a scientific question with a scientific answer. It doesn't suggest that we are superior or that you are inferior. It suggests, however, that your birth or your origin is from the black people of this earth: superiority and inferiority is determined by our righteousness and not by our color."

Pressed by Russert on whether he agreed with Elijah Muhammad's preaching that whites are blue-eyed devils, Farrakhan responded:

Elijah Muhammad addressing followers

> "Well, you have not been saints in the way you have acted toward the darker peoples of the world and toward even your own people. But, in truth, Mr. Russert, any human being who gives themself over to the doing of evil could be considered a devil. In the Bible, in the Book of Revelation, it talks about the fall of Babylon. It says Babylon is fallen because she has become the habitation of devils. We believe that that ancient Babylon is a symbol of a modern Babylon, which is America."

While Malcolm X was a member of the Nation of Islam, he preached that black people were genetically superior to white people but were dominated by a system of white supremacy.

> Thoughtful white people know they are inferior to Black people. Even [Senator James] Eastland knows it. Anyone who has studied the genetic phase of biology knows that white is considered recessive and black is considered dominant. ..The entire American economy is based on white supremacy. Even the religious philosophies, in essence, white supremacy. A white Jesus. A white Virgin. White angels. White everything. But a black Devil, of course. The "Uncle Sam" political foundation is based on white supremacy, relegating nonwhites to second–class citizenship. It goes without saying that the social philosophy is strictly white supremacist. And the educational system perpetuates white supremacy.

The Nation of Islam teaches that intermarriage or race mixing should be prohibited. This is point 10 of the official platform, "What the Muslims Want" published 1965.[citation needed]

The Mother Plane and Ezekiel's Wheel

Elijah Muhammad taught his followers about a Mother Plane or Wheel, a UFO that was seen and described in the visions of the prophet Ezekiel in the Book of Ezekiel, in the Hebrew Bible.

> "Now as I looked at the living creatures, I saw a wheel on the earth beside the living creatures, one for each of the four of them. As for the appearance of the wheels and their construction: their appearance was like the gleaming of beryl. And the four had the same likeness, their appearance and construction being as it were a wheel within a wheel. When they went, they went in any of their four directions without turning as they went. And their rims were tall and awesome, and the rims of all four were full of eyes all around."

—Book of Ezekiel Chapter 1:15–18, Bible, English Standard Version

Louis Farrakhan, commenting on his teacher's description said the following:

"The Honorable Elijah Muhammad told us of a giant Mother Plane that is made like the universe, spheres within spheres. White people call them unidentified flying objects (UFOs). Ezekiel, in the Old Testament, saw a wheel that looked like a cloud by day but a pillar of fire by night. The Honorable Elijah Muhammad said that that wheel was built on the island of Nippon, which is now called Japan, by some of the Original scientists. It took $15 billion in gold at that time to build it. It is made of the toughest steel. America does not yet know the composition of the steel used to make an instrument like it. It is a circular plane, and the Bible says that it never makes turns. Because of its circular nature it can stop and travel in all directions at speeds of thousands of miles per hour. He said there are 1,500 small wheels in this Mother Wheel, which is a half mile by a half mile [800 m by 800 m]. This Mother Wheel is like a small human-built planet. Each one of these small planes carry three bombs.

"The Honorable Elijah Muhammad said these planes were used to set up mountains on the earth. The Qur'an says it like this: We have raised mountains on the earth lest it convulse with you. How do you raise a mountain, and what is the purpose of a mountain? Have you ever tried to balance a tire? You use weights to keep the tire balanced. That's how the earth is balanced, with mountain ranges. The Honorable Elijah Muhammad said that we have a type of bomb that, when it strikes the earth a drill on it is timed to go into the earth and explode at the height that you wish the mountain to be. If you wish to take the mountain up a mile [1.6 km], you time the drill to go a mile in and then explode. The bombs these planes have are timed to go one mile down and bring up a mountain one mile high, but it will destroy everything within a 50-square-mile [130 km²] radius. The white man writes in his above top secret memos of the UFOs. He sees them around his military installations like they are spying.

"That Mother Wheel is a dreadful-looking thing. White folks are making movies now to make these planes look like fiction, but it is based on something real. The Honorable Elijah Muhammad said that Mother Plane is so powerful that with sound reverberating in the atmosphere, just with a sound, she can crumble buildings."

—Minister Louis Farrakhan, *The Divine Destruction of America: Can She Avert It?*

Criticisms

The first book analyzing the Nation of Islam was *The Black Muslims in America* (1961) by C. Eric Lincoln. Lincoln describes the use of doctrines during religious services.

Often the minister reads passages from well-known historical, sociological, or anthropological works, and finds in them inconspicuous references to the Blackman's true history in the world.... Occasionally the minister chides the audience for its skepticism: "I know you don't believe me because I happen to be a Black man. Well, you can look it up in a book I'm going to tell you about that was written by a white man." He then reads off references that his hearers are challenged to check.

The 1975 death of Elijah Muhammad

Some members of The Nation of Islam have long denied the fact of Elijah Muhammad's death to the extent of proposing that he escaped a death plot, was restored to health, and is aboard "that huge wheel-like plane that is even now flying over our heads" and that among other passengers on the Mother Wheel is Allah otherwise known as Wallie Dodd. As witnessed by some 20000 people at his funeral service on February 28, 1975, he is buried in Mount Glenwood Cemetery in Thornton, Illinois.

Antisemitism

Main article: Nation of Islam and antisemitism

A number of Jewish organizations, Christian organizations, and academics consider the Nation of Islam to be antisemitic. Professor David W. Leinweber, Ph.D. of Emory University asserts that the Nation Of Islam has engaged in revisionist and antisemitic interpretations of the Holocaust and that they exaggerate the role of Jews in the trans-Atlantic slave trade.

The charges are based on statements such as the following by Farrakhan:

> "German Jews financed Hitler right here in America...International bankers financed Hitler and poor Jews died while big Jews were at the root of what you call the Holocaust...Little Jews died while big Jews made money. Little Jews [were] being turned into soap while big Jews washed themselves with it. Jews [were] playing violin, Jews [were] playing music, while other Jews [were] marching into the gas chambers...."
>
> —

The Anti-Defamation League (ADL) alleges that NOI Health Minister, Abdul Alim Muhammad, has accused Jewish doctors of injecting Blacks with the AIDS virus, an allegation that Dr. Abdul Alim Muhammad has denied.

The Nation of Islam has repeatedly denied charges of anti-Semitism, and NOI leader Minister Louis Farrakhan has stated, "The ADL .. uses the term 'anti-Semitism' to stifle all criticism of Zionism and the Zionist policies of the State of Israel and also to stifle all legitimate criticism of the errant behavior of some Jewish people toward the non-Jewish population of the earth."

Responding to the widely reported assertion that he referred to Judaism as a dirty and "gutter religion", Farrakhan wrote a June 18, 1997 letter to a former *Wall Street Journal* associate editor, Jude Wanniski, stating in part:

> "Over the centuries, the evils of Christians, Jews and Muslims have dirtied their respective religions. True Faith in the laws and Teaching of Abraham, Jesus and Muhammad is not dirty, but, practices in the name of these religions can be unclean and can cause people to look upon the misrepresented religion as being unclean."

Wanniski also defended the Nation of Islam writing, "I've met dozens of men and women who belong to the Nation of Islam, attended many of their conferences, and prayed with them in their Chicago mosque to the God of Abraham, Moses, Jesus and Muhammed. I've concluded beyond any reasonable doubt that there is not an ounce of anti-Semitism or bigotry in Farrakhan."

The Nation of Islam has had friendly relations with the Neturei Karta, a small, controversial Jewish group that is well-known for its association with and support for anti-Zionists.

Comparison with traditional Islam

The Nation of Islam preaches adherence to the Five Pillars of the Islamic Faith, however these are sometimes avoided, for example the Friday prayers, which are obligatory for men, are rarely practiced, furthermore prayers are conducted in temples on seated chairs in church-fashion, instead of mosques and without prostration. The NOI also teaches morality and personal decorum, emphasizing modesty, mutual respect, and discipline in dress and comportment. NOI adherents do not consume pork, frown upon the consumption of alcohol, drugs, and tobacco, and stress a healthy diet and physical fitness. However, the Nation of Islam argues that because of the unique experience of the oppression and degradation of slavery, Elijah Muhammad used unique methods for introducing Islam to his people. Traditional Islamic beliefs however, stand in stark opposition to the entire theological and creedal foundation of the Nation of Islam.

Other doctrines of the Nation of Islam are disputed, specifically:

A mosque of Nation of Islam in Baton Rouge, Louisiana, United States, 2005.

- God's incarnation:

  - NOI teaches that "Allah (God) appeared in the Person of Master W. Fard Muhammad, July 1930; the long-awaited Messiah of the Christians and the Mahdi of the Muslims."

  - Traditional Sunni and Shi'a Muslim doctrine is that it is heretical and blasphemous to believe that God would manifest Himself in human form. Likening any individual(s) to God is a form of *shirk*—a major sin in Islam.

- Relations with whites:

  - NOI teaches that the Black man is the original man, and from him came all brown, yellow, and white people. By using a special method of birth control law (the Yakub teaching), the Blackman was able to produce the white race. NOI does not believe that whites are worthy to be evangelized, and thus does not accept them into the NOI.[citation needed]

- Traditional Islam teaches that all races are equal, and any person of any race can convert to Islam. Islam recognizes the Biblical and Qur'anic figure, the patriarch Jacob, but this Jacob is viewed by Muslims as a prophet, not the Yakub featured in Nation of Islam theology.
- Perspectives on the Quran:
  - The NOI states that they believe in the Qur'an and the writings of all the prophets of God. The NOI believes there are truths in the Bible but it is tampered material and "must be reinterpreted so that mankind will not be snared by the falsehoods that have been added to it."
  - The vast majority of Muslims, worldwide, believe that the Quran is Allah's final revelation to mankind and that it was given to the Islamic Prophet Muhammad between the years of 610 and 632. Islam believes in the previous scriptures (such as the Bible and Torah) but holds firm the belief that they have been manipulated.
- Status of the Islamic prophet Muhammad vs. other prophets:
  - The Nation of Islam believes that Elijah Muhammad was a messenger and was taught by God Himself, who the NOI claim as "Master" Fard Muhammad (W. D. Fard).
  - Islam teaches that Muhammad was the **last** of the messengers that Allah has sent to mankind — there would be no more and all Muslims are to follow the teachings of the Quran and accept monotheism
- Practice of Friday prayers:
  - The Nation of Islam ignores Jumuah, as a pillar of practice for Muslims. This was changed briefly in 2002, when W. Deen Mohammed, a Muslim in opposition of black separatism, delivered the Friday sermon at the Los Angeles Convention Center. The practice of Jumuah prayer for the NOI has since stopped in place of a traditional "Christian" Sunday service.
  - Islam dedicates Friday as the congregational prayer (salat) that Muslims hold every Friday, just after noon in lieu of dhuhr (noon prayer).

Table of comparison of Traditional Islam and Nation of Islam:

Belief	Traditional Islam	Nation of Islam
God	Allah is one, who has no partners	Wallace D. Fard came as God incarnate (God is man)
Muhammad	The final prophet of Islam, no one comes after him	Elijah Muhammad is the prophet to tell about incarnation of Fard
Race	All are equal regardless of color of skin, judged on behavior	The original black race of man is superior, especially to the white man: a race of "blue-eyed devils" created by the black man
Creation	Allah created the universe, first humans were Adam and Eve	Black scientists created the plan which repeats every 25,000 years
Qur'an	Revealed to Muhammad from God through the Angel Gabriel	Black scientists created and revealed the Bible and the Qur'an

Sharia law	Sacred rules and laws of Islamic life, based on Qur'an and Sunnah	Not followed, own-created such as 4-6pm meal or avoid white flour cake meals

- Translation of the Qur'an:

The Nation of Islam generally uses the Maulana Muhammad Ali English translation of the Qur'an. The most common and most well-known English translation of the Qur'an, however, is by Abdullah Yusuf Ali. Maulana Muhammad Ali was a leading figure of the Ahmadiyya movement (citation #42).

Actions and programs

The NOI has a do-for-self philosophy that resulted in the NOI owning and operating hundreds of businesses nationwide, employing thousands of people. The NOI has purchased and now operates food-industry services, bakeries, and restaurants. It owns a large amount of farmland in Georgia. It owns and operates hair-care shops. Some of these business ventures have been success stories. Others have been criticized as Amway-style marketing schemes that have not benefited most of their employees.

NOI preacher in 1999, in England.

The NOI has worked to clean up drug addicts, reform prostitutes, and keep black youth out of gangs. It has helped some newly released ex-convicts make a new start and stay out of jail.

In *The Fire Next Time*, James Baldwin wrote:

> Elijah Muhammad has been able to do what generations of welfare workers and committees and resolutions and reports and housing projects and playgrounds have failed to do: to heal and redeem drunkards and junkies, to convert people who have come out of prison and to keep them out, to make men chaste and women virtuous, and to invest both the male and the female with pride and a serenity that hang about them like an unfailing light. He has done all these things, which our

A Nation of Islam member sells copies of the Final Call newspaper and what appears to be assorted oils and perfumes.

Christian church has spectacularly failed to do. (James Baldwin, *The Fire Next Time*, New York: Vintage International/Random House, 1963)

During the 1980s when crack cocaine became very common, the United States Department of Housing and Urban Development employed several private firms run by members of the Nation of Islam to provide security in housing projects in black neighborhoods. The Anti-Defamation League successfully lobbied Congress to sever the HUD contracts.

Noted current and former members and associates of Nation of Islam

- Elijah Muhammad
- Tynetta Muhammad
- Louis Farrakhan
- Khalid Abdul Muhammad
- Khadijah Farrakhan
- Malcolm X - Later converted to Sunni Islam
- Muhammad Ali – Later converted to Sufism
- Warith Deen Mohammed – Later converted to Sunni Islam
- MC Ren – Later converted to Islam
- KAM- member of the Nation Of Islam and former associate of Ice Cube
- John Allen Muhammad – The Beltway Sniper, Gulf war veteran, former NOI member
- Benjamin Chavis Muhammad
- JT The Bigga Figga
- Paris
- Kemi Seba
- Snoop Dogg

Subsidiaries

Main article: The Nation of Gods and Earths

The Nation of Gods and Earths is an offshoot of the Nation of Islam founded in 1964 in the Harlem section of the borough of Manhattan in New York City by Clarence Smith, known most commonly to the public at large as Clarence 13X. Gods and Earths hold events known as Universal Parliaments in various cities—usually once a month—to build on their interpretation of the Supreme Mathematics, lessons, and to discuss business concerning the Nation.

See also

- Black separatism
- Black supremacy
- Afrocentrism
- The Final Call
- Fruit of Islam (FOI)
- The Hate That Hate Produced
- History of the Nation of Islam
- Islam in the African diaspora
- List of topics related to Black and African people
- Moorish Science Temple of America
- Muslim Girls Training (MGT)
- The Nation of Gods and Earths
- Nation of Islam and antisemitism
- Zebra Murders
- UFO religion

External links

- Official Website The Nation of Islam [1] (N.O.I.)
- Messenger Elijah Muhammad Web Resources Center, Online books, audio, and video [2]
- Nation of Islam affiliated Final Call Newspaper website [3]
- Official Website of the United Kingdom Branch of the Nation of Islam [4]
- Walker, Dennis Searching for African American Nationhood: Looking Into the Nation of Islam (Interview) [5]
- "Nation of Islam" [6], Federal Bureau of Prisons, *Technical Reference Manual on Inmate Beliefs and Practices*

1. REDIRECT Template:Navboxes

Black Panther Party

Black Panther Party	
Founded	1966
Dissolved	c. 1976
Ideology	Marxism-Leninism, Maoism, internationalism, black nationalism, socialism
Political position	Far left
International affiliation	Algeria, Cuba, France
Official colors	Black, Light Blue
Politics of the United States Political parties Elections	

The **Black Panther Party** (originally the **Black Panther Party for Self-Defense**) was an African-American revolutionary organization working for the self-defense of black people. It was active in the United States from the mid-1960s into the 1970s. The Black Panther Party achieved national and international impact through their deep involvement in the Black Power movement and in US politics of the 1960s and 70s, as the intense anti-racism of the time is today considered one of the most significant social, political and cultural currents in US history. The group's "provocative rhetoric, militant posture, and cultural and political flourishes permanently altered the contours of American Identity."

Founded in Oakland, California, by Bobby Seale and Huey P. Newton on October 15, 1966, the organization initially set forth a doctrine calling primarily for the protection of African American neighborhoods from police brutality. But the Black Panther Party's objectives and philosophy expanded and evolved rapidly during the party's existence. The organization's leaders passionately espoused socialist and communist (largely Maoist) doctrines, but the Party's black nationalist reputation attracted an ideologically diverse membership. Ideological consensus within the party was difficult to achieve, and some prominent members openly disagreed with the views of the leaders.

The organization's official newspaper, *The Black Panther*, was first circulated in 1967. Also that year, the Black Panther Party marched on the California State Capitol in Sacramento in protest of a selective ban on weapons. By 1968, the party had expanded into many cities throughout the United States, including New Orleans, Chicago, Los Angeles, Detroit, San Diego, Denver, Newark, New York City, Boston, Dallas, Philadelphia, Pittsburgh, Cleveland, Seattle, Washington, D.C., and Baltimore. Membership reached 5,000 and their newspaper, under the editorial leadership of Eldridge Cleaver, had a circulation of 250,000. The group created a Ten-Point Program, a document that called for "Land,

Bread, Housing, Education, Clothing, Justice and Peace", as well as exemption from conscription for African-American men, among other demands. With the Ten-Point program, "What we Want, What We Believe", the Black Panther Party captured in uncompromising language the collective economic and political grievances articulated by black radicals and many black liberals since the 1930s.

Gaining national prominence, the Black Panther Party became an icon of the counterculture of the 1960s. Ultimately, the Panthers condemned black nationalism as "black racism" and became more focused on socialism without racial exclusivity. They instituted a variety of community social programs designed to alleviate poverty and improve health among communities deemed most needful of aid. It also recognized that different minority communities (those it deemed oppressed by the US government) needed to organize around their own set of issues and encouraged alliances with such organizations.

The Black Panther Party's most influential and widely known programs were its armed citizens' patrols to evaluate behavior of police officers and its Free Breakfast for Children program. However, the group's political goals were often overshadowed by their confrontational, militant, and sometimes violent tactics against police.

Federal Bureau of Investigation Director J. Edgar Hoover called the party "the greatest threat to the internal security of the country," and he supervised an extensive program (COINTELPRO) of surveillance, assassination, infiltration, police harassment, perjury, and a laundry list of other tactics designed to incriminate party members and drain the organization of resources and manpower. Through these tactics, it was thought that their potential for further advancement would diminish and probability of continuing to serve as a threat to the general power structure of the US, or maintain a presence as a strong undercurrent would shrink." While party membership started to decline during Huey Newton's 1968 manslaughter trial, the Black Panther Party collapsed altogether in the early 1970s. Scholars such as Angela Davis and Ward Churchill have alleged that law enforcement officials went to great lengths to discredit and destroy the organization, including assassination.

Origins

In 1966, Huey P. Newton was released from jail. With his friend Bobby Seale from Oakland City College, he joined a black power group called the Revolutionary Action Movement (RAM). RAM had a chapter in Oakland and followed the writings of Robert F. Williams. Williams had been the president of the Monroe, North Carolina branch of the NAACP and later published a newsletter called *The Crusader* from China, where he fled to escape kidnapping charges.

They worked at the North Oakland Neighborhood Anti-Poverty Center, where they also served on the advisory board. To combat police brutality, the advisory board obtained 5,000 signatures in support of the City Council's setting up a police review board to review complaints. Newton was also taking classes at the City College and at San Francisco Law School. Both institutions were active in the North Oakland Center. Thus the pair had numerous connections with whom they talked about a new organization. Inspired by the success of the Lowndes County Freedom Organization and Stokely

Carmichael's calls for separate black political organizations, they wrote their initial platform statement, the Ten-Point Program. With the help of Huey's brother Melvin, they decided on a uniform of blue shirts, black pants, black leather jackets, black berets, and openly displayed loaded shotguns (in his studies, Newton had discovered a California law that allowed carrying a loaded rifle or shotgun in public, as long as it was publicly displayed and pointed at no one).

What became standard Black Panther discourse emerged from a long history of urban activism, social criticism and political struggle by African Americans. "As inheritors of the discipline, pride, and calm self-assurance preached by Malcolm X, the panthers became national heroes in African American communities by infusing abstract nationalism with street toughness-by joining the rhythms of black working-class youth culture to the interracial élan and effervescence of Bay Area New Left politics." There is often debate about the impact that the Black Panther Party had on the greater society, or even their local environment. Some feel as though their only impact was one of contention against law enforcement, as facilitators of violence, and outspoken misguided radicals. "Beyond their immediate and material impact, though, the survival programs aimed at deeper spiritual and ideological transformations among neighborhood men and women whom the Party hoped to mobilize. As models of black self-determination and pride, the programs combined self-help and education in revolutionary diction with the free-spirited, animated public displays of political commitment that had become the sine qua non of Left culture in the Bay Area." "In 1966, the Panthers defined Oakland's ghetto as a territory, the police as interlopers, and the Panther mission as the defense of community. The Panthers' famous "policing the police" drew attention to the spatial remove that White Americans enjoyed from the state violence that had come to characterize life in black urban communities."

The Ten Point Program

The Ten Point Program was as follows:

1. WE WANT FREEDOM. WE WANT POWER TO DETERMINE THE DESTINY OF OUR BLACK AND OPPRESSED COMMUNITIES. We believe that Black and oppressed people will not be free until we are able to determine our destinies in our own communities ourselves, by fully controlling all the institutions which exist in our communities.
2. WE WANT FULL EMPLOYMENT FOR OUR PEOPLE. We believe that the federal government is responsible and obligated to give every person employment or a guaranteed income. We believe that if the American businessmen will not give full employment, then the technology and means of production should be taken from the businessmen and placed in the community so that the people of the community can organize and employ all of its people and give a high standard of living.
3. WE WANT AN END TO THE ROBBERY BY THE CAPITALISTS OF OUR BLACK AND OPPRESSED COMMUNITIES. We believe that this racist government has robbed us and now we are demanding the overdue debt of forty acres and two mules. Forty acres and two mules were promised 100 years ago as restitution for slave labor and mass murder of Black people. We will

accept the payment in currency which will be distributed to our many communities. The American racist has taken part in the slaughter of our fifty million Black people. Therefore, we feel this is a modest demand that we make.

4. WE WANT DECENT HOUSING, FIT FOR THE SHELTER OF HUMAN BEINGS. We believe that if the landlords will not give decent housing to our Black and oppressed communities, then housing and the land should be made into cooperatives so that the people in our communities, with government aid, can build and make decent housing for the people.

5. WE WANT DECENT EDUCATION FOR OUR PEOPLE THAT EXPOSES THE TRUE NATURE OF THIS DECADENT AMERICAN SOCIETY. WE WANT EDUCATION THAT TEACHES US OUR TRUE HISTORY AND OUR ROLE IN THE PRESENT-DAY SOCIETY. We believe in an educational system that will give to our people a knowledge of the self. If you do not have knowledge of yourself and your position in the society and in the world, then you will have little chance to know anything else.

6. WE WANT COMPLETELY FREE HEALTH CARE FOR ALL BLACK AND OPPRESSED PEOPLE. We believe that the government must provide, free of charge, for the people, health facilities which will not only treat our illnesses, most of which have come about as a result of our oppression, but which will also develop preventive medical programs to guarantee our future survival. We believe that mass health education and research programs must be developed to give all Black and oppressed people access to advanced scientific and medical information, so we may provide our selves with proper medical attention and care.

7. WE WANT AN IMMEDIATE END TO POLICE BRUTALITY AND MURDER OF BLACK PEOPLE, OTHER PEOPLE OF COLOR, ALL OPPRESSED PEOPLE INSIDE THE UNITED STATES. We believe that the racist and fascist government of the United States uses its domestic enforcement agencies to carry out its program of oppression against black people, other people of color and poor people inside the United States. We believe it is our right, therefore, to defend ourselves against such armed forces and that all Black and oppressed people should be armed for self defense of our homes and communities against these fascist police forces.

8. WE WANT AN IMMEDIATE END TO ALL WARS OF AGGRESSION. We believe that the various conflicts which exist around the world stem directly from the aggressive desire of the United States ruling circle and government to force its domination upon the oppressed people of the world. We believe that if the United States government or its lackeys do not cease these aggressive wars it is the right of the people to defend themselves by any means necessary against their aggressors.

9. WE WANT FREEDOM FOR ALL BLACK AND OPPRESSED PEOPLE NOW HELD IN U. S. FEDERAL, STATE, COUNTY, CITY, AND MILITARY PRISONS AND JAILS. WE WANT TRIALS BY A JURY OF PEERS FOR ALL PERSONS CHARGED WITH SO-CALLED CRIMES UNDER THE LAWS OF THIS COUNTRY. We believe that the many Black and poor oppressed people now held in United States prisons and jails have not received fair and impartial trials under a racist and fascist judicial system and should be free from incarceration. We believe in

the ultimate elimination of all wretched, inhuman penal institutions, because the masses of men and women imprisoned inside the United States or by the United States military are the victims of oppressive conditions which are the real cause of their imprisonment. We believe that when persons are brought to trial they must be guaranteed, by the United States, juries of their peers, attorneys of their choice and freedom from imprisonment while awaiting trial.

10. WE WANT LAND, BREAD, HOUSING, EDUCATION, CLOTHING, JUSTICE, PEACE AND PEOPLE'S COMMUNITY CONTROL OF MODERN TECHNOLOGY. When, in the course of human events, it becomes necessary for one people to dissolve the political bonds which have connected them with another, and to assume, among the powers of the earth, the separate and equal station to which the laws of nature and nature's God entitle them, a decent respect to the opinions of mankind requires that they should declare the causes which impel them to the separation. We hold these truths to be self-evident, that all men are created equal; that they are endowed by their Creator with certain unalienable rights; that among these are life, liberty, and the pursuit of happiness. That to secure these rights, governments are instituted among men, deriving their just powers from the consent of the governed; that, whenever any form of government becomes destructive of these ends, it is the right of the people to alter or to abolish it, and to institute a new government, laying its foundation on such principles, and organizing its powers in such form as to them shall seem most likely to effect their safety and happiness. Prudence, indeed, will dictate that governments long established should not be changed for light and transient causes; and, accordingly, all experience hath shown that mankind are most disposed to suffer, while evils are sufferable, than to right themselves by abolishing the forms to which they are accustomed. But, when a long train of abuses and usurpation, pursuing invariably the same object, evinces a design to reduce them under absolute despotism, it is their right, it is their duty, to throw off such government, and to provide new guards for their future security.

Action

"This country is a nation of thieves. It stole everything it has, beginning with black people. The U.S. cannot justify its existence as the policeman of the world any longer. I do not want to be a part of the American pie. The American pie means raping South Africa, beating Vietnam, beating South America, raping the Philippines, raping every country you've been in. I don't want any of your blood money. I don't want to be part of that system. We must question whether or not we want this country to continue being the wealthiest country in the world at the price of raping everybody else."

— Stokely Carmichael, Honorary Prime Minister

Survival programs

Inspired by Mao Zedong's advice to revolutionaries in *The Little Red Book*, Newton called on the Panthers to "serve the people" and to make "survival programs" a priority within its branches. The most famous and successful of their programs was the Free Breakfast for Children Program, initially run out of an Oakland church.

Other survival programs were free services such as clothing distribution, classes on politics and economics, free medical clinics, lessons on self-defense and first aid, transportation to upstate prisons for family members of inmates, an emergency-response ambulance program, drug and alcohol rehabilitation, and testing for sickle-cell disease.

The BPP also founded the "Intercommunal Youth Institute" in January 1971, with the intent of demonstrating how black youth ought to be educated. Ericka Huggins was the director of the school and Regina Davis was an administrator. The school was unique in that it didn't have grade levels but instead had different skill levels so an 11 year old could be in second-level English and fifth-level science. Elaine Brown taught reading and writing to a group of 10 to 11 year olds deemed "uneducable" by the system. At the school children were given free busing; breakfast, lunch, and dinner; books and school supplies; children were taken to have medical checkups; and many children were given free clothes.

Political activities

The Party briefly merged with the Student Nonviolent Coordinating Committee, headed by Stokely Carmichael (later Kwame Ture). In 1967, the party organized a march on the California state capitol to protest the state's attempt to outlaw carrying loaded weapons in public after the Panthers had begun exercising that right. Participants in the march carried rifles. In 1968, BPP Minister of Information Eldridge Cleaver ran for Presidential office on the Peace and Freedom Party ticket. They were a big influence on the White Panther Party, that was tied to the Detroit/Ann Arbor band MC5 and their manager John Sinclair, author of the book *Guitar Army* that also promulgated a ten-point program.

Conflict with law enforcement

As the Black Panther Party was beginning to gain a national presence, the government began a crackdown on the party and its activities. Huey P. Newton was arrested for an alleged murder, which sparked a "free Huey" campaign, organized by Eldridge Cleaver to help Newton's legal defense. Newton was convicted for voluntary manslaughter, though his conviction was overturned in the 1970s.

In April 1968, the party was involved in a gun battle, in which Bobby Hutton, a Panther, was killed. Cleaver later said that he had led the Panther group on a deliberate ambush of the police officers, thus provoking the shoot-out. In Chicago, two Panthers were killed in a police raid.

One of the central aims of the BPP was to stop abuse by local police departments. When the party was founded in 1966, only 16 of Oakland's 661 police officers were African American. Accordingly, many members questioned the Department's objectivity and impartiality. This situation was not unique to Oakland, California. Most police departments in major cities did not have proportional membership by African Americans. Throughout the 1960s, race riots and civil unrest broke out in impoverished African-American communities subject to policing by disproportionately white police departments. The work and writings of Robert F. Williams, Monroe, North Carolina NAACP chapter president and author of *Negroes with Guns*, also influenced the BPP's tactics.

The BPP sought to oppose police brutality through neighborhood patrols (an approach since adopted by groups such as Copwatch). Police officers were often followed by armed Black Panthers who sought at times to aid African-Americans who were victims of police brutality and racial prejudice. Both Panthers and police died as a result of violent confrontations. By 1970, 34 Panthers had died as a result of police raids, shoot-outs and internal conflict. Various police organizations claim the Black Panthers were responsible for the deaths of at least 15 law enforcement officers and the injuries of dozens more. During those years, juries found several BPP members guilty of violent crimes.

From 1966 to 1972, when the party was most active, several departments hired significantly more African-American police officers. During this time period, many African American police officers started to form organizations of their own to become more protective of the African American citizenry and to increase black representation on police forces. However, in many police departments, African American officers often received promotions through brutality against other African Americans, causing many of them to play prominent roles in shutting down the Panthers' activities. In Chicago in 1969 for example, Panthers Mark Clark and Fred Hampton were both killed in a police raid (In which five of the officers present were African American) by Sergeant James Davis, an African American officer. In cities such as New York City, black police officers were used to infiltrate Panther meetings. By 1972, when the party disbanded, almost every major police department in the US was integrated.

Prominent member H. Rap Brown is serving life imprisonment for the 2000 murder of Ricky Leon Kinchen, a Fulton County, Georgia sheriff's deputy, and the wounding of another officer in a gunbattle. Both officers were black.

Conflict with COINTELPRO

In August 1967, the Federal Bureau of Investigation (FBI) instructed its program "COINTELPRO" to "neutralize" what the FBI called "black nationalist hate groups" and other dissident groups. In September 1968, FBI Director J. Edgar Hoover described the Black Panthers as "the greatest threat to the internal security of the country." By 1969, the Black Panthers were the primary target of COINTELPRO. They were the target of 233 of the 295 authorized "Black Nationalist" COINTELPRO actions. The goals of the program were to prevent the unification of militant black nationalist groups and to weaken the power of their leaders, as well as to discredit the groups to reduce their support and growth. The initial targets included the Southern Christian Leadership Conference, the Student Nonviolent Coordinating Committee, the Revolutionary Action Movement and the Nation of Islam. Leaders who were targeted included the Rev. Martin Luther King, Jr., Stokely Carmichael, H. Rap Brown, Maxwell Stanford and Elijah Muhammad.

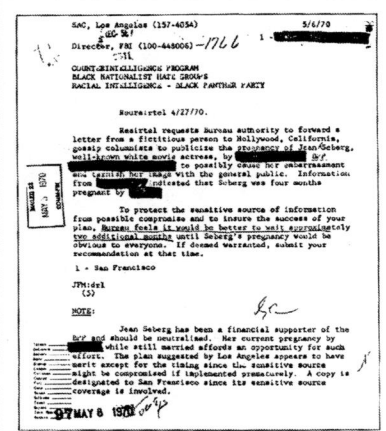

COINTELPRO document outlining the FBI's plans to 'neutralize' Jean Seberg for her support for the Black Panther Party, by attempting to publicly "cause her embarrassment" and "tarnish her image"

Although COINTELPRO was commissioned ostensibly to prevent violence, it used some tactics to foster violence. For instance, the FBI tried to "intensify the degree of animosity" between the Black Panthers and the Blackstone Rangers, a Chicago gang. They sent an anonymous letter to the Ranger's gang leader claiming that the Panthers were threatening his life, a letter whose intent was to induce "reprisals" against Panther leadership. In Southern California similar actions were taken to exacerbate a "gang war" between the Black Panther Party and a group called the US Organization. Violent conflict between these two groups, including shootings and beatings, led to the deaths of at least four Black Panther Party members. FBI agents claimed credit for instigating some of the violence between the two groups.

On January 17, 1969, Los Angeles Panther Captain Bunchy Carter and Deputy Minister John Huggins were killed in Campbell Hall on the UCLA campus, in a gun battle with members of US Organization stemming from a dispute over who would control UCLA's black studies program. Another shootout between the two groups on March 17 led to further injuries. It was alleged that the FBI had sent a provocative letter to US Organization in an attempt to create antagonism between US and the Panthers.

One of the most notorious actions was a Chicago Police raid of the home of Panther organizer Fred Hampton on December 4, 1969. The raid had been orchestrated by the police in conjunction with the FBI. The FBI was complicit in many of the actions. The people inside the home had been drugged by an FBI informant, William O'Neal, and were asleep at the time of the raid. Hampton was shot and killed, as was the guard, Mark Clark. The others were dragged into the street, beaten, and subsequently charged with assault. These charges were later dropped. The Chicago Police and FBI were never investigated or charged for their role in the event.

In May 1969, party members tortured and murdered Alex Rackley, a 19-year-old member of the New York chapter of the Black Panther party, because they suspected him of being a police informant. Three party officers — Warren Kimbro, George Sams, Jr., and Lonnie McLucas — later admitted taking part. Sams, who gave the order to shoot Rackley at the murder scene, turned state's evidence and testified that he had received orders personally from Bobby Seale to carry out the execution. After this betrayal, party supporters alleged that Sams was himself the informant and an agent provocateur employed by the FBI. The case resulted in the New Haven, Connecticut Black Panther trials of 1970, memorialized in the courtroom sketches of Robert Templeton. The trial ended with a hung jury, and the prosecution chose not to seek another trial.

Widening support

Awareness of the group continued to grow, especially after the May 2, 1967 protest at the California State Assembly and the arrest of Newton in the fall of 1967.

Black Panther convention, Lincoln Memorial, June 19, 1970.

> *In May 1967, the Panthers invaded the State Assembly Chamber in Sacramento, guns in hand, in what appears to have been a publicity stunt. Still, they scared a lot of important people that day. At the time, the Panthers had almost no following. Now, [a year later] however, their leaders speak on invitation almost anywhere radicals gather, and many whites wear "Honkeys for Huey" buttons, supporting the fight to free Newton, who has been in jail since last Oct. 28, [1967] on the charge that he killed a policeman..."*

On February 17, 1968, a large rally was held for Huey in the Oakland Auditorium. The speakers included Stokely Carmichael, H. Rap Brown, and James Forman. After this event, membership grew rapidly. The structure of the group became more defined. New members had to attend a six-week training program and political education classes, largely based on Mao's *Little Red Book*.

In 1968, the group shortened its name to the Black Panther Party and sought to focus directly on political action. Members were encouraged to carry guns and to defend themselves against violence.

An influx of college students joined the group, which had consisted chiefly of "brothers off the block." This created some tension in the group. Some members were more interested in supporting the Panther's social programs, while others wanted to maintain their "street mentality". For many Panthers, the group was little more than a type of gang.

Panther slogans and iconography spread. At the 1968 Summer Olympics, Tommie Smith and John Carlos, two American medalists, gave the black power salute during the playing of the American national anthem. The International Olympic Committee banned them from the Olympic Games for life. Some Hollywood celebrities, such as Jane Fonda, became involved in their leftist program. She publicly supported Huey Newton and the Black Panthers in the early 1970s. The Black Panthers attracted a wide variety of left-wing revolutionaries and political activists, including writer Jean Genet, former *Ramparts Magazine* editor David Horowitz and left-wing lawyer Charles R. Garry, who often acted as their counsel. Survival Committees and coalitions were organized with several groups across the United States. Chief among these in Chicago was the first Rainbow Coalition formed by Fred Hampton and the Black Panthers which included Young Patriots and a Latino youth gang turned political:the Young Lords.

Controversy

Violence

From the beginning the Black Panther Party's focus on militancy came with a reputation for violence. They employed a California law which permitted carrying a loaded rifle or shotgun as long as it was publicly displayed and pointed at no one. Carrying weapons openly and making threats against police officers, for example, chants like "The Revolution has co-ome, it's time to pick up the gu-un. Off the pigs!", helped create the Panthers' reputation as a violent organization.

On October 17, 1967, Oakland police officer John Frey was shot to death in an altercation with Huey P. Newton during a traffic stop. In the stop, Newton and backup officer Herbert Heanes also suffered gunshot wounds. Newton was convicted of voluntary manslaughter at trial. This incident gained the party even wider recognition by the radical American left, and a "Free Huey" campaign ensued. Newton was released after three years, when his conviction was reversed on appeal.

On May 2, 1967, the California State Assembly Committee on Criminal Procedure was scheduled to convene to discuss what was known as the "Mulford Act", which would ban public displays of loaded firearms. Cleaver and Newton put together a plan to send a group of about 30 Panthers led by Seale from Oakland to Sacramento to protest the bill. The group entered the assembly carrying their weapons, an incident which was widely publicized, and which prompted police to arrest Seale and five others. The group pled guilty to misdemeanor charges of disrupting a legislative session.

On April 7, 1968, Panther Bobby Hutton was killed, and Cleaver was wounded in a shootout with the Oakland police. Each side called the event an ambush by the other. Two policemen were shot in the incident.

From the fall of 1967 through the end of 1970, nine police officers were killed and 56 were wounded, and ten Panther deaths and an unknown number of injuries resulted from confrontations. In 1969 alone, 348 Panthers were arrested for a variety of crimes. On February 18, 1970 Albert Wayne Williams was shot by the Portland Police Bureau outside the Black Panther party headquarters in Portland, Oregon. Though his wounds put him in a critical condition, he made a full recovery.

Death of Betty van Patter

When Panther bookkeeper Betty van Patter was murdered in 1974, David Horowitz became certain that Black Panther members were responsible and denounced the Panthers. When Huey Newton was shot to death 15 years later, Horowitz characterized Newton as a killer. When a former colleague at *Ramparts* alleged that Horowitz himself was responsible for the death of van Patter by recommending her for the position of Black Panther accountant, Horowitz counter-alleged that "the Panthers had killed more than a dozen people in the course of conducting extortion, prostitution and drug rackets in the Oakland ghetto." He said further that the organization was committed "to doctrines that are false and to causes that are demonstrably wrongheaded and even evil." Former chairperson Elaine Brown also questioned Horowitz's motives in recommending van Patter to the Panthers; she suspected espionage.

Decline

While part of the organization was already participating in local government and social services, another group was in constant conflict with the police. For some of the Party's supporters, the separation between political action, criminal activity, social services, access to power, and grass-roots identity became confusing and contradictory as the Panthers' political momentum was bogged down in the criminal justice system. Disagreements among the Party's leaders over how to confront these challenges led to a significant split in the Party. Some Panther leaders, such as Huey Newton and David Hilliard, favored a focus on community service coupled with self-defense; others, such as Eldridge Cleaver, embraced a more confrontational strategy. Eldridge Cleaver deepened the inevitable schism in the party when he publicly criticized the Party for adopting a "reformist" rather than "revolutionary" agenda and called for Hilliard's removal. Cleaver was expelled from the Central Committee but went on to lead a splinter group, the Black Liberation Army, which had previously existed as an underground paramilitary wing of the Party.

The Party eventually fell apart due to rising legal costs and internal disputes. In 1974, Huey Newton appointed Elaine Brown as the first Chairwoman of the Party. Under Brown's leadership, the Party became involved in organizing for more radical electoral campaigns, including Brown's 1975 unsuccessful run for Oakland City Council and Lionel Wilson's successful election as the first Black mayor of Oakland. Although many scholars and activists date the Party's downfall before Brown became the leader, an increasingly smaller cadre continued to exist well into the late 1970s.

In addition to changing the Party's direction towards more involvement in the electoral arena, Brown also increased the influence of women Panthers by placing them in more visible roles within the male-dominated organization. Brown's attempt to battle this previously pervasive sexism within the Party was very stressful for her and led to her dependence on Thorazine as a way to escape the pressures of leading the Party.

In 1977, after Newton returned from Cuba and ordered the beating of a woman Panther who organized many of the Party's social programs, Brown decided she needed a break and left the Party.

Aftermath

In October 2006, the Black Panther Party held a 40-year reunion in Oakland, California.

In January 2007, a joint California state and Federal task force charged eight men with the 1971 murder of a California police officer. The defendants have been identified as former members of the Black Liberation Army. Two have been linked to the Black Panthers. In 1975 a similar case was dismissed when a judge ruled that police gathered evidence through the use of torture. On June 29, 2009 Herman Bell pleaded guilty to voluntary manslaughter in the death of

Black Panther 40th Reunion 2006

Sgt. Young. In July 2009, charges were dropped against four of the accused: Ray Boudreaux, Henry W. Jones, Richard Brown and Harold Taylor. Also that month Jalil Muntaquim pleaded no contest to conspiracy to commit voluntary manslaughter becoming the second person to be convicted in this case.

New Black Panther Party

See also: New Black Panther Party

In 1989, a group calling itself the "New Black Panther Party" was formed in Dallas, Texas. Ten years later, the NBPP became home to many former Nation of Islam members when the chairmanship was taken by Khalid Abdul Muhammad.

The Anti-Defamation League and The Southern Poverty Law Center consider the New Black Panthers as a hate group. Members of the original Black Panther Party have insisted that this New Black Panther Party is illegitimate and have strongly objected that there "is no new Black Panther Party".

The National Alliance of Black Panthers

The National Alliance of Black Panthers was formed on July 31, 2004. It was inspired by the grassroots activism of the original organization but not otherwise related. Its chairwoman is Shazza Nzingha.

See also

- 1960s counterculture
- Black anarchism
- Black feminism
- George Jackson Brigade
- Gun Control Act of 1968
- I Wor Kuen
- List of former members of the Black Panther Party
- Mark Essex
- MC5
- Nation of Islam
- New Communist Movement
- New Left
- The Patriot Party
- Protests of 1968
- Rainbow Coalition (Fred Hampton)
- Red Guard Party (United States)
- Red power
- Rice/Poindexter Case
- Renault Robinson
- Student Nonviolent Coordinating Committee
- Students for a Democratic Society (1960 organization)
- Symbionese Liberation Army
- US Organization
- Up Against the Wall Motherfuckers
- Weather Underground
- World communism
- Young Lords

References

Bibliography

- Austin, Curtis J. (2006). *Up Against the Wall: Violence in the Making and Unmaking of the Black Panther Party*. University of Arkansas Press. ISBN 1-55728-827-5
- Brown, Elaine. (1993). *A Taste of Power: A Black Woman's Story*. Anchor Books. ISBN 0-679-41944-6
- Churchill, Ward and Vander Wall, Jim (1988). *Agents of Repression: The FBI's Secret War Against the Black Panther Party and the American Indian Movement*. South End Press. ISBN 0-89608-294-6
- Dooley, Brian. (1998). *Black and Green: The Fight for Civil Rights in Northern Ireland and Black America*. Pluto Press.
- Forbes, Flores A. (2006). *Will You Die With Me? My Life and the Black Panther Party*. Atria Books. ISBN 0-7434-8266-2
- Hilliard, David, and Cole, Lewis. (1993). *This Side of Glory: The Autobiography of David Hilliard and the Story of the Black Panther Party*. Little, Brown and Co. ISBN 0-316-36421-5

- Hughey, Matthew W. (2009). "Black Aesthetics and Panther Rhetoric – A Critical Decoding of Black Masculinity in The Black Panther, 1967-1980." *Critical Sociology*, 35(1): 29-56.
- Hughey, Matthew W. (2007). "The Pedagogy of Huey P. Newton: Critical Reflections on Education in his Writings and Speeches." *Journal of Black Studies*, 38(2): 209-231.
- Hughey, Matthew W. (2005). "The Sociology, Pedagogy, and Theology of Huey P. Newton: Toward a Radical Democratic Utopia." *Western Journal of Black Studies*, 29(3): 639-655.
- Joseph, Peniel E. (2006). *Waiting 'Til the Midnight Hour: A Narrative History of Black Power in America*. Henry Holt and Company. ISBN 0-8050-7539-9
- Lewis, John. (1998). *Walking with the Wind*. Simon and Schuster, p. 353. ISBN 0-684-81065-4
- Ogbar, Jeffrey O. G. (2004). *Black Power: Radical Politics and African American Identity*. The Johns Hopkins University Press.
- Pearson, Hugh. (1994) *The Shadow of the Panther: Huey Newton and the Price of Black Power in America* De Capo Pres. ISBN 0-201-48341-6
- Phu, T. N. (2008). "Shooting the Movement: Black Panther Party Photography and African American Protest Traditions". *Canadian Review of American Studies* **38** (1): 165–189. doi:10.3138/cras.38.1.165 [1].
- Shames, Stephen. "The Black Panthers," Aperture, 2006. A photographic essay of the organization, allegedly suppressed due to Spiro Agnew's intervention in 1970.
- Street, Joe, "The Historiography of the Black Panther Party," Journal of American Studies (Cambridge), 44 (May 2010), 351–75.

External links

- BlackPanther.org [2] official website according to the Dr. Huey P. Newton Foundation.
- "The Black Panther Party for Self Defense" [3], *Libcom.org*
- "The Black Panther Party" [4], *Marxists Internet Archive*

News articles

- Children of the Revolutionary [5] 2007 LA Weekly feature on the 1969 UCLA shootout that killed John Huggins and Bunchy Carter.
- "The strange history of the Black Panthers in the Triad" [6] By Jordan Green, *Yes! Weekly*. Greensboro NC. Published April 11, 2006. Retrieved April 14, 2006.
- Film on the Black Panthers wins praise [7], by Streetgangs.Com, March 17, 2010
- Stern, Sol. "Ah, those Black Panthers! How Beautiful! [8]" from *City Journal*, 27 May 2003. Retrieved March 13, 2006.

Archives

- UC Berkeley Social Activism Online Sound Recordings: The Black Panther Party [9]
- Hartford Web Publishing collection of BPP documents [10]

- Robert Templeton Drawings and sketches related to the Black Panthers trial of Bobby Seale and Erica Huggins, New Haven, Connecticut [11]. From the collection of the Beinecke Rare Book and Manuscript Library at Yale University [12]

New Left

The **New Left** was a term used mainly in the United Kingdom and United States in reference to activists, educators, agitators and others in the 1960s and 1970s who sought to implement a broad range of reforms, in contrast to earlier leftist or Marxist movements that had taken a more vanguardist approach to social justice and focused mostly on labor unionization and questions of social class.

In the U.S., the "New Left" was associated with the Hippie movement and college campus protest movements. The British "New Left" sought to correct the perceived errors of "Old Left" parties in the post-World War II period.

Herbert Marcuse, associated with the Frankfurt School of critical theory, is celebrated as the "Father of the New Left".

Origins

The confused response of the Communist Party of the USA and the Communist Party of Great Britain to the Hungarian Revolution of 1956 led some Marxist intellectuals to develop a more democratic approach to politics, opposed to what they saw as the centralised and authoritarian politics of the pre-war leftist parties. Those Communists who became disillusioned with Communism due to its authoritarian character eventually formed the "new left", first among dissenting Communist Party intellectuals and campus groups in the United Kingdom, and later alongside campus radicalism in the US and elsewhere.

In Britain

As a result of Khrushchev's Secret Speech denouncing Stalin and the Soviet invasion of Hungary in 1956, many abandoned the Communist Party of Great Britain (CPGB) and began to rethink its orthodox Marxism. Some joined various Trotskyist groupings or the Labour Party.

The Marxist historians E. P. Thompson and Ralph Miliband established the Communist Party Historians Group and a dissenting journal within the CPGB called *Reasoner*. Once expelled from the party, they began the *New Reasoner* from 1957. In 1960, this journal merged with the *Universities and Left Review* to form the *New Left Review*. These journals attempted to synthesise a theoretical position of a revisionist, humanist, socialist Marxism, departing from orthodox Marxist theory. This publishing effort made the ideas of culturally oriented theorists available to an undergraduate reading audience. In this early period, many on the New Left were involved in the Campaign for Nuclear Disarmament, formed in 1957. According to Robin Blackburn, "The decline of CND by late 1961, however, deprived the New Left of much of its momentum as a movement, and uncertainties and divisions within the Board of the journal led to the transfer of the Review to a younger and less experienced group in 1962."

Under the long-standing editorial leadership of Perry Anderson, the *New Left Review* popularised the Frankfurt School, Antonio Gramsci, Louis Althusser and other forms of Marxism. Other periodicals like *Socialist Register*, started in 1964, and *Radical Philosophy*, started in 1972, have also been associated with the New Left, and published a range of important writings in this field.

As the campus orientation of the American New Left became clear in the mid to late 1960s, the student sections of the British New Left began taking action. The London School of Economics became a key site of British student militancy. The influence of protests against the Vietnam War and of the May 1968 events in France were also felt strongly throughout the British New Left. Some within the British New Left joined the International Socialists, which later became Socialist Workers Party while others became involved with groups such as the International Marxist Group. Trotskyist Tariq Ali, who played a role in some of the New Left protests of this era, documents his involvement in his book *Street Fighting Years*. The politics of the British New Left can be contrasted with Solidarity, UK, which continued to focus primarily on industrial issues.

1960s in the United States

In the United States, the "New Left" was the name loosely associated with liberal, sometimes radical, political movements that took place during the 1960s, primarily among college students. At the core of this was the Students for a Democratic Society, or SDS. The New Left can be defined as 'a loosely organized, mostly white student movement that promoted participatory democracy, crusaded for civil rights and various types of university reforms and protested against the Vietnam war.'

The term "New Left" was popularised in the US in an open letter written in 1960 by sociologist C. Wright Mills entitled *Letter to the New Left*. Mills argued for a new leftist ideology, moving away from the traditional ("Old Left") focus on labor issues, towards issues such as opposing alienation, anomie, and authoritarianism. Mills argued for a shift from traditional leftism, toward the values of the counter-culture. According to David Burner, C Wright Mills claimed that the proletariat were no longer the revolutionary force; the new agent of revolutionary change were young intellectuals around the world.

The New Left opposed what it saw as the prevailing authority structures in society, which it termed "The Establishment", and those who rejected this authority became known as "anti-Establishment". The New Left did not seek to recruit industrial workers,[citation needed] but rather concentrated on a social activist approach to organization, convinced that they could be the source for a better kind of social revolution.

Most New Left thinkers in the U.S. were influenced by the Vietnam War and the Chinese Cultural Revolution. Like the British New Left, they also believed that the Secret Speech drew attention to problems with the Soviet Union, but unlike the British New Left, they did not turn to Trotskyism or social democracy. Some in the U.S. New Left argued that since the Soviet Union could no longer be considered the world center for proletarian revolution, new revolutionary Communist thinkers had to be substituted in its place, such as Mao Zedong, Ho Chi Minh and Fidel Castro.

Other elements of the U.S. New Left were anarchist and looked to libertarian socialist traditions of American radicalism, the Industrial Workers of the World and union militancy. This group coalesced around the historical journal *Radical America*. American Autonomist Marxism was also a child of this stream, for instance in the thought of Harry Cleaver. Murray Bookchin and Noam Chomsky were also part of the anarchist stream of the New Left, as were the Yippies.

The U.S. New Left drew inspiration from black radicalism, particularly the Black Power movement and the more explicitly left-wing Black Panther Party. The Panthers in turn influenced other similar militant groups, like the Young Lords, the Brown Berets and the American Indian Movement. The New Left was also inspired by SNCC, Student Non-violent Coordinating Committee. Students immersed themselves into poor communities building up support with the locals. The New Left sought to be a broad based, grass roots movement.

It could be argued that the New Left's most successful legacy was the rebirth of feminism. As the leaders of the New Left were largely white men, women reacted to the lack of progressive gender politics with their own social intellectual movement.

The New Left was also marked by the invention of the modern environmentalist movement, which clashed with the Old Left's disregard for the environment in favor of preserving the jobs of union workers. Environmentalism also gave rise to various other social justice movements such as the environmental justice movement, which aims to prevent the toxification of the environment of minority and disadvantaged communities.

Students for a Democratic Society

Main article: Students for a Democratic Society (1960 organization)

The organization that really came to symbolize the core of the New Left was the Students for a Democratic Society (SDS). By 1962, the SDS had emerged as the most important of the new campus radical groups; soon it would be regarded as virtually synonymous with the 'New Left'. In 1962, Tom Hayden wrote its founding document, the Port Huron Statement, which issued a call for "participatory democracy" based on non-violent civil disobedience. This was the idea that individual citizens could help make 'those social decisions determining the quality and direction' of their lives. The SDS marshalled anti-war, pro-civil rights and free speech concerns on campuses, and brought together liberals and more revolutionary leftists.

The SDS became the leading organization of the anti-war movement on college campuses during the Vietnam War. As the war escalated the membership of the SDS also increased greatly as more people were willing to scrutinise political decisions in moral terms. During the course of the war, the people became increasingly militant. As opposition to the war grew stronger, the SDS became a nationally prominent political organization, with opposing the war an overriding concern that overshadowed many of the original issues that had inspired SDS. In 1967 the old statement in Port Huron was abandoned for a new call for action, which would inevitably lead to the destruction of the SDS.

In 1968 and 1969, as its radicalism reached a fever pitch, the SDS began to split under the strain of internal dissension and increasing turn towards Maoism. Along with adherents known as the New Communist Movement, some extremist illegal factions also emerged, such as the Weather Underground Organization.

The SDS suffered the difficulty of wanting to change the world while 'freeing life in the here and now.' This caused confusion between short term and long term goals. The sudden growth due to the successful rallies against the Vietnam War meant there were more people wanting action to end the Vietnam war, whereas the original New Left had wanted to focus on critical reflection. In the end it was the anti-war sentiment that dominated the SDS.

International movements

The Prague Spring was legitimised by the Czechoslovak government as a socialist reform movement. The 1968 events in the Czechoslovakia were driven forward by industrial workers, and were explicitly theorized by active Czechoslovak unionists as a revolution for workers' control.

The driving force of near-revolution in France in May 1968 were students inspired by the ideas of the Situationist International, which in turn had been inspired by Socialisme ou Barbarie. Both of these groups emphasised culture as a form of production.

While the Autonomia in Italy have been called New Left, it is more appropriate to see them as the result of traditional, industrially oriented, communism re-theorising its ideas and methods. Unlike most of the New Left, Autonomia had a strong blue-collar arm, active in regularly occupying factories.

The Provos were a Dutch counter-cultural movement of mostly young people with anarchist influences.

Criticism of the legacy

As many of those who supported the New Left in the 1960s are now in charge of the kinds of institutions they once opposed, conservative opponents argue that their assumptions - sometimes described as politically correct multiculturalism— are now the establishment orthodoxy.

In what has been described as the culture wars, conservative critics of this orthodoxy such as Allan Bloom and Roger Scruton claim that New Left radical egalitarianism is motivated by anti-Western nihilism.

Inspirations and influences

- Albert Camus
- Guy Debord
- Frantz Fanon
- Allen Ginsberg
- Emma Goldman
- Che Guevara
- Peter Kropotkin
- R. D. Laing
- Henri Lefebvre
- Vladimir Lenin
- Rosa Luxemburg
- Herbert Marcuse
- George Orwell
- Bertrand Russell
- Jean-Paul Sartre
- Malcolm X

Key figures

- Stew Albert
- Bill Ayers
- Rudolf Bahro
- Charles Bettelheim
- Stokely Carmichael
- Daniel Cohn-Bendit
- Angela Davis
- Régis Debray
- Rudi Dutschke
- Deniz Gezmiş
- Abbie Hoffman
- David Horowitz
- Tom Nairn
- Carl Oglesby
- Ronald Radosh
- Jerry Rubin
- Mark Rudd
- Mario Savio

Other associated people

- César Chávez
- David Dellinger
- Joschka Fischer
- Michel Foucault
- Norman Fruchter
- Karl Hess
- William Mandel
- A. J. Muste
- Nicos Poulantzas
- Charles Taylor

See also

- Chinese New Left
- New Left 95
- New Right

Further reading

General

- Interview with André Gorz, about The New Left [1]
- Teodori, Massimo, ed., *The New Left: A documentary History*. London: Jonathan Cape (1970).
- Oglesby, Carl (ed.) *The New Left Reader* Grove Press (1969). ISBN 83-456-1536-8. Influential collection of texts by Mills, Marcuse, Fanon, Cohn-Bendit, Castro, Hall, Althusser, Kolakowski, Malcolm X, Gorz & others.
- Michael R. Krätke,Otto Bauer and the early "Third Way" to Socialism [2]
- Detlev Albers u.a. (Hg.), Otto Bauer und der "dritte" Weg. Die Wiederentdeckung des Austromarxismus durch Linkssozialisten und Eurokommunisten, Frankfurt/M 1979

Canada

For a discussion on the rise and fall of the 60s movement in Canada, USA and Germany see: Levitt, C. (1984). *Children of Privilege*. University of Toronto Press, Toronto, Ontario.

Japan

- Miyazaki, Manabu (2005). *Toppamono: Outlaw, Radical, Suspect: My Life in Japan's Underworld*. Tōkyō: Kotan Publishing. ISBN 978-0970171627. Includes an account of the author's days as a student activist and street fighter for the Japanese Communist Party, 1964–1969.

United Kingdom

- Ali, Tariq. *Street Fighting Years: An Autobiography of the Sixties* London: Collins, 1987. ISBN 0-00-217779-X.
- Hock, Paul and Vic Schoenbach. *LSE: the natives are restless, a report on student power in action* London: Sheed and Ward, 1969. ISBN 0-7220-0596-2.
- Scruton, Roger *Thinkers of the New Left* (Claridge Press, 1985).
- *The New Left's renewal of Marxism* [3] an account by Paul Blackledge from *International Socialism*

British New Left periodicals

- "The New Reasoner" [4]. *indexed articles online*. 1957–1959. Retrieved 2006-10-16.
- "Marxism Today" [5]. *indexed articles online*. Communist Party of Great Britain and Marxism Today. 1980–1991 & 1998 special issue. Retrieved 2006-10-16.
- "New Left Review" [6]. *indexed articles online*. Retrieved 2007-03-24.
- "Socialist Register" [7]. *indexed articles online*. 1964–1999. Retrieved 2006-10-16.
- "Universities & Left Review" [8]. *indexed articles online*. 1957–1959. Retrieved 2006-10-16.

British New Left articles

- Mills, C. Wright (September–October 1960). "Letter to the New Left" [9]. *New Left Review* (5). Retrieved 2006-10-16.
- "Placating Mr. Jenkins" [10]. *Article discussing online archiving of four British New Left publications Universities & Left Review, Marxism Today, The New Reasoner and Socialist Register.* October 16, 2006. Retrieved 2006-10-16.

United States

Archives

- *New Left Movement: 1964–1973.* Archive # 88-020. Title: New Left Movement fonds. 1964–1973. 51 cm of textual records. Trent University Archives. Peterborough, Ontario, Canada. Online guide retrieved April 12, 2005 [11].
- *Russ Gilbert "New Left" Pamphlet Collection: An inventory of the collection at the University of Illinois at Chicago.* Online guide retrieved October 8, 2005 [12]

Reference

- Albert, Judith Clavir, and Albert, Stewart Edward. *The Sixties Papers: Documents of a Rebellious Decade* (New York: Praeger, 1984). ISBN 0-275-91781-9
- Breines, Wini. *Community Organization in the New Left, 1962–1968: The Great Refusal*, reissue edition (Rutgers University Press, 1989). ISBN 0-8135-1403-7.
- Cohen, Mitchell, and Hale, Dennis, eds. *The New Student Left* (Boston: Beacon Press, 1966).
- Evans, Sara. *Personal Politics: The Roots of Women's Liberation in the Civil Rights Movement & the New Left* (Vintage, 1980). ISBN 0-394-74228-1.
- Frost, Jennifer. *"An Interracial Movement of the Poor": Community Organizing & the New Left in the 1960s* (New York University Press, 2001). ISBN 0-8147-2697-6.
- Gosse, Van. *The Movements of the New Left, 1950–1975: A Brief History with Documents* (Bedford/St. Martin's, 2004). ISBN 0-312-13397-9.
- Isserman, Maurice. *If I had a Hammer: the Death of the Old Left and the Birth of the New Left*, reprint edition (University of Illinois Press, 1993). ISBN 0-252-06338-4.
- Long, Priscilla, ed. *The New Left: A Collection of Essays* (Boston: Porter Sargent, 1969).
- Mattson, Kevin, *Intellectuals in Action: The Origins of the New Left and Radical Liberalism, 1945-1970* [13] (Penn State Press, 2002). ISBN 0-271-02206-X
- McMillian, John and Buhle, Paul (eds.). *The New Left Revisited* (Temple University Press, 2003). ISBN 1-56639-976-9.
- Novack, George; writing as "William F. Warde" (1961). "Who Will Change The World? The New left and the Views of C. Wright Mills" [14]. *International Socialist Review* (USFI) **22** (3): pp. 67–79. Retrieved 2006-10-16. * Rand, Ayn. *The New Left: The Anti-Industrial Revolution* (New York: Penguin Books, 1993, 1975). ISBN 0452011256.
- Rossinow, Doug. *The Politics of Authenticity: Liberalism, Christianity, and the New Left in America* (Columbia University Press, 1998). ISBN 0-231-11057-x.
- Rubenstein, Richard E. *Left Turn: Origins of the Next American Revolution* (Boston: Little, Brown, 1973).
- Young, C. A. *Culture, Radicalism, and the Making of a US Third Wold Left* (Duke University Press, 2006).

Publications

- Munk, Michael. *The New Left: What It Is ... Where It's Going ... What Makes it Move.* 22pp A National Guardian Pamphlet. New York. n.d. [1965]. Stapled softcover. Photos.

Legacy

J. Edgar Hoover Building

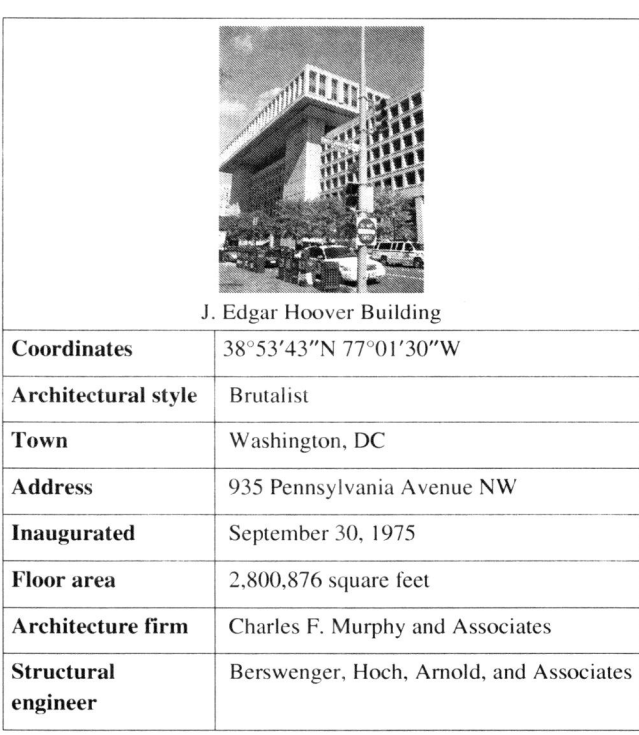

J. Edgar Hoover Building

Coordinates	38°53′43″N 77°01′30″W
Architectural style	Brutalist
Town	Washington, DC
Address	935 Pennsylvania Avenue NW
Inaugurated	September 30, 1975
Floor area	2,800,876 square feet
Architecture firm	Charles F. Murphy and Associates
Structural engineer	Berswenger, Hoch, Arnold, and Associates

The **J. Edgar Hoover Building** is located in Washington, D.C.. It is the headquarters of the Federal Bureau of Investigation (FBI). The building, named for former FBI director J. Edgar Hoover, is located at 935 Pennsylvania Avenue NW. The building received its official name, the J. Edgar Hoover F.B.I. Building, through Public Law 92-520, which President Richard Nixon signed May 4, 1972, two days after Director Hoover's death. President Gerald Ford dedicated the building September 30, 1975.

Planning

Since 1935, as an element of the United States Department of Justice, the FBI had been headquartered in the Department of Justice Building. In April 1962, Congress approved the construction of a separate building for the FBI. The General Services Administration allocated funding for the project, and design began. The GSA appointed Berswenger, Hoch, Arnold, and Associates for engineering, and Charles F. Murphy and Associates as an architectural firm.

The design was finalized in 1964, and construction began on December 6, 1967. The naming was authorized by President Richard Nixon on May 4, 1972, two days after Hoover's death. Employees moved into the facility between June 28, 1974, and June 1977. President Gerald Ford officially dedicated the building on September 30, 1975. J. Edgar Hoover.

Architecture

The building was constructed in a Brutalist architectural style, the entire exterior having been constructed from poured concrete. Like most Brutalist buildings, it has suffered criticism for aesthetics and functionality. *Washingtonian* magazine named it one of the "Buildings I'd Tear Down," along with the Kennedy Center. According to the plans, the building contains 2,800,876 square feet (260,201 m²) of floor space for 7,090 employees.

External links

- The History of FBI Headquarters [1]
- Google 3D model [2]

National Security Medal

National Security Medal	
National Security Medal	
Type	Individual Award
Status	Active
Statistics	
Last awarded	January 16,2009
Precedence	
Equivalent	National Intelligence Distinguished Service Medal
National Security Ribbon	

The **National Security Medal** was a decoration of the United States of America officially established by President Harry S. Truman in Executive Order 10431 of January 19, 1953. The medal was awarded to any person, without regard to nationality, for distinguished achievement or outstanding contribution on or after July 26, 1947, in the field of intelligence relating to the national security of the United States.

The National Security Medal is authorized to both civilians and personnel of the United States military and is an authorized decoration for display on active duty uniforms of the United States armed forces. In such cases, the National Security Medal is worn after all U.S. military personal decorations and unit awards and before any military campaign/service awards and foreign decorations.

Additional decorations of the National Security Medal are denoted by a bronze oak leaf cluster.

Upon establishment of the National Intelligence Awards Program by the United States Intelligence Community, this highest award has been replaced with the National Intelligence Distinguished Service Medal.

Notable recipients

- Major General William Joseph Donovan
- Allen Dulles
- Robert Gates
- Richard Helms
- Lawrence R. Houston
- Clarence Leonard Johnson
- Frank Rowlett
- Adm. William O. Studeman, USN
- Adm. John Scott Redd
- Walter Bedell Smith

See also

- Awards and decorations of the United States government

Awards of the United States Department of State

The **United States Department of State**, like other agencies of the U.S. federal government, gives civilian decorations for outstanding service, sacrifice, or heroism. The criteria for the awards are set down in 3 FAM 4820 - *Foreign Affairs Manual*, 3 FAM - Personnel, section 3 FAM 4800 Department Awards Program.

The *Foreign Affairs Manual* described the purpose of Department of State honor awards as to "bestow recognition on an individual or group who has made a significant contribution to the agency's mission" and states that "The honor awards vary in scope and magnitude. The impact of the act or deed which precipitates the nomination must be carefully examined, and consideration given to whether the act to be recognized benefits the post or bureau, the area, the agency, or the Federal Government as a whole."

Secretary's Distinguished Service Award

The **Secretary's Distinguished Service Award** is presented at the discretion of the Secretary of State in recognition of exceptionally outstanding leadership, professional competence, and significant accomplishment over a sustained period of time in the field of foreign affairs. Such achievementsmust be of notable national or international significance and have made an important contribution to the advancement of U.S. national interests.

The award is personally authorized by the Secretary of State provided that one of the criteria eligibility in Foreign Affairs Manual is met. It may be presented to members of the foreign affairs communities.

The award consists of a gold medal set and a certificate signed by the Secretary. Upon authorization, members of the U.S. military may wear the medal and ribbon in the appropriate order of precedence as a *U.S. non-military personal decoration.*

Nominations for the Secretary's Distinguished Service Award are normally initiated by the Secretary of State. However, officials at assistant secretary or higher level who wish to recommend an individual for this award may do so by submitting a memorandum of justification, cleared by the Director General, to the Executive Secretary of the Department.

Secretary's Award

The **Secretary's Award** is "presented to employees of State, USAID, and Marine guards assigned to diplomatic and consular facilities in recognition of sacrifice of health or life, in the performance of official duties."

The award consists of a medal set and a certificate signed by the Secretary.

Nominations for the Secretary's Award are submitted through supervisory channels to the Joint Country Awards Committee for review and recommendation to the chief of mission. Approved nominations will be forwarded through the appropriate area awards committee to the Department Awards Committee for final action. Nominations initiated in Washington are submitted through the appropriate area awards committee to the Department Awards Committee for final action.

Award for Heroism

The Award for Heroism is given "recognition of acts of courage or outstanding performance under unusually difficult or dangerous circumstances, whether or not in connection with the performance of assigned duties."

It may be granted for: (1) Sustained superior performance while under threat of physical attack or harassment; or (2) An individual act of courage or exceptional performance at the risk of personal safety.

The award consists of a medal set and a certificate signed by the Secretary.

Nominations for the Award for Heroism are submitted through supervisory channels to the Joint Country Awards Committee for review and recommendation to the chief of mission. Approved nominations will be forwarded through the appropriatearea awards committee to the Department Awards Committee for final action. Nominations initiated in Washington are submitted through the appropriate area awards committee to the Department Awards Committee for final action.

Thomas Jefferson Star for Foreign Service

The **Thomas Jefferson Star for Foreign Service** "recognizes those individuals who, while traveling or serving abroad on official business, are killed or incur a serious illness or injury that results in death, permanent incapacity or disability."

a. The Thomas Jefferson Star for Foreign Service recognizes those individuals who, while traveling or serving abroad on official business, are killed or incur a serious illness or injury that results in death, permanent incapacity or disability.

b. The award consists of a Foreign Service Star Medal and a certificate signed by the President and the Secretary.

c. Posthumous awards shall be issued to the recipient employee's next of kin.

Eligibility

Any civilian employee of any agency, including Foreign Service Nationals (appointed under Section 303 of the Foreign Service Act), non-family member U.S. citizen employees hired at post (appointed under Section 303 and appointed under Section 311 (a) of the Foreign Service Act), and U.S. citizens and foreign nationals serving under a Personal Services Contract or Personal Services Agreement (if eligibility for the award is authorized in their contracts), are eligible for the Foreign Service Star Award as long as the employee is:

(1) Under the administrative direction of State or USAID;

(2) Employed at, or assigned permanently or temporarily to an official mission abroad, or while traveling abroad on official business; and

(3) Killed or incurs a serious illness or injury which requires hospitalization or similar treatment and which results in incapacity or disability that prevents the employee from performing his or her official duties or adversely affects his or her ability to obtain medical clearance, while the employee:

(a) Is performing official duties;

(b) Is located on the premises of a U.S. mission abroad; or alternatively,

(c) By reason of the individual's status as U.S. Government employee.

Criteria

a. Selection of award recipients will be based on:

(1) The nexus between the death, illness or injury and the act of serving abroad in an official capacity. The death, illness or injury must be linked to the official duties of the employee. This may be by reason of location at the U.S. mission, by reason of the employee's status as a U.S. Government of-ficial, or by reason of the fact that the employee is performing, or en-route to

perform official duties; and

(2) The seriousness of the illness or injury. An illness or injury is "serious" if it requires hospitalization or similar treatment and results in incapacity or disability that prevents the employee from performing his other official duties or adversely affects his or her ability to obtain medical clearance.

b. Examples of employees meeting the selection criteria include, but are not limited to:

(1) The United States as the target of hostile action:

(a) Mission as target while performing official duty, hostile fire kills or wounds a U.S. civilian employee who is accompanying U.S. peacekeepers abroad;

(b) Employee as target, but not while on official duty, a commercial airliner flying abroad is hijacked and an employee, by reason of his or her status as a U.S. Government official, is subjected to mistreatment resulting in death, injury or serious illness.

(2) Accidents occurring in a hostile environment or crisis situation:

(a) Employee is killed or wounded by "friendly" fire launched to counter or respond to hostile action.

(b) Employee is killed or wounded in an automobile or airplane accident caused by a hostile action or crisis situation.

(c) Employee is killed or wounded by a land mine, trap, bomb or chemical/biological agent, even if not targeted at the employee or the United States.

(3) Natural disasters linked to service:

(a) Employee is killed or wounded while away from the mission, but while performing official duties, e.g., an earthquake abroad causes a building to collapse, killing several employees who are negotiating an arms control treaty; or

(b) Employee is killed or injured at the mission, e.g., a flood strikes a U.S. Embassy compound, killing and injuring dozens of employees.

(4) Nothing in this Foreign Affairs Manual shall limit the discretion of the Secretary to recommend the Foreign Service Star Award for an otherwise eligible and deserving employee.

Nominating and Approval Procedures

Nominations for the Thomas Jefferson Star for Foreign Service must beinitiated by the chief of mission or by an assistant secretary, cleared by the Medical Director, as appropriate, and then submitted to the Department Awards Committee for review and recommendation to the Secretary. The Secretary shall make final recommendations to the President.

Effective Date

The effective date for the *Thomas Jefferson Star for Foreign Service* shall be August 7, 1998.

An employee or surviving next of kin may petition the Department Awards Committee to consider individuals who are eligible and deserving of the Thomas Jefferson Star for Foreign Service notwithstanding the fact that the illness, injury or death occurred prior to the effective date.

Distinguished Honor Award

The **Distinguished Honor Award** is awarded to individuals or groups that provide:

(1) Exceptionally outstanding service to the agencies or the U.S. Government resulting in achievements of marked national or international significance;

(2) Exceptionally outstanding service and/or leadership in the administration of one or more agency programs that results in the highly successful accomplishment of mission, or in a major attainment of objectives or specific accomplishment to meet unique or emergency situations; and

(3) Outstanding accomplishments over a prolonged period that involve the exercise of authority or judgment in the public interest.

The award consists of a medal set and a certificate signed, as appropriate, by the Secretary of State.

Superior Honor Award

The **Superior Honor Award** is presented to groups or individuals in recognition of a special act or service or sustained extraordinary performance covering a period of one year or longer. The following criteria are applicable to granting a Superior Honor Award:

Ribbon of the Superior Honor Award

(1) Contributions, which had a substantial impact on the accomplishment of the agency's missions, goals, or objectives;

(2) Accomplishments, which substantially contributed to the advancement of U.S. Government interests;

(3) Exceptional performance in one or more areas of the employee's official duties as defined in the Work Requirements Statement (Foreign Service) or Performance Plan (Civil Service);

(4) Innovation and creativity in accomplishing long-term tasks or projects;

(5) Contributions that resulted in increased productivity and efficiency, and economy of operations at agency level; and/or

(6) Exceptional devotion to duty under adverse conditions.

The award consists of a medal set and a certificate signed by an assistant secretary or an official of equivalent rank.

Meritorious Honor Award

The **Meritorious Honor Award** is presented to groups or individuals in recognition of a special act or service or sustained outstanding performance. The following criteria are applicable to granting a Meritorious Honor Award:

(1) Outstanding service in support of a one-time event (e.g., support for a major conference or summit meeting);

(2) Innovation and creativity in accomplishing short-term tasks or projects;

(3) Outstanding performance in one or more areas of the employee's official duties as defined in the Work Requirements Statement (Foreign Service) or Performance Plan (Civil Service); and/or

(4) Contributions that resulted in increased productivity and efficiency, and economy of operations at post or bureau level.

The award consists of a medal set and a certificate signed, by an assistant secretary, an official of equivalent rank or the chief of mission.

State funerals in the United States

See also: State funeral

State funerals in the United States are public funerals containing military spectacle, ceremonial pomp, and religious observance. Held in the nation's capital, Washington D.C., a state funeral is the highest honor bestowed upon a person posthumously. Offered and granted by federal law to a President-elect of the United States as well as to the sitting and any former President of the United States, state funerals allow an opportunity for the general public to

Ronald Reagan, 40th President of the United States, lying in state in the United States Capitol Rotunda as spectators and mourners file past his flag draped coffin, 2004.

mourn and pay homage to their legacy. In the past, state funerals have also been accorded to other notable individuals, such as retired military officers of 4-star or 5-star rank who served in the United States Armed Forces. Administered and executed by the Military District of Washington (MDW), state funerals are greatly influenced by protocol, steeped in tradition, and rich in history. However, the overall planning as well as the decision itself to have a state funeral, is largely determined by the President and the First Family.

History and development

See also: Lincoln Catafalque and Black Jack (horse)

The pomp, grandeur, and splendor of state funerals were eschewed by the Founding Fathers of the United States, who believed them to be too reminiscent of British rule. The first general mourning proclaimed in the United States came upon the death of Benjamin Franklin in 1790, followed by the death of George Washington in 1799. Upon hearing the news of President Washington's death, Napoleon Bonaparte ordered ten days of mourning throughout France while in the United States, thousands of mourners wore black clothing for months. Though there was mourning across the nation and around the world after President Washington's death, his funeral was a local affair at

Military units seen marching down Pennsylvania Avenue in Washington D.C. during a ceremonial procession for Abraham Lincoln, 1865.

his Virginia plantation, Mount Vernon. President Washington's Masonic lodge prepared the funeral arrangements. The ceremonial procession consisted of the coffin mounted on and using a limbers and caissons, foot soldiers, clergy, and a caparisoned, riderless horse. Upon arrival at a red brick tomb on a hillside in the environs of Mount Vernon, the coffin was placed on a wood bier for grieving mourners to gather around for a final viewing and clergy to conduct funeral rites. The first major state funeral was for William Henry Harrison in 1841, the first sitting president to die in office. Alexander Hunter, a Washington merchant, was commissioned to plan the ceremony. Alexander Hunter had the White House draped in black ribbon and ordered a curtained, upholstered black and white carriage to carry President Harrison's coffin. Another famous state funeral was for Dolley Madison on July 17, 1849.

It was not until the assassination of Abraham Lincoln in 1865 that the United States experienced a period of national mourning which was made possible by advances in innovative technologies such as the railroad and telegraph. On the Easter Sunday after President Lincoln's death, clergymen around the nation praised President Lincoln in their sermons. Millions of people witnessed President Lincoln's funeral procession in Washington, D.C. on April 19, 1865, and as his coffin was transported 1700 miles (2700 km) through New York City to Springfield, Illinois. Abraham Lincoln was the first president to lie in state in the United States Capitol Rotunda.

Subsequent state funerals over the years have henceforth been loosely modeled on the Lincoln state funeral, the most notable being the state funeral of John F. Kennedy in 1963. Upon hearing the news of the assassination of John F. Kennedy, military and federal government officials immediately began planning for a state funeral. The extensive research uncovered on President Lincoln's state funeral was accomplished on the evening of November 23, 1963 by Professor James Robertson, the executive director of the United States Civil War Centennial Commission as well as David Mearns, the director of the Library of Congress. The two men went to the

The flag-draped coffin of John F. Kennedy lying in repose in the East Room of the White House, 1963.

government repository where the lights were inoperative because they were connected to a timer switch and would only operate during the time the Library of Congress was scheduled to be opened the following morning. Using flashlights they found copies of Frank Leslie's *Illustrated* and *Harper's Weekly* which depicted the Lincoln state funeral in full graphic detail. Using this information, the East Room of the White House was quickly transformed into a venue for President Kennedy's remains to lie in repose, which matched the exact description of what it was like nearly a century earlier for President Lincoln.

Eleven presidents, including the four presidents who were assassinated, have been honored by having their remains lie in state in the United States Capitol Rotunda and on the Lincoln Catafalque, a bier made of pine wood purpose-built for Abraham Lincoln's coffin over 140 years ago. Growing in popularity, many presidents in recent years have been interred at their presidential libraries around the nation while other presidents in history, have been interred in cemeteries, tombs, crypts, vaults, in the grounds at a place of residence, and inside cathedrals. Some examples include the following. The remains of George Washington were interred in a tomb at his Virginia plantation, Mount Vernon, in 1799. After falling into disrepair as well as grave robbers attempting to steal the remains of President Washington, a new and more secure vault was constructed at Mount Vernon in 1831. Thomas Jefferson was interred at his Virginia plantation, Monticello, in 1826. The remains of Abraham Lincoln were exhumed and moved a total of seventeen times, the first exhumation occurring in 1865, before the ornate and lavish Lincoln Tomb was finally built for final interment in 1901 at Oak Ridge Cemetery located in Springfield, Illinois. Ulysses S. Grant, who died in 1885, was interred in Riverside Park in New York City where eventually, the construction of Grant's Tomb housing the former president's remains was finally completed and dedicated in 1897. The remains of Woodrow Wilson were interred in a sarcophagus inside Washington National Cathedral in 1924. William Howard Taft and John F. Kennedy were interred at Arlington National Cemetery in the years 1930 and 1963 respectively.

Major components

See also: Military funeral

In the United States, a sitting president while in office will immediately issue a presidential proclamation allowing for the flag of the United States to be flown at half-staff upon the death of principal figures in the federal government, such as a former president, and others, as a mark of respect to their memory. When such a proclamation is issued, all government buildings, offices, public schools and military bases are to fly their flags at half-staff. Under federal law (4 U.S.C. § 7(f)), the flags of states, cities, localities, and pennants of societies, shall never be placed above the flag of the United States. Thus, all other flags also fly at half-staff when the flag of the United States has been ordered to fly at half-staff.

A limbers and caissons carrying the remains of Warren G. Harding at the North Portico entrance of the White House before its procession down Pennsylvania Avenue enroute to the United States Capitol Building, 1923.

Protocol dictates that flags will be flown at half-staff for a period of thirty days for a former president, beginning at the time a presidential proclamation is made effective. At the discretion of the sitting president, he will also issue an executive order which authorizes the closure of all federal departments, agencies, and buildings on a national day of mourning during a state funeral.

On the day after the death of a president, a former president, or a president-elect unless the day falls on a Sunday or holiday, in which case the honor will be rendered the following day, the commanders of Army installations with the necessary personnel and material traditionally order that one gun be fired every half hour, beginning at reveille and ending at retreat. On the day of interment for a president, a 21-gun salute traditionally is fired starting at noon at all military installations with the necessary personnel and material. Guns will be fired at one minute intervals. Also on the day of interment, those installations will fire a 50-gun salute with one round for each of the fifty states and at five-second intervals immediately following a lowering of the flag. 19-gun salutes are reserved for deputy heads of state, chiefs of staff, cabinet members, and 5-star generals. For each flag rank junior to a five-star officer, two guns are subtracted for each.

The commanding general of the Military District of Washington (MDW) will act as a military escort for the president's family from the time of the official announcement of death until interment occurs.

One example of this role was by Major General Galen B. Jackman who escorted former First Lady Nancy Reagan during the state funeral of Ronald Reagan in 2004.

Most state funerals include a nine-person honor guard acting as pallbearers (also known as body bearers) from all five branches of the United States Armed Forces, a series of gun salutes using artillery pieces from the Presidential Salute Guns Battery of the 3rd United States Infantry Regiment "The Old Guard", various musical selections performed by military bands and choirs, a military chaplain for the immediate family, and a flag-draped coffin or pall.

Sitting presidents who die while in office may lie in repose in the East Room of the White House. Former presidents may lie in repose in their home or adopted state, usually at their presidential library, before traveling to Washington, D.C. when thereafter, lying in state in the United States Capitol Rotunda will occur. Dwight D. Eisenhower was an exception to this general rule. Following his death at Walter Reed Army Hospital in 1969, President Eisenhower lay in repose at Washington National Cathedral, rather than his presidential library in Abilene, Kansas.

Funeral procession

A ceremonial procession uses a four-wheeled limbers and caissons to transport the flag-draped coffin, which was originally intended to carry a 75mm cannon when it was built in 1918. The limbers and caissons is drawn by a draft-mix of six same colored horses with three riders and a section chief mounted on a separate horse from the United States Army Caisson Platoon of the 3rd United States Infantry Regiment "The Old Guard". In addition, two sets of four body bearers (eight total) will march on foot alongside both sides of the limbers and caissons transporting the flag-draped coffin. The entire ceremonial procession is composed of the National Guard, reserve, active-duty, and academy personnel that represent the five branches of the United States Armed Forces. Moving at 20 miles per hour, the ceremonial procession begins in sight of the White House and travels to the United States Capitol Building. For former presidents, the coffin is unloaded from a hearse and transferred to a limbers and caissons at 16th Street and Constitution Avenue in view of the South Lawn. The ceremonial procession then proceeds down Constitution Avenue. For sitting presidents, the coffin is transferred at the North Portico entrance of the White House. Thereafter, the ceremonial procession proceeds down Pennsylvania Avenue. One rare exception for this ceremonial procession was during the state funeral of Gerald Ford in 2006. President Ford's coffin was transported in a hearse to the United States Capitol Building and en route, stopped at the National World War II Memorial in order to pay tribute to his service in the United States Navy during World War II. President Ford himself requested the 'Pause of Mutual Tribute' as his personal wishes deemed a ceremonial procession unnecessary.

Each march unit is led by a military band. Positioned directly in front of the limbers and caissons, three color guards will march on foot, with the center color guard having responsibility for holding the national colors, the flag of the United States. Following immediately behind the limbers and caissons, a single color guard will march on foot holding the presidential colors, the flag of the President of the United States. Next, a single honor guard will march on foot holding the reins of a caparisoned, riderless horse with a set of boots reversed in the stirrups, symbolizing a fallen warrior who will never ride again which also betokens the commander's parting look on his troops, who march behind.

The riderless horse named Sergeant York, during the funeral procession for Ronald Reagan, with a ceremonial sword attached to the saddle and a pair of the president's boots reversed in the stirrups, 2004.

This inclusion of a riderless horse in a ceremonial procession dates back to the death of George Washington in 1799 when a caparisoned, riderless horse carried President Washington's saddle, holsters, and pistol during the president's funeral. In 1865, Abraham Lincoln was honored by the inclusion of a riderless horse at his state funeral. When President Lincoln's funeral train reached Springfield, Illinois, his horse "Old Bob", who was draped in a black mourning blanket, followed the ceremonial procession and led mourners to the president's burial plot. The most famous riderless horse was "Black Jack" who was foaled January 19, 1947, and was the last of the Quartermaster-issue horses branded with the Army's "US" brand. He was named after General of the Armies John J. "Black Jack" Pershing. He participated in the state funerals of John F. Kennedy, Herbert Hoover, and Lyndon B. Johnson, as well as the state funeral of General of the Army Douglas MacArthur. The deceased president's family, who are accompanied by federal government officials, will follow behind the ceremonial procession in a presidential motorcade.

The ceremonial procession traditionally ends at the center steps on the east front of the United States Capitol Building. Exceptions were made for Lyndon B. Johnson, Ronald Reagan, and Gerald Ford. President Johnson's coffin was carried up the Senate wing steps because the center steps were blocked with construction scaffolding from the second inauguration of Richard Nixon which occurred just days earlier. President Reagan, as former Governor of California, requested that his coffin be carried up the steps which face west, overlooking California. President Ford, as a former member of the United States House of Representatives, requested that his coffin be carried up the House wing steps. Honor guards, a military band, and a 21 gun salute will all be present during the coffin's arrival, at whichever steps of the United States Capitol Building it is planned to be carried up.

Lying in state

Shortly after the coffin is moved onto the floor of the United States Capitol Rotunda and placed on top of the Lincoln Catafalque, the state funeral itself, is administered by members of the United States Congress. A program which includes a eulogy, benediction, prayers, and the laying of floral wreaths will be conducted. Afterward, the president's remains lie in state or an honoree's remains lie in honor for public viewing. Although lying in state continues for a period of at least 24 hours, it differs from lying in honor. Five honor guards, each representing a branch of the United States Armed Forces, will face the

James A. Garfield's coffin lying in state on the Lincoln Catafalque in the United States Capitol Rotunda, 1881.

flag-draped coffin while holding their rifles with their right hand and keeping the rifle butt resting on the floor. These honor guards will periodically rotate in order to relieve previous honor guards during their constant vigil over the coffin. A mass public viewing is permitted during the lying in state until one hour before the next departure ceremony begins. For the remains of those deceased who are designated to lie in honor, a civilian honor guard derived from the United States Capitol Police will form a vigil over the coffin in the United States Capitol Rotunda.

National funeral service

A national funeral service, with a religious theme, is traditionally held at Washington National Cathedral in Washington D.C. or at another church or cathedral, depending on the president's religious faith. Two notable exceptions were for John F. Kennedy and Lyndon B. Johnson. President Kennedy's funeral service was held at the Cathedral of St. Matthew the Apostle, as he was a Roman Catholic, while President Johnson's was at National City Christian Church, as he worshipped there often while president. Both an arrival ceremony held before as well as a departure ceremony held after the funeral service ends, will be accompanied by honor guards, a military band, and a 21 gun salute at whichever venue in the Washington D.C. area was chosen for the funeral service to be conducted.

Various foreign dignitaries, heads of state, royalty, and government officials attend. On the matter of seating arrangements, the family of the deceased is immediately followed by federal government officials, and then by foreign heads of state who are arranged alphabetically by the English spelling of the countries in which they represent. Royalty representing heads of state, such as princes and dukes, come next, followed by heads of government, such as prime ministers and premiers. During the funeral service, military top brass sit in the north transept and extended family members sit in the south transept, if the funeral service is held at Washington National Cathedral.

Immediately after the national funeral service is completed, the coffin travels to its final resting place for interment. Before the mid 20th century, the coffin was moved long distances across the nation by a funeral train procession, where thousands of mourners would line the railroad tracks to pay homage. VIP transport in recent decades between the deceased president's home state and Washington, D.C. has been aboard one of the two Boeing VC-25 jets (tail codes SAM 28000 and SAM 29000) in the presidential fleet which are operated by the United States Air Force. As protocol dictates, any deceased president whose remains are flown on an air force jet are not entitled to use the call sign *Air Force One* since this call sign is exclusively reserved for any aircraft in the air force with a sitting and living president aboard. The departure and arrival ceremonies held at Andrews Air Force Base as well as at the final destination of interment are met with honor guards, a military band, and a 21 gun salute as the coffin is loaded on and unloaded off the aft section of a Boeing VC-25. Because of air transportation in the modern era, it has now become possible for a funeral service and interment to be completed within the same day, as seen during the state funerals of Lyndon B. Johnson, Ronald Reagan, and Gerald Ford. However, one notable exception occurred in 1969. Instead of using a Boeing VC-137C jet (tail code SAM 26000) which at the time typically served the role as *Air Force One*, a funeral train was used to carry and transport the coffin of Dwight D. Eisenhower. Departing from Union Station in Washington D.C. on March 31, 1969, President Eisenhower's funeral train arrived in his hometown of Abilene, Kansas on April 2, 1969. Interment inside a small chapel located on the grounds of the Eisenhower Presidential Library occurred later that day.

Burial service

More reminiscent of a military funeral during interment, presidents are automatically accorded full military honors in recognition of their role as Commander-in-Chief of the United States Armed Forces. A 3-volley salute is fired over the gravesite by seven honor guards who form a rifle party. This however, does *not* constitute a 21-gun salute. *Taps*, a bugle call sounded over the grave dating from the era of the American Civil War is performed by one lone bugler from the United States Marine Band, thirty to fifty yards away. Immediately thereafter, the United States Marine Band will perform William Whiting's *Eternal Father, Strong to Save* as the "Final Salute" is given and the flag of the United States draped over the coffin is meticulously folded by a total of eight honor guards, four on each side of the coffin.

Flag presentation

Next, an honor guard representing one of the five branches of the United States Armed Forces will present the flag to the next-of-kin by kneeling in front of the recipient, holding the folded flag waist high with the straight edge facing the recipient, while leaning toward the recipient. Depending on the service of the selected honor guard chosen to present the flag to the next-of-kin, each of the five military branches uses slightly different wording.

An honor guard representing the United States Army would present the flag to the next-of-kin by saying:

> On behalf of the President of the United States and the people of a grateful nation, may I present this flag as a token of appreciation for the honorable and faithful service your loved one rendered this nation.

An honor guard representing the United States Navy would present the flag to the next-of-kin by saying:

> On behalf of the President of the United States and the Chief of Naval Operations, please accept this flag as a symbol of our appreciation for your loved one's service to this Country and a grateful Navy.

An honor guard representing the United States Marine Corps would present the flag to the next-of-kin by saying:

> On behalf of the President of the United States, the Commandant of the Marine Corps, and a grateful nation, please accept this flag as a symbol of our appreciation for your loved one's service to Country and Corps.

An honor guard representing the United States Air Force would present the flag to the next-of-kin by saying:

> On behalf of the President of the United States, the Department of the Air Force, and a grateful nation, we offer this flag for the faithful and dedicated service of (Service member's rank and name).

- (NOTE: If the next-of-kin has expressed a religious preference or belief, the Air Force honor guard will add: "God bless you and this family, and God bless the United States of America.")

An honor guard representing the United States Coast Guard would present the flag to the next-of-kin by saying:

> On behalf of the President of the United States, the Commandant of the Coast Guard, and a grateful nation, please accept this flag as a symbol of our appreciation for your loved one's service to Country and the Coast Guard.

A final component of a state funeral is a series of flyovers of fighter aircraft by the United States Air Force in missing man formation, the first flyover in Washington D.C. during the ceremonial procession to the United States Capitol Building and the last flyover during interment at the place of burial.

Music

See also: United States military bands

For the numerous arrival and departure ceremonies conducted throughout the entire course of a state funeral for a deceased president, four *ruffles and flourishes* are rendered, followed by *Hail to the Chief* which is performed by a United States military band from one of the five branches of the United States Armed Forces. Other religious and patriotic music such as Antonín Dvořák's *New World Symphony* (popularly known as *"Goin' Home"*), Daniel C. Robert's *God of Our Fathers*, Irving Berlin's *God Bless America*, Sarah Fuller Flower Adams' *Nearer My God to Thee*, and John Newton's *Amazing Grace* may be performed as an accompaniment during the arrival and departure ceremonies. For a ceremonial procession, the musical selections vary. As a tradition that began during the state funeral of John F. Kennedy in 1963 and used in most subsequent state funerals thereafter, Frédéric Chopin's *Piano Sonata No. 2 "The Funeral March"* has been performed by a military band, usually the 99-piece United States Marine Band, while marching down either Constitution or Pennsylvania Avenue. The use of muffled drums and bagpipes are common as well. During a national funeral service, such as those held at Washington National Cathedral, the Cathedral Choir or the Armed Forces Choir will sing a selection of religious and patriotic music. Solo artists who are internationally acclaimed have also performed during a funeral service, a recent example being Irish tenor Ronan Tynan who sang *Amazing Grace* and Franz Schubert's *Ave Maria* at Washington National Cathedral during the state funeral of Ronald Reagan in 2004.

Lying in state and honor

See also: Lying in state and Lying in repose

The main difference between lying in state and lying in honor is the designated honor guard that keeps watch over the coffin. When lying in state, five honor guards, each representing the five branches of the United States Armed Forces, will periodically rotate and relieve the preceding set of honor guards who watch over the coffin around the clock in what is known as a vigil. When lying in honor, the United States Capitol Police will act as a civilian honor guard. No law, written rule, or regulation specifies who may lie in state. Use of the United States Capitol Rotunda is controlled by concurrent action of the

When not in use, the Lincoln Catafalque is displayed in the Exhibition Hall at the United States Capitol Visitor Center.

United States House of Representatives and the United States Senate. Any person who has rendered distinguished service to the nation may lie in state if the family so wishes and the United States

Congress approves. In the case of unknown soldiers, the president or the appropriate branch of the armed forces initiates the action.

- People to have lain in state in the United States Capitol Rotunda are as follows:

  - Henry Clay (July 1, 1852)
  - Abraham Lincoln (April 19–21, 1865)
  - Thaddeus Stevens (August 13–14, 1868)
  - Charles Sumner (March 13, 1874)
  - Henry Wilson (November 25–26, 1875)
  - James A. Garfield (September 21–23, 1881)
  - John Alexander Logan (December 30–31, 1886)
  - William McKinley (September 17, 1901)
  - Pierre Charles L'Enfant (April 28, 1909)
  - George Dewey (January 20, 1917)
  - Unknown Soldier of World War I (November 9–11, 1921)
  - Warren Harding (August 8, 1923)
  - William Howard Taft (March 11, 1930)
  - John Joseph Pershing (July 18–19, 1948)
  - Robert Alphonso Taft (August 2–3, 1953)
  - Unknown Soldiers of World War II and the Korean War (May 28–30, 1958)
  - John F. Kennedy (November 24–25, 1963)
  - Douglas MacArthur (April 8–9, 1964)
  - Herbert Hoover (October 23–25, 1964)
  - Dwight D. Eisenhower (March 30–31, 1969)
  - Everett McKinley Dirksen (September 9–10, 1969)
  - J. Edgar Hoover (May 3–4, 1972)
  - Lyndon B. Johnson (January 24–25, 1973)
  - Hubert Humphrey (January 14–15, 1978)
  - Unknown Soldier of the Vietnam War, later identified as Michael J. Blassie (May 25–28, 1984)
  - Claude Denson Pepper (June 1–2, 1989)
  - Ronald Reagan (June 9–11, 2004)
  - Gerald Ford (December 30, 2006 – January 2, 2007)

- People to have lain in honor in the United States Capitol Rotunda are as follows:

  - Jacob Chestnut and John Gibson (July 28, 1998)
  - Rosa Parks (October 30–31, 2005)

- People to have lain in state in the Herbert C. Hoover Building are as follows:

  - Ronald H. Brown (April 9–10, 1996)

- Supreme Court Justices to have lain in state in the Supreme Court Room at the United States Capitol Building are as follows:
  - Salmon P. Chase (May 11, 1873)
- Supreme Court Justices to have lain in state in the Great Hall at the United States Supreme Court Building are as follows:
  - Earl Warren (July 11–12, 1974)
  - Thurgood Marshall (January 27, 1993)
  - Warren E. Burger (June 28, 1995)
  - William J. Brennan, Jr. (July 28, 1997)
  - Harry A. Blackmun (March 8, 1999)
  - William H. Rehnquist (September 6–7, 2005)

Funeral arrangements

Since state funerals in the United States are elaborate affairs which are in itself rare occurrences, they are planned years in advance. Each living president, sitting or former, is generally expected to have funeral plans in place on becoming president. However, these details become more important after a president leaves office, and serves to reduce stress for the president's family in an era of worldwide media scrutiny.

The Military District of Washington (MDW) has primary responsibility in overseeing state funerals and in all cases, must strictly follow a 138-page planning document. Detailed funeral arrangements have emerged for two former presidents, Jimmy Carter and George H.W. Bush. A 411-page document outlining a state funeral for President Carter has been filed with the Military District of Washington, including a public viewing of the president's remains at the Carter Center in Atlanta, Georgia as well as final interment to occur in the president's hometown of Plains, Georgia. President Carter has stated that he will be buried in the front yard of the Carter family's residence, which is now a component of the Jimmy Carter National Historic Site. President Bush has filed a 211-page document with the Military District of Washington, which contains a request for an aerial flyover of fighter jets in missing man formation by the United States Air Force during his state funeral as well as final interment and burial to occur at the George Bush Presidential Library in College Station, Texas. President Bush has also indicated that he does not want the presidential fanfare, *Hail to the Chief*, to be performed during final interment and burial. In addition, Presidents Carter and Bush have made plans for a national funeral service to be held at Washington National Cathedral in Washington D.C. No funeral arrangements for two other former presidents, Bill Clinton and George W. Bush, or for the current sitting president, Barack Obama, have been filed with the Military District of Washington.

Security measures

In the aftermath of the events of September 11, 2001, the Secretary of Homeland Security has declared state funerals to be a National Security Special Event. Thus, these occasions are of great importance to the nation which are in itself, a potential target for terrorists. This designation authorizes the United States Secret Service to implement all security arrangements and protection of all federal government officials.

Gallery

The funeral train of Abraham Lincoln departing Washington D.C. enroute to Springfield, Illinois for interment, 1865.

A drawing depicting Abraham Lincoln's funeral procession in New York City en route from Washington D.C. to Springfield, Illinois, 1865.

A drawing which shows the coffin of Abraham Lincoln being prepared for the first of many of his interments in Illinois, 1865.

A limbers and caissons carrying the coffin of William McKinley past the United States Treasury Building on Pennsylvania Avenue enroute to the United States Capitol Building, 1901.

Honor guards during an arrival ceremony carrying the coffin of William McKinley up the east steps of the United States Capitol Building, 1901.

A departure ceremony held on the center steps at the United States Capitol Building as honor guards carry the coffin of the Unknown Soldier of World War I to a limbers and caissons, 1921.

A limbers and caissons carrying the remains of Franklin D. Roosevelt proceeds down Pennsylvania Avenue towards Union Station for the journey to Hyde Park, New York, 1945.

The remains of John F. Kennedy lying in repose in the East Room of the White House, 1963.

Robert F. Kennedy and Jean Kennedy seen following Jacqueline Kennedy as she leaves the United States Capitol Buolding with John Kennedy Jr. and Caroline Kennedy, after viewing the lying in state of John F. Kennedy, 1963.

The caparisoned, riderless horse named "Black Jack" during a departure ceremony held at the United States Cspitol Building in conjunction with the state funeral of John F. Kennedy, 1963.

Honor guards carrying the remains of Dwight D. Eisenhower down the center steps located on the east front of the United States Capitol Building, 1969.

The coffins of Jacob Chestnut and John Gibson 'lying in honor' in the United States Capitol Rotunda as the United States Capitol Police act as an honor guard, 1998.

A limbers and caissons carrying the remains of Ronald Reagan down Constitution Avenue enroute to the United States Capitol Building, 2004.

The flag of the United States flying at half-staff outside the United States Capitol Building while honoring the life of Ronald Reagan, 2004.

The caparisoned, riderless horse named Sergeant York during the ceremonial funeral procession of Ronald Reagan, with a ceremonial sword attached to the saddle and a pair of the president's boots reversed in the stirrups, 2004.

The coffin of Gerald Ford lying in state in the United States Capitol Rotunda during the president's state funeral, 2006.

The memorial service celebrating and honoring the life of Gerald Ford at Washington National Cathedral, 2006.

See also

- Abraham Lincoln's burial and exhumation
- Death and funeral of Richard Nixon
- Death and state funeral of Gerald Ford
- Death and state funeral of Ronald Reagan
- List of United States presidential assassination attempts and plots
- List of United States Presidents who died in office
- State funeral of John F. Kennedy
- State funerals in Canada

Further reading

- Mossman, B.C.; Stark, M.W. (1991). *The Last Salute: Civil and Military Funerals 1921-1969* [1]. Department of the Army. CMH Pub 90-1.
- Sandburg, Carl (1936). *Abraham Lincoln: The War Years IV*. Harcourt, Brace & World. ISBN 0781261716.
- Swanson, James (2006). *Manhunt: The 12-Day Chase for Lincoln's Killer*. Harper Collins. ISBN 9780060518493.

External links

- "STATE, OFFICIAL, AND SPECIAL MILITARY FUNERALS" by the U.S. Army [2]
- *The Last Salute* by the U.S. Army [3]
- 1/3 Battalion HHC Caisson Platoon, 3rd United States Infantry Regiment "The Old Guard" [4]

Article Sources and Contributors

J. Edgar Hoover *Source*: http://en.wikipedia.org/?oldid=390561068 *Contributors*: 1 anonymous edits

Federal Bureau of Investigation *Source*: http://en.wikipedia.org/?oldid=390437480 *Contributors*:

Eastern Market, Washington, D.C. *Source*: http://en.wikipedia.org/?oldid=387160019 *Contributors*:

Library of Congress *Source*: http://en.wikipedia.org/?oldid=390469819 *Contributors*: 1 anonymous edits

George Washington University *Source*: http://en.wikipedia.org/?oldid=390447748 *Contributors*: 0wendy33

Anthony Comstock *Source*: http://en.wikipedia.org/?oldid=390512063 *Contributors*: Gsf

William J. Burns *Source*: http://en.wikipedia.org/?oldid=382963080 *Contributors*: Dudeman5685

Teapot Dome scandal *Source*: http://en.wikipedia.org/?oldid=390281770 *Contributors*: North Shoreman

John Dillinger *Source*: http://en.wikipedia.org/?oldid=389959209 *Contributors*: 1 anonymous edits

Little Bohemia Lodge *Source*: http://en.wikipedia.org/?oldid=388731161 *Contributors*: 1 anonymous edits

Biograph Theater *Source*: http://en.wikipedia.org/?oldid=374782997 *Contributors*: Pauljeffersonks

Alvin Karpis *Source*: http://en.wikipedia.org/?oldid=388941482 *Contributors*:

Machine Gun Kelly *Source*: http://en.wikipedia.org/?oldid=389085475 *Contributors*: John of Reading

Walter Winchell *Source*: http://en.wikipedia.org/?oldid=388685346 *Contributors*:

Venona project *Source*: http://en.wikipedia.org/?oldid=388417082 *Contributors*:

COINTELPRO *Source*: http://en.wikipedia.org/?oldid=390198260 *Contributors*:

Socialist Workers Party (United States) *Source*: http://en.wikipedia.org/?oldid=388829132 *Contributors*: Kuralyov

Ku Klux Klan *Source*: http://en.wikipedia.org/?oldid=390533965 *Contributors*: Charles Edward

Nation of Islam *Source*: http://en.wikipedia.org/?oldid=390209222 *Contributors*: 1 anonymous edits

Black Panther Party *Source*: http://en.wikipedia.org/?oldid=390487614 *Contributors*: William Avery

New Left *Source*: http://en.wikipedia.org/?oldid=389495993 *Contributors*: 1 anonymous edits

J. Edgar Hoover Building *Source*: http://en.wikipedia.org/?oldid=377323469 *Contributors*: 1 anonymous edits

National Security Medal *Source*: http://en.wikipedia.org/?oldid=382146661 *Contributors*: Hawkeye7

Awards of the United States Department of State *Source*: http://en.wikipedia.org/?oldid=372242376 *Contributors*: Eastlaw

State funerals in the United States *Source*: http://en.wikipedia.org/?oldid=390199250 *Contributors*: Yoganate79

Image Sources, Licenses and Contributors

Image:Anti-kkk-cartoon.jpg *Source*: http://bibliocm.bibliolabs.com/mwAnon/index.php?title=File:Anti-kkk-cartoon.jpg *License*: Public Domain *Contributors*: Cartoon from 1868

Image:NathanBedfordForrest.jpg *Source*: http://bibliocm.bibliolabs.com/mwAnon/index.php?title=File:NathanBedfordForrest.jpg *License*: Public Domain *Contributors*: Frieda, Red devil 666

Image:Mississippi ku klux.jpg *Source*: http://bibliocm.bibliolabs.com/mwAnon/index.php?title=File:Misissippi_ku_klux.jpg *License*: Public Domain *Contributors*: Chowbok, GeorgHH, Howcheng, Infrogmation, KAMiKAZOW, Oxam Hartog, 8 anonymous edits

Image:BenFrankButler.jpg *Source*: http://bibliocm.bibliolabs.com/mwAnon/index.php?title=File:BenFrankButler.jpg *License*: Public Domain *Contributors*: Original uploader was The Mystery Man at en.wikipedia

Image:NCG-WilliamHolden.jpg *Source*: http://bibliocm.bibliolabs.com/mwAnon/index.php?title=File:NCG-WilliamHolden.jpg *License*: Public Domain *Contributors*: Original uploader was Seth Ilys at en.wikipedia

Image:Birth-of-a-nation-poster-color.jpg *Source*: http://bibliocm.bibliolabs.com/mwAnon/index.php?title=File:Birth-of-a-nation-poster-color.jpg *License*: Public Domain *Contributors*: Feydey, Infrogmation, KAMiKAZOW, Pitke, Quadell, R-41, Snek01, Thib Phil, TwoWings, Vanjagenije, 1 anonymous edits

Image:The-clansman-cropped.jpg *Source*: http://bibliocm.bibliolabs.com/mwAnon/index.php?title=File:The-clansman-cropped.jpg *License*: Public Domain *Contributors*: Original uploader was Bcrowell at en.wikipedia

Image:President Woodrow Wilson portrait December 2 1912.jpg *Source*: http://bibliocm.bibliolabs.com/mwAnon/index.php?title=File:President_Woodrow_Wilson_portrait_December_2_1912.jpg *License*: Public Domain *Contributors*: Pach Brothers, New York

Image:William-joseph-simmons2.jpg *Source*: http://bibliocm.bibliolabs.com/mwAnon/index.php?title=File:William-joseph-simmons2.jpg *License*: Public Domain *Contributors*: Original uploader was Bcrowell at en.wikipedia Later versions were uploaded by Pixel23 at en.wikipedia.

Image:Stonemtn2.jpg *Source*: http://bibliocm.bibliolabs.com/mwAnon/index.php?title=File:Stonemtn2.jpg *License*: GNU Free Documentation License *Contributors*: Author and original uploader was Kkmd (Kelvin Kay) at en.wikipedia

Image:Burning-cross2.jpg *Source*: http://bibliocm.bibliolabs.com/mwAnon/index.php?title=File:Burning-cross2.jpg *License*: Public Domain *Contributors*: Denver News

Image:klan-sheet-music.jpg *Source*: http://bibliocm.bibliolabs.com/mwAnon/index.php?title=File:Klan-sheet-music.jpg *License*: Public Domain *Contributors*: Original uploader was Bcrowell at en.wikipedia

File:Good Citizen Pillar of Fire Church July 1926.jpg *Source*: http://bibliocm.bibliolabs.com/mwAnon/index.php?title=File:Good_Citizen_Pillar_of_Fire_Church_July_1926.jpg *License*: unknown *Contributors*: Original uploader was Buz lightning at en.wikipedia. Later version(s) were uploaded by Beao at en.wikipedia.

Image:Ballot1.jpg *Source*: http://bibliocm.bibliolabs.com/mwAnon/index.php?title=File:Ballot1.jpg *License*: unknown *Contributors*: Bishop Alma White. Original uploader was Buz lightning at en.wikipedia

File:D. C. Stephenson Grand Dragon of the Klu Klux Klan in Indiana, c 1922.jpg *Source*: http://bibliocm.bibliolabs.com/mwAnon/index.php?title=File:D._C._Stephenson_Grand_Dragon_of_the_Klu_Klux_Klan_in_Indiana,_c_1922.jpg *License*: Public Domain *Contributors*: Charles Edward, Kilom691, 1 anonymous edits

Image:Kkk1928.jpg *Source*: http://bibliocm.bibliolabs.com/mwAnon/index.php?title=File:Kkk1928.jpg *License*: Public Domain *Contributors*: User:Bcrowell

Image:Poster35.jpg *Source*: http://bibliocm.bibliolabs.com/mwAnon/index.php?title=File:Poster35.jpg *License*: Public Domain *Contributors*: Alex Bakharev, GDW13, Goldfritha, Infrogmation, Membershiped, Pomeranian, Shakko, Syrcro, Ustas, 2 anonymous edits

Image:Kkk-march-violence.jpg *Source*: http://bibliocm.bibliolabs.com/mwAnon/index.php?title=File:Kkk-march-violence.jpg *License*: Public Domain *Contributors*: Original uploader was Bcrowell at en.wikipedia

Image:Noi flag 2.svg *Source*: http://bibliocm.bibliolabs.com/mwAnon/index.php?title=File:Noi_flag_2.svg *License*: Public Domain *Contributors*: User:Pmx

File:Elijah Muhammad NYWTS-2.jpg *Source*: http://bibliocm.bibliolabs.com/mwAnon/index.php?title=File:Elijah_Muhammad_NYWTS-2.jpg *License*: unknown *Contributors*: New York World-Telegram and the Sun staff photographer: Wolfson, Stanley, photographer.

File:Farrakhan.jpg *Source*: http://bibliocm.bibliolabs.com/mwAnon/index.php?title=File:Farrakhan.jpg *License*: Public Domain *Contributors*: Christophe cagé, Kenmayer, Yahel Guhan

File:Fruits-of-islam-1964.jpg *Source*: http://bibliocm.bibliolabs.com/mwAnon/index.php?title=File:Fruits-of-islam-1964.jpg *License*: unknown *Contributors*: New York World-Telegram and the Sun staff photographer: Wolfson, Stanley, photographer.

File:20051030-161112-08-E-Nation-of-Islam-mosque.jpg *Source*: http://bibliocm.bibliolabs.com/mwAnon/index.php?title=File:20051030-161112-08-E-Nation-of-Islam-mosque.jpg *License*: Creative Commons Attribution-Sharealike 2.5 *Contributors*: (Warmbucket)

File:Noi.PNG *Source*: http://bibliocm.bibliolabs.com/mwAnon/index.php?title=File:Noi.PNG *License*: Creative Commons Attribution-Sharealike 2.5 *Contributors*: Ardfern, Christophe cagé, EugeneZelenko, J 1982, Kenmayer, Man vyi, Nrive, Oneblackline, Yahel Guhan, 2 anonymous edits

File:Nation of islam seller.jpg *Source*: http://bibliocm.bibliolabs.com/mwAnon/index.php?title=File:Nation_of_islam_seller.jpg *License*: Creative Commons Attribution 2.0 *Contributors*: ChicagoEye / Lee Bey

File:COINTELPRO - Jean Seberg.jpg *Source*: http://bibliocm.bibliolabs.com/mwAnon/index.php?title=File:COINTELPRO_-_Jean_Seberg.jpg *License*: Public Domain *Contributors*: Richard W. Held

File:Black Panther convention2.jpg *Source*: http://bibliocm.bibliolabs.com/mwAnon/index.php?title=File:Black_Panther_convention2.jpg *License*: Public Domain *Contributors*: O'Halloran, Thomas J., photographer.; Leffler, Warren K., photographer. For US News and World Report.

Image:BPP REUNION 2006.JPG *Source*: http://bibliocm.bibliolabs.com/mwAnon/index.php?title=File:BPP_REUNION_2006.JPG *License*: GNU Free Documentation License *Contributors*: User:TalkAbout. Original uploader was TalkAbout at en.wikipedia

File:Herbert Marcuse in Newton, Massachusetts 1955.jpeg *Source*: http://bibliocm.bibliolabs.com/mwAnon/index.php?title=File:Herbert_Marcuse_in_Newton,_Massachusetts_1955.jpeg *License*: GNU Free Documentation License *Contributors*: Copyright holder: Marcuse family, represented by Harold Marcuse

File:J edgar hoover bldg.jpg *Source*: http://bibliocm.bibliolabs.com/mwAnon/index.php?title=File:J_edgar_hoover_bldg.jpg *License*: Creative Commons Attribution-Sharealike 2.5 *Contributors*: AgnosticPreachersKid, Aude, Mattes, Ric36, Rootology, SchuminWeb, Stunteltje, WhisperToMe

File:Nationalsecuritymedal.jpeg *Source*: http://bibliocm.bibliolabs.com/mwAnon/index.php?title=File:Nationalsecuritymedal.jpeg *License*: Public Domain *Contributors*: US Federal Government

CPSIA information can be obtained at www.ICGtesting.com
Printed in the USA
BVOW061936021111

275149BV00003B/33/P

9 781240 442805